IMAGES
of America

MONTICELLO

On the Cover: Two men stand in front of the Pepsin Syrup Company in the 1920s. The men are most probably assistant sales manager Maxwell Hott (left) and assistant treasurer Donn Piatt. The vans read, "Dr. Caldwell's Syrup Pepsin—The Family Laxative." Smaller lettering by the tire reads, "Advertising Car No. 27." (Courtesy of the Piatt County Historical and Genealogical Society.)

IMAGES
of America

MONTICELLO

Maureen Holtz

ARCADIA
PUBLISHING

ISBN 978-0-7385-9982-3

Published by Arcadia Publishing
Charleston, South Carolina

Printed in the United States of America

Library of Congress Control Number: 2012954812

For all general information, please contact Arcadia Publishing:
Telephone 843-853-2070
Fax 843-853-0044
E-mail sales@arcadiapublishing.com
For customer service and orders:
Toll-Free 1-888-313-2665

Visit us on the Internet at www.arcadiapublishing.com

This book is dedicated to my husband, Michael, and to my parents, who instilled in me a love of history.

CONTENTS

Acknowledgments

This book would not have been possible without the incredible assistance provided by Allerton Public Library director Lisa Winters and Piatt County Historical and Genealogical Society president Dee Lund. Other Monticello citizens supporting this effort included Juanita Gale, Susan Galt, Sharon Williams, Richard Skagenberg, Donna Catlin, Walter Cresap, Sandra Rosenfield, and John Heider. Many of the photographs are from the Francis Brooks and Samuel Roane collections found at Allerton Public Library and the Piatt County Historical and Genealogical Society. The source of each image is shown at the end of each caption using the abbreviations noted below. Thanks are also extended to all the people who captivated me with their stories. Due to name-spelling variations found in my research, I kept the most prevalent or preferred spelling.

(APL): Courtesy of Allerton Public Library
(APL-HS): From the Harold Scott Collection, courtesy of Allerton Public Library
(APL-SR): From the Samuel Roane Collection, courtesy of Allerton Public Library
(DC): Courtesy of Donna Catlin
(JG): Courtesy of Juanita Gale
(MH): Courtesy of Michael Holtz
(PCHGS): Courtesy of the Piatt County Historical and Genealogical Society
(PCHGS-FP): From the Frances Perkins Collection, courtesy of the Piatt County Historical and Genealogical Society
(PCCC): Courtesy of the Piatt County Clerk's Office
(RS): Courtesy of Richard Skagenberg
(SG): Courtesy of Susan Galt
(SR): Courtesy of Sandra Rosenfield; photograph by Harold Scott
(SW): Courtesy of Sharon Williams
(WC): Courtesy of Walter Cresap

INTRODUCTION

By car, Monticello lies 30 minutes from both Decatur and Champaign-Urbana. But many people in and near Monticello are not aware of the interesting history of the small city sitting at the bottom of a bowl of prairie. Since its beginnings in 1822 with a handful of people, the town had grown to a population of approximately 5,600 as of 2011.

The first pioneers who traveled west to this territory of Kickapoo and Potawatomi Indians arrived by wagon train and camped by the Sangamon River. They considered the area an immense garden, and many chose to build homes on prime farmland left behind after glaciers swept through Illinois thousands of years ago. They fed on abundant deer, elk, buffalo, wolves, coyotes, beaver, and smaller animals.

Early settlers included people by the name of Piatt, Haneline, Rhoades, Dighton, and Marquiss. Many descendants of the early pioneers still live in and around Monticello. As the population increased, other names became prominent, such as Lodge, Kirby, England, Moore, Allerton, and Hott.

As a newcomer of only 20-plus years in Monticello, I became fascinated by stories I learned since we moved here: Such as how Abraham Lincoln met up with Stephen A. Douglas on the edge of town in 1858 and planned their debates that later won Lincoln the presidency. Or how several Monticello dwellings hosted Lincoln as he journeyed the Eighth Judicial Circuit during his law practice. Or how Monticello became the "patent medicine capital of the world" when Dr. Caldwell's Pepsin Syrup Company's tasty laxative was sold worldwide. Or how a number of Monticello's entrepreneurs grew so wealthy from their business ventures that the street on which they lived was nicknamed "Millionaires' Row." Or the fantastical rumor that Robert Allerton shipped a boxcar full of snakes to spread around his estate on Monticello's outskirts to intimidate intruders.

Throughout the decades, even as local companies closed down, farmland around Monticello continued to feed not just the community but also the wallet. A great number of those who gained from their investments, either through land or industry, have been generous to the city. They donated a school gymnasium, land and funds for a hospital, assisted-living facilities, a 4-H camp, and at least four parks: Allerton, Lodge, Valentine, and the forest preserve.

I hope the photographs in this book entertain and enrich your understanding of, and appreciation for, Monticello's intriguing history.

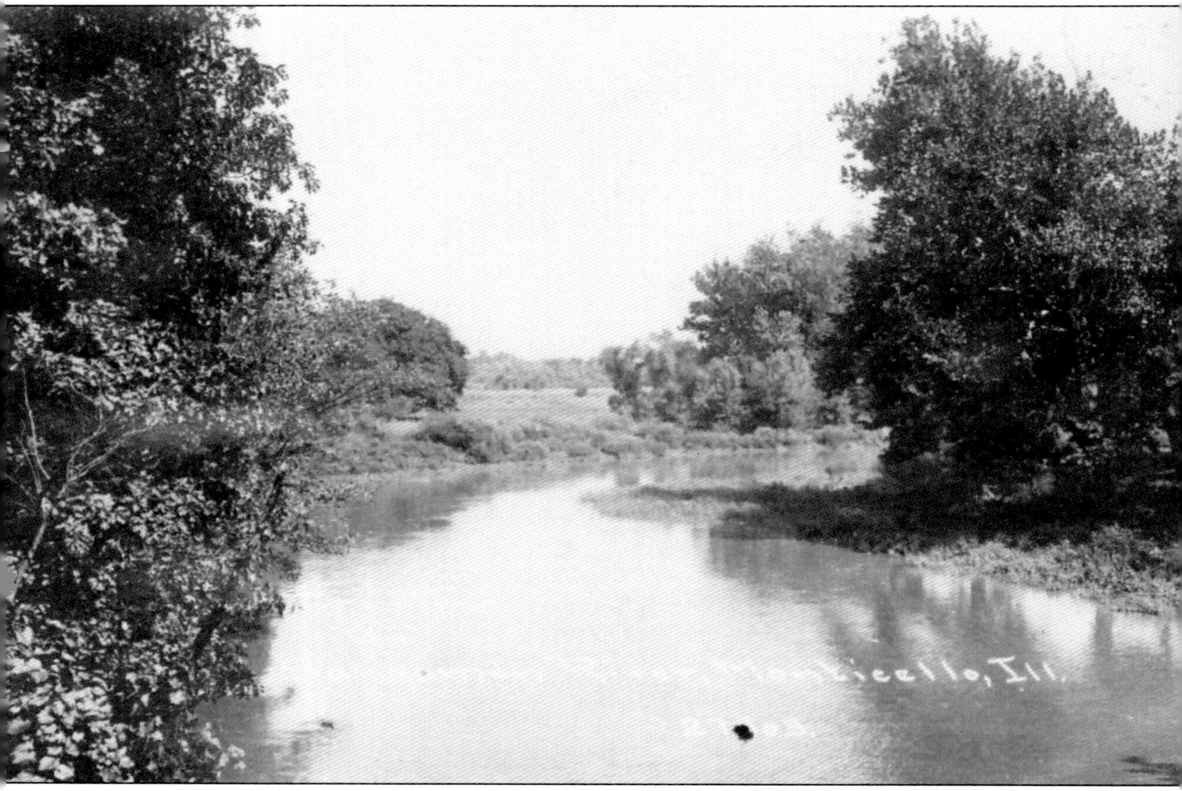

The Sangamon River meanders for approximately 246 miles and drains the agricultural area between Peoria and Springfield. The name Sangamon comes from the Potawatomi word *sain-guee-mon*, which means "where there is plenty to eat." Kickapoo Indians settled along the river in the 1700s. The river area flowing through Allerton Park and Recreation Center was named a National Natural Landmark in 1971. (APL.)

One

From Settlement to City 1822–1872

The first settlers trickling into the Monticello area were George Hayworth in 1822, followed by James Martin, who erected a cabin on property that is now 1124 North State Street. Abraham Haneline arrived in 1824, then James A. and Jemima Piatt and their family in 1829. In 1833, Abraham Marquiss arrived via wagon train with 21 relatives.

Decatur and Champaign were many hours away. The pioneers worked together to battle heat, wolves, and bad winters. Snow began during the autumn of 1830 and continued through the winter, accumulating layers of snow and sleet four feet deep. In time, the "Deep Snow" of 1830 served as a milestone for a person's longevity (and thus esteem) in the community. The year 1836 became known as the "Sudden Freeze" when the fast-dropping temperature combined with a heavy rain to freeze people and animals in their tracks.

In 1837, Abraham Marquiss, James Piatt, William Barnes, and Maj. James McReynolds formed a committee to find the best site on which to establish a town. After examining areas along the Sangamon River, they picked the existing settlement on Piatt's land as the most appealing site. The four men created a stock company and bought the land from Piatt. McReynolds, raised in Virginia, paid homage to Thomas Jefferson's estate by choosing Monticello as the town's name. On July 1, 1837, the town's plat was recorded in Macon County. Founders picked July 4 as the town's birthday.

In 1841, after frustration with the arduous journey to the Macon county seat in Decatur, citizens circulated petitions requesting that a new county be created. They named their new county Piatt to honor one of the first settlers and selected Monticello—the only town actually established at that time—as the county seat.

Like many Illinois sites, Monticello had its connection to Abraham Lincoln. It was there that he met up with Stephen Douglas outside of town in 1858 and agreed to plan a series of debates.

In 1872, with a population of 1,060, Monticello was incorporated as a city. As the year ended, smallpox broke out in town.

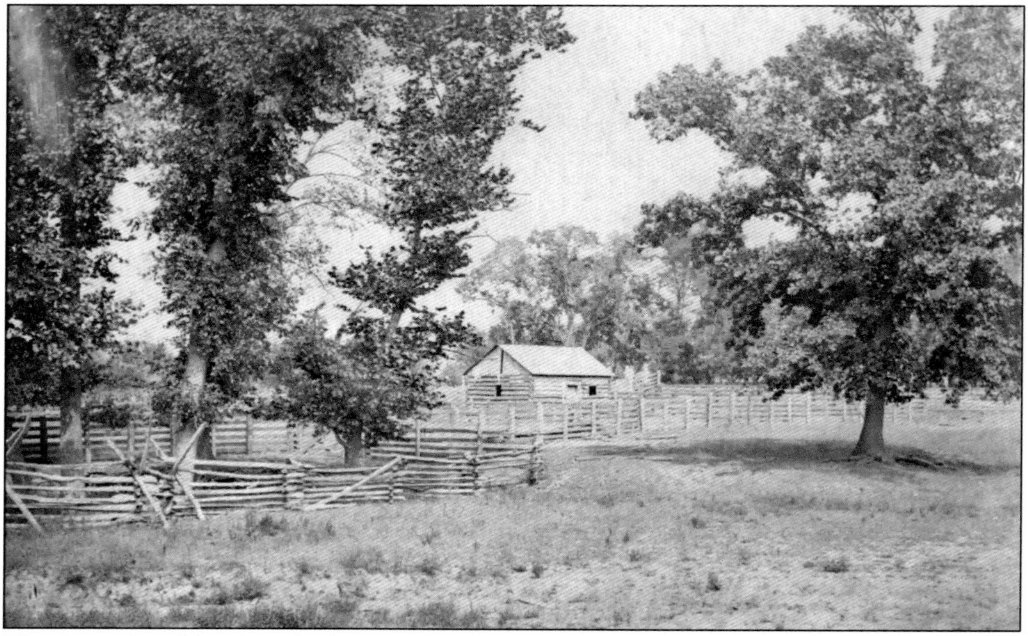

The first cabin (photographed in 1880) in Piatt County was built in 1822 by Quaker George Hayworth. The government sent him to persuade the Indians to sign over their land and leave. In 1829, James Piatt bought the cabin, which stood just north of where the Illinois Central ran under the Wabash tracks. In 1917, William F. Lodge moved it to his estate, where it burned down shortly afterwards. (PCHGS.)

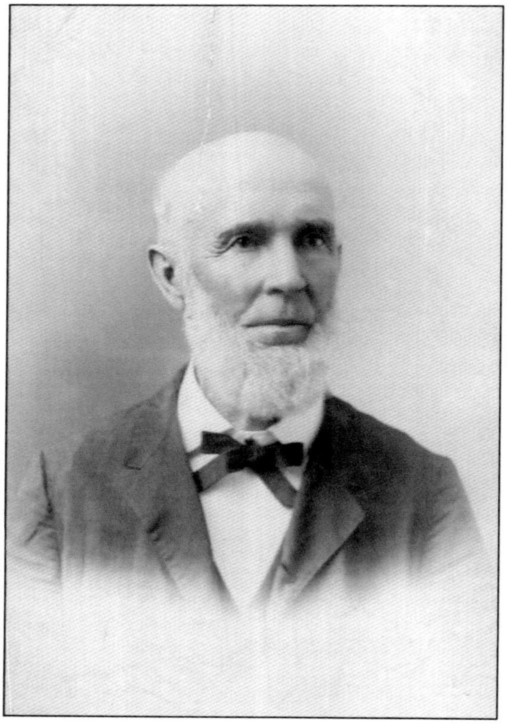

William H. Piatt, the eldest son of James A. and Jemima Ford Piatt's seven children, was born in 1816 and married Clarinda Marquiss in 1838. They lived briefly on the site of the present State Street Forest Preserve and then moved to Goose Creek. Piatt became wealthy through land and livestock investments. Their daughter Emma Piatt (Llewellyn) wrote a history of Piatt County. He died in 1906. (PCHGS.)

Born in 1819, Clarinda Marquiss, daughter of Elizabeth Barnes and Abraham Marquiss, arrived with 21 members of her family in a wagon train in 1833. In 1836, she rode her horse through the night to make a claim on property, barely arriving before another claimant. She died in June 1893 of typhoid pneumonia after having visited her daughter and the World's Columbian Exposition in Chicago. (APL.)

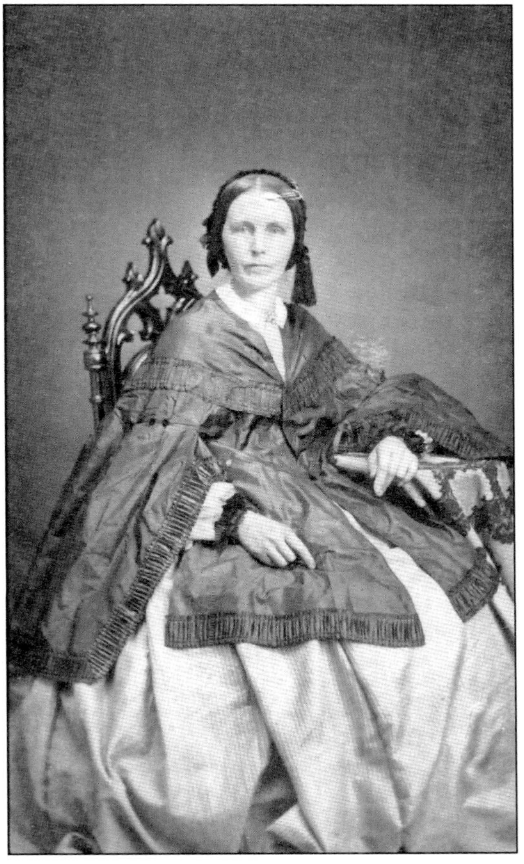

In 1845, Jacob Tenbrook, second cousin to James A. Piatt, built a one-room log cabin as a blacksmith shop on what is now the northwest corner of Washington and Market Streets. In 1847, his widowed sister Ann Tenbrook Honselman and her four children moved into the cabin. Born in Pennsylvania on February 14, 1806, she died in October 1901. In 1920, the Honselman cabin was dismantled and moved to the country. (APL-SR.)

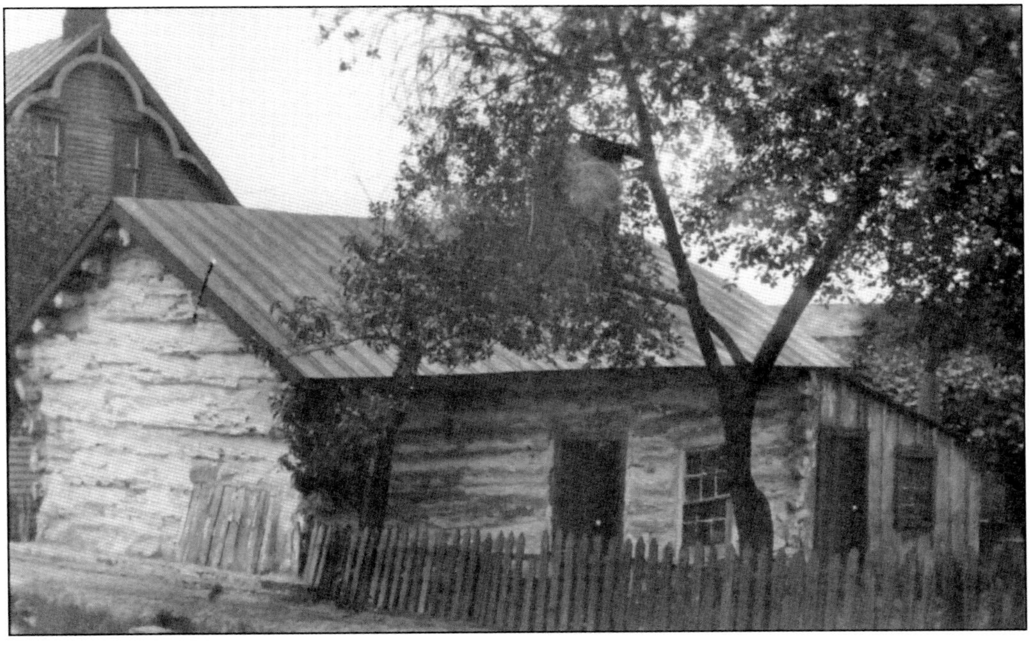

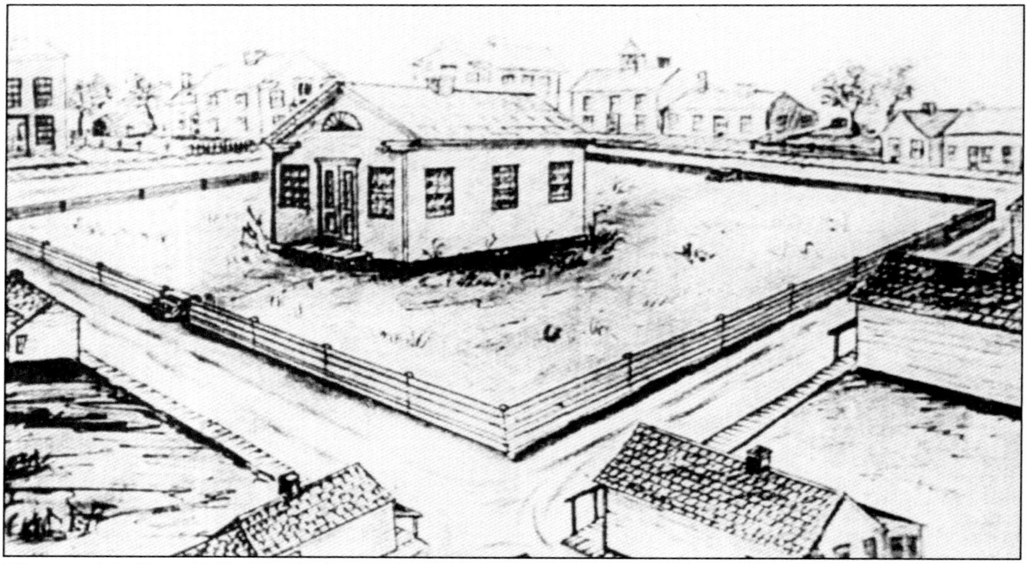

Thomas Moffit's 1860 sketch shows the first courthouse in Piatt County. The wooden structure was built on Monticello's square in 1843 by Judge Ricketts on land donated by William H. Piatt. It also doubled as a school and hosted church meetings until it was replaced in 1856. It was relocated to approximately 110 South Charter Street, where it served as a grocery store until destroyed by fire in 1874. (PCHGS.)

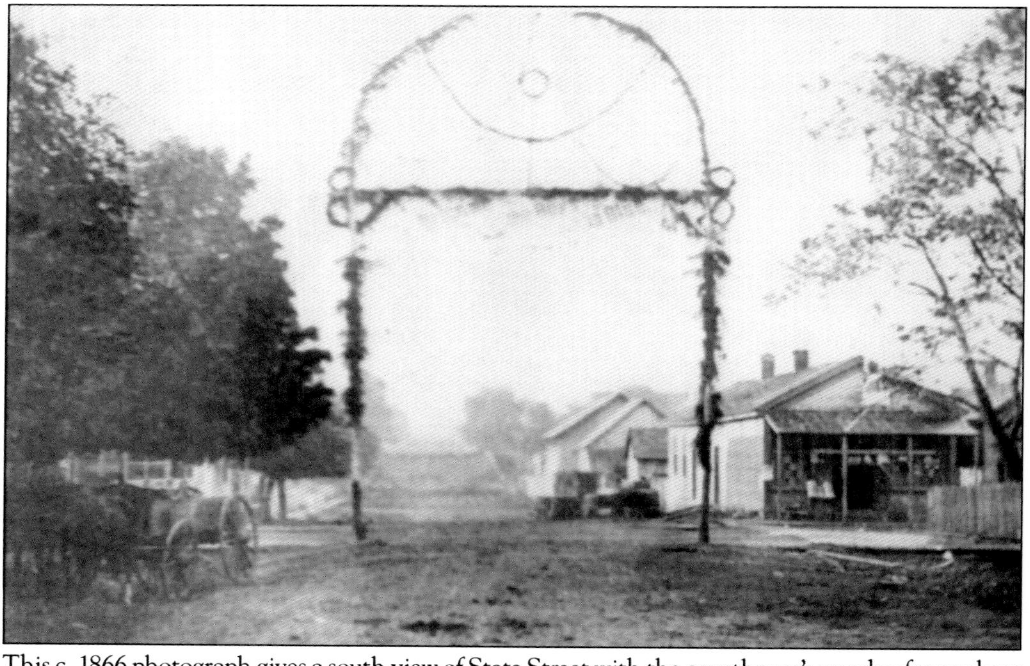

This c. 1866 photograph gives a south view of State Street with the courthouse's wooden fence along the right side. The Tenbrook (also "Tinbrook") Hotel sits across the street from the courthouse on the southwest corner of Main and State Streets. Begun as a one-room log house, it was later enlarged to eight rooms. Abraham Lincoln visited between 1847 and 1859 as he traveled the Eighth Judicial Circuit. (PCHGS.)

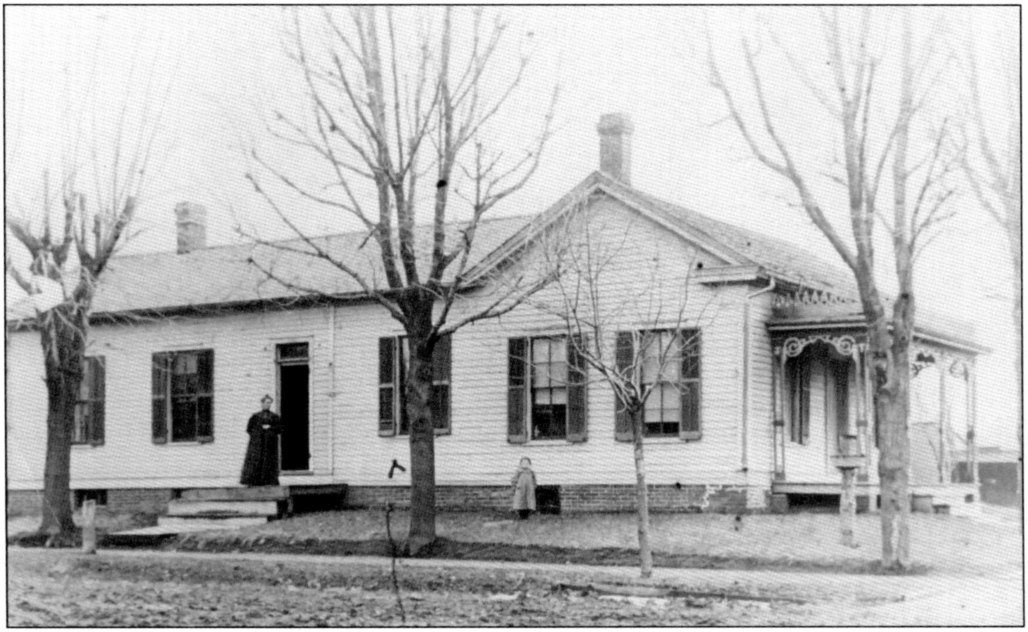

On September 17, 1856, Abraham Lincoln arrived to speak at Monticello's courthouse in support of Republican John C. Fremont's campaign for the presidency. Lincoln joined R.M. Guy, Ezra Marquiss, and a gentleman named Burnham in carrying a Fremont banner to the courthouse. Lincoln spent the night at Guy's home at 303 South Independence Street. The house was significantly remodeled by later owner Ross Cresap and his son Walter. (WC.)

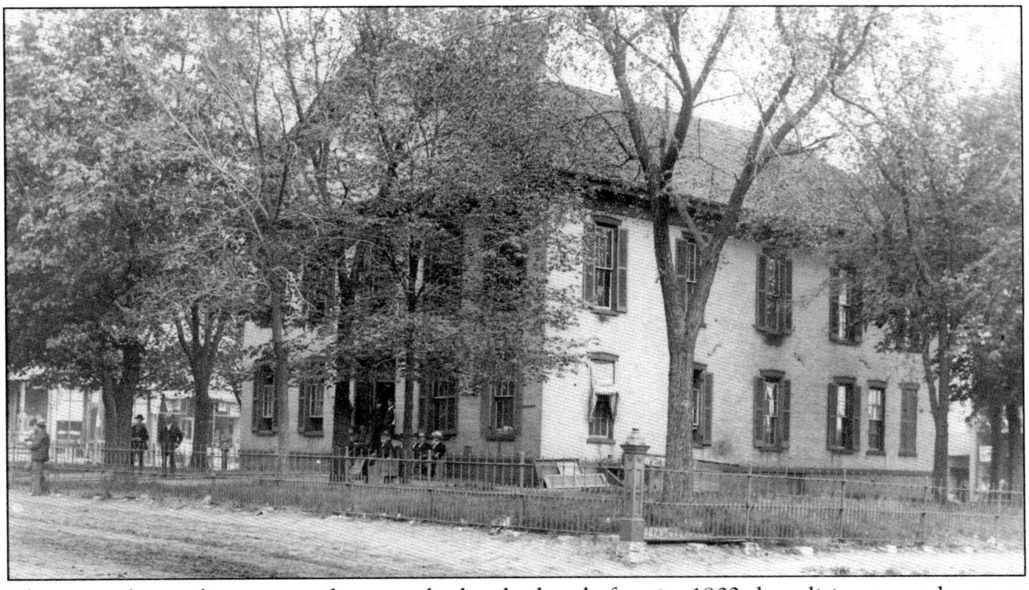

The second courthouse was photographed only days before its 1903 demolition to make room for Monticello's third and current courthouse. Built in 1856–1857, the two-story structure with attic was originally crowned with a cupola, but an 1871 storm destroyed the cupola. William F. Lodge bought the brick structure for $138.01 and used it to build a blacksmith and wagon shop on West Main Street. (PCHGS.)

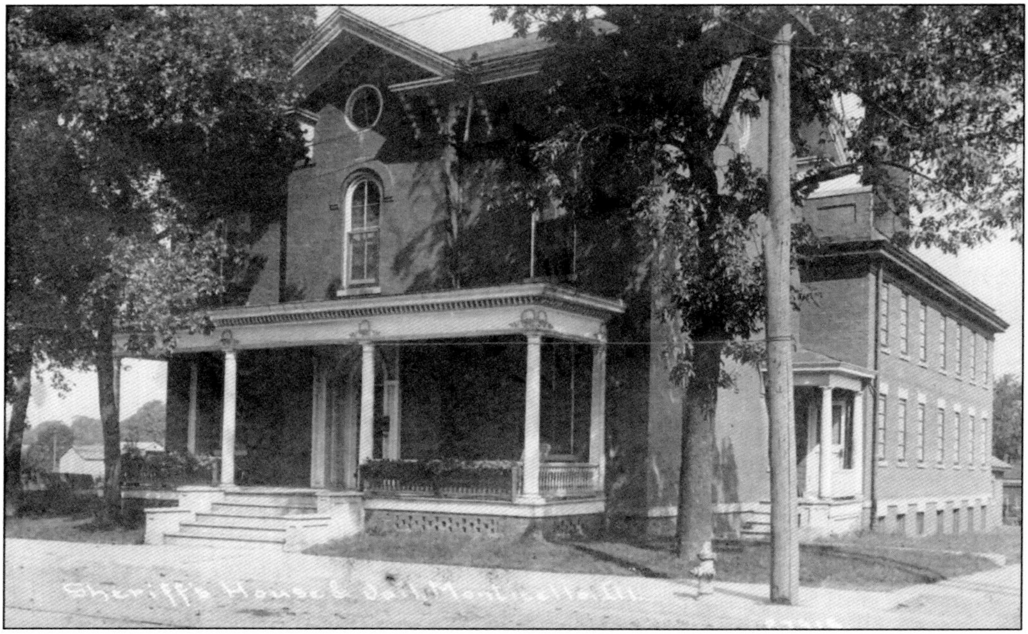

Constructed in 1867 at Livingston and Charter Streets, the Piatt County Jail also served as the sheriff's home. In 1886, a mob (rumored to be Ku Klux Klan) dragged murderer Henry Wildman from jail and shot him nine times while lynching him from one of the property's trees. Until May 2004, the building was the second-oldest jail in Illinois still holding prisoners. It was razed in November 2004. (APL-SR.)

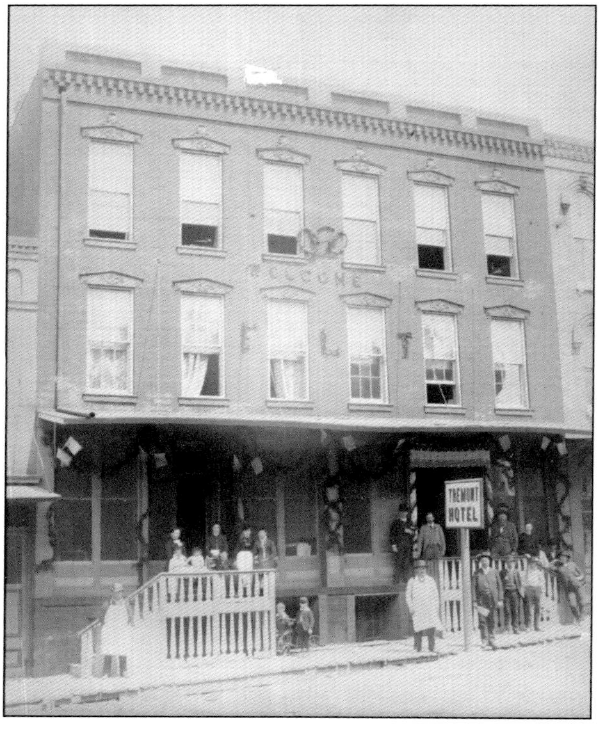

In 1858 Jonathan C. Johnson built the Tremont Hotel, one of the first brick buildings in town, at what is now 204–206 West Washington Street. Johnson eventually became postmaster, justice of the peace, circuit clerk, sheriff, and also opened an icehouse. Subsequent owners named the hotel, among others, the Pierson and Motherspaw Hotel, the Royal Hotel, the National Hotel, and Tinder House. (PCHGS.)

In 1856, Christian Wengenroth established Monticello's first undertaking and furniture business in an existing building at 212 West Washington Street. He built a brick home in 1862 near the southwest corner of Market and Washington Streets. In 1971, the Illinois Pioneer Heritage Center owned it and moved it 60 feet west in order for Amoco to expand its service station. The house now sits at 315 West Washington Street. (MH.)

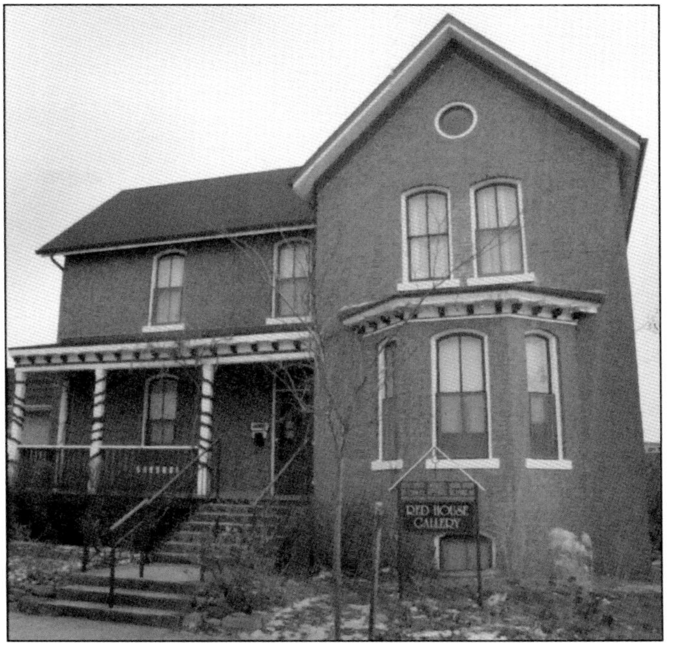

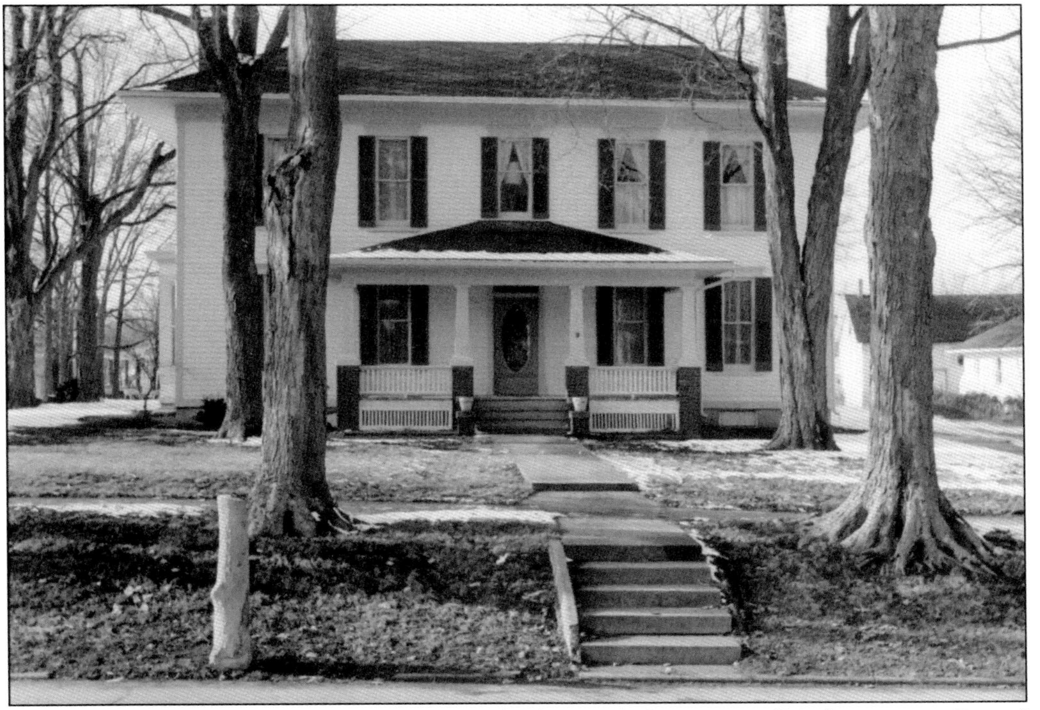

The house at 420 South Charter Street was built c. 1855 by Monticello's first mayor, Daniel Stickel, and his wife, Annabelle (James Piatt's daughter). The Tatmans moved there in 1870. Their two daughters walked the cows from a field behind the house to a pasture in the current Weather Oaks subdivision. Upon the 1977 death of their daughter Eva, her estate established Tatman Village on the edge of Monticello. (APL.)

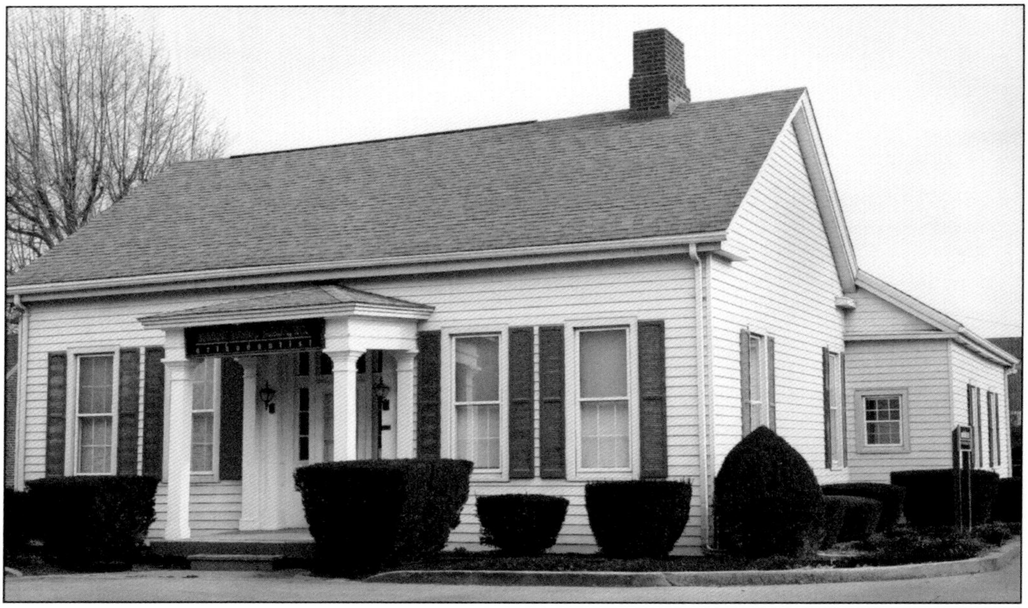

One of the oldest existing houses in Monticello, 817 South Charter Street was home to Mary Jane Piatt Bryden, daughter of James Piatt. She married Monticello merchant William Bryden in 1860, about the time the house was built. In 1858, while Lincoln was visiting her brother Jacob, she helped serve lunch to the future president. The Monticello school district later owned the house and used it for office space. (MH.)

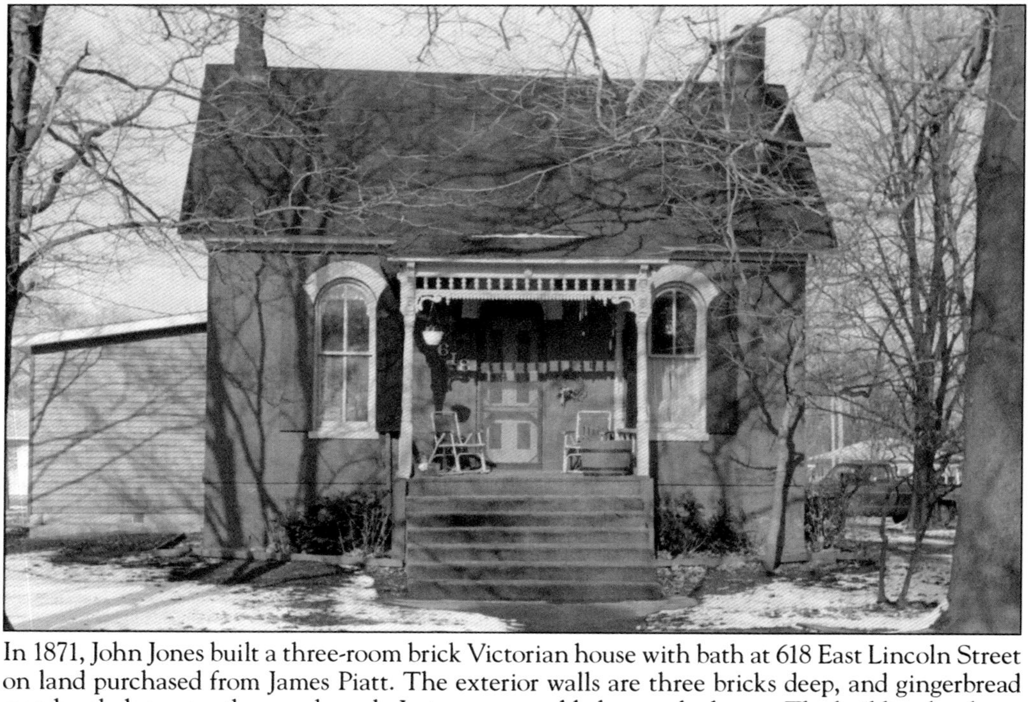

In 1871, John Jones built a three-room brick Victorian house with bath at 618 East Lincoln Street on land purchased from James Piatt. The exterior walls are three bricks deep, and gingerbread woodwork decorates the wood porch. Later owners added on to the house. The building has been placed on the Historical Preservation Board list. (APL.)

The brick Gothic Revival and Italianate house at 404 South Charter Street was built around 1872 for Dr. J.W. Coleman, a Monticello doctor and Piatt County's first superintendent of schools. At one time, a tower dominated the house. From 1912 until 1949, another superintendent of schools, Charles McIntosh, and his family lived there. Painted gray for years, the house was sandblasted down to the original red brick in 1992. (APL.)

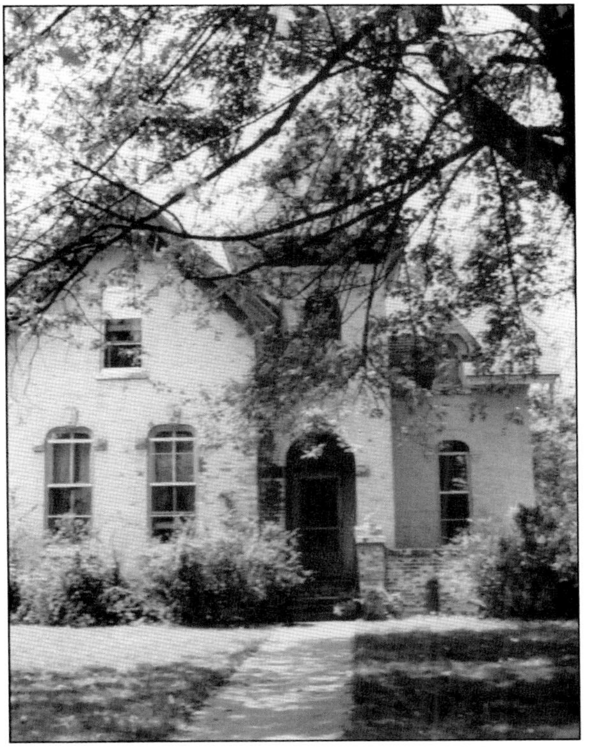

Built in the 1860s, this house at 405 West William Street was owned by Dr. William B. Noecker, who had also owned what is now 603 East Center Street. This 10-room house's circular walnut staircase was difficult to build and unusual for the times. With barn and outbuildings, the home sat on almost seven acres and was sold for $4,700 in 1924 after the death of Noecker's widow, Ella. (PCHGS.)

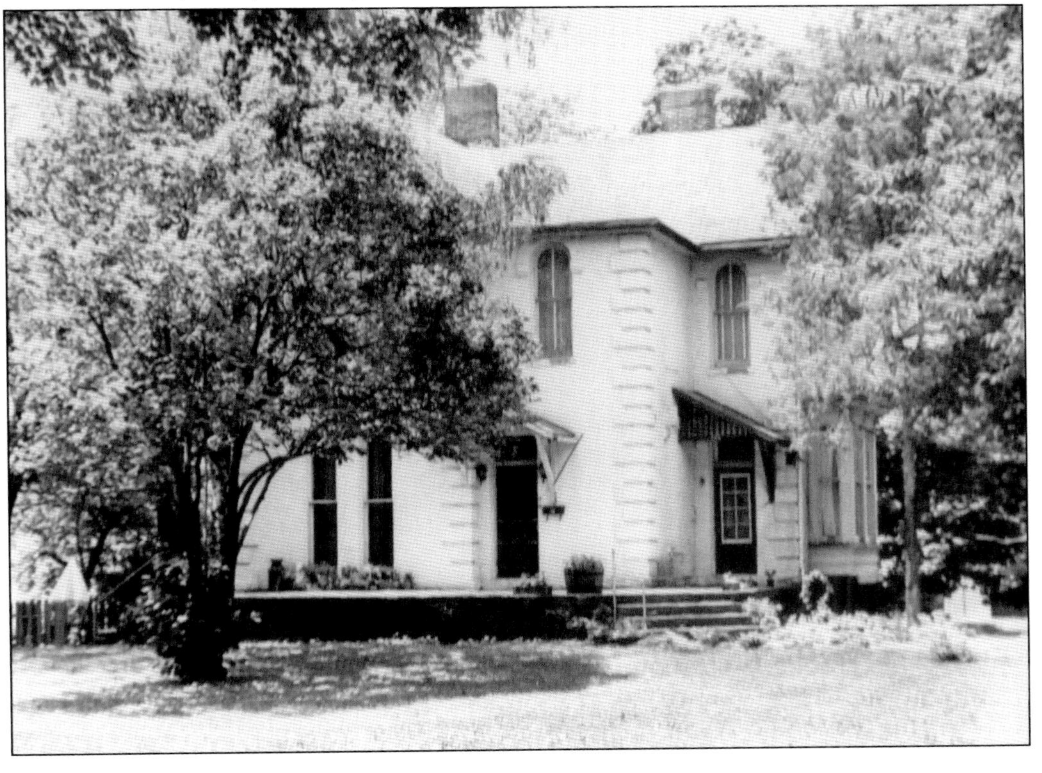

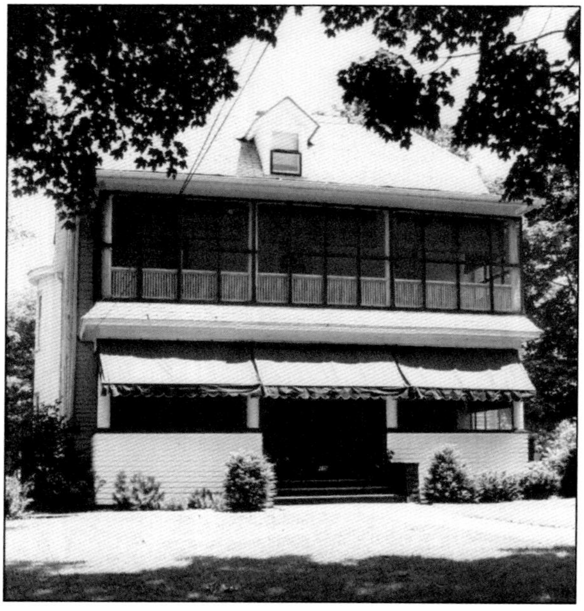

One of the first houses on the street, 419 South Charter Street was built around 1873. A tower once graced the rear corner of the house, but owners in the 1940s removed it. When early resident Martha Porter became an invalid, a newly-installed hand-operated elevator allowed her access from the basement to the second floor. Dry goods merchant H.P. Martin lived there after the Porters. (APL.)

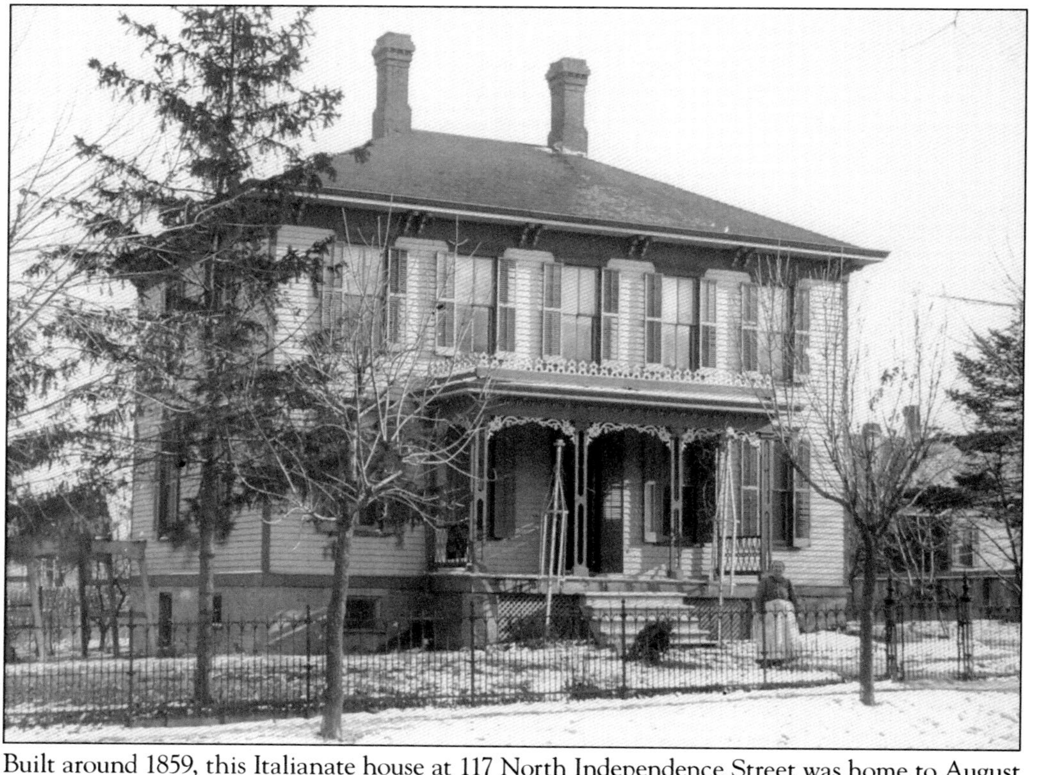

Built around 1859, this Italianate house at 117 North Independence Street was home to August and Elizabeth Louise (Hammerschmidt) Zybell. They married in St. Louis in 1857, and the next year they settled in Monticello, where he established the first shoe business in Piatt County. The woman is most probably Elizabeth Louise. Sharon and Edward Williams joined the house to their Leiper Furniture store in 1985. (SW.)

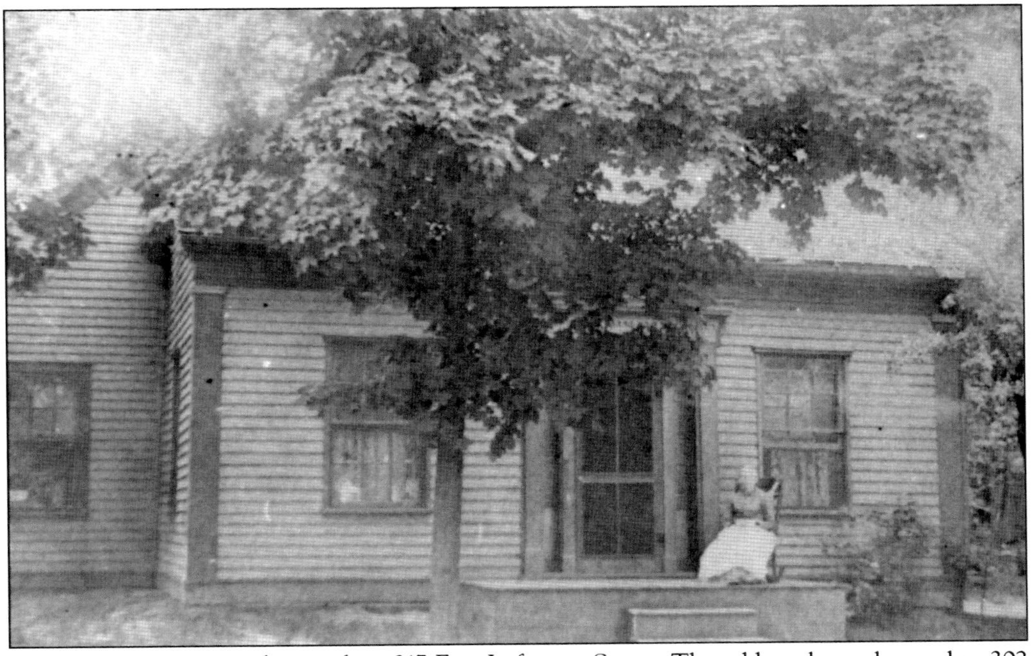

Martha Barnes sits on the porch at 217 East Lafayette Street. The address later changed to 302 South Hamilton Street, and the front door now looks out upon Hamilton Street. Prior to post office facilities being located inside businesses on the square, the two front rooms of this house served as Monticello's post office. The post office was inside a store at 108 West Washington Street in 1869. (PCHGS.)

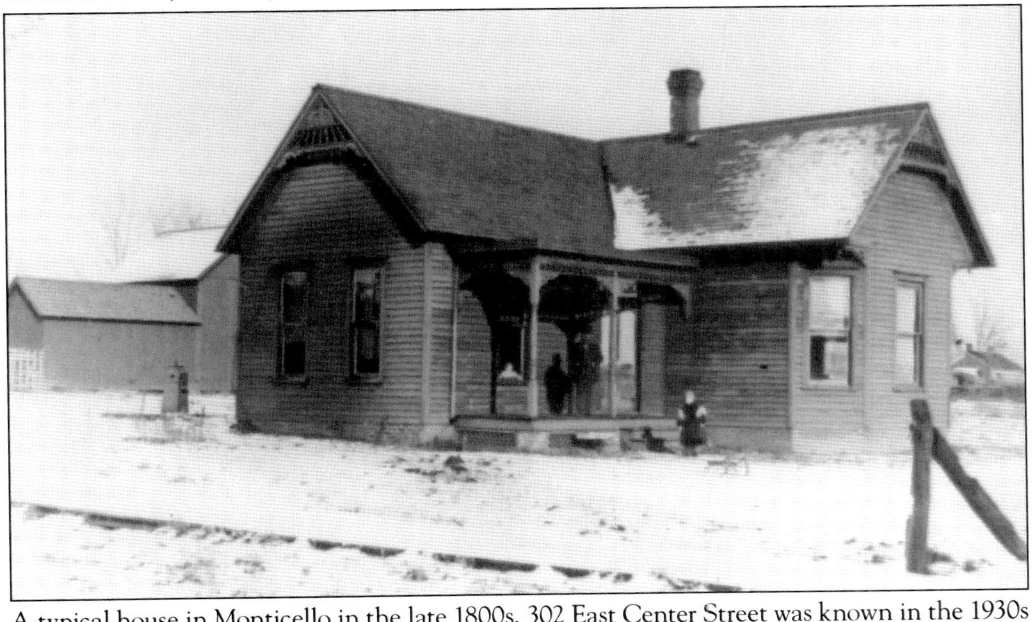

A typical house in Monticello in the late 1800s, 302 East Center Street was known in the 1930s as the "Little Doc Jones" house although, at the time, carpenter Fred B. Fitzwater owned it (from 1935 until 1940). Richard Jones stands on the porch. Other owners included L. Hammerschmidt and A.C. Ahlrich. (SR.)

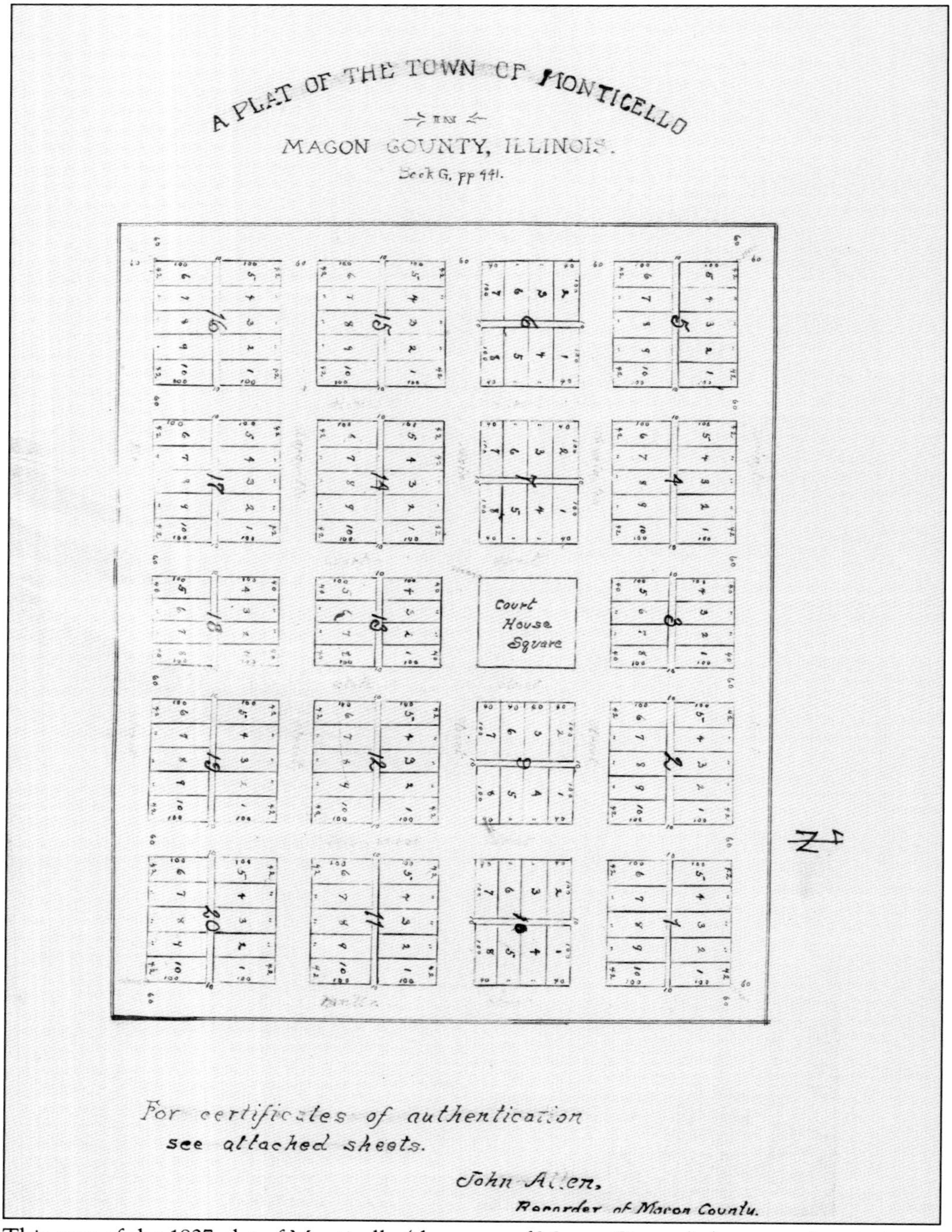

This map of the 1837 plat of Monticello (then part of Macon County) shows north pointing to the right, with Livingston Street running along that side. Block one appears in the lower right corner, incrementally moving up along Washington Street, then down to Hamilton Street, which runs across the bottom of the image. There are 20 blocks in the "Original Town." (PCCC.)

Two

Courthouse Square and Community 1870s–1900

From the 1870s onward, businesses flourished in Monticello. Attorneys, restaurants, shoe stores, meat markets, hotels, groceries, dry goods, and furniture and undertaking businesses clustered around the square on Washington, Main, Charter (known briefly in 1889 as "Englewood"), and State Streets.

The first Monticello bank, H.R. Huston and Company, opened in 1870 with H.V. Moore as a partner. The new Monticello Railroad to Champaign was being finished in 1871. That same year, residents suffered from smoke and haze wafting south from the Great Chicago Fire.

Nathan Rhoades excited townspeople in 1873 when he built the Rhoades Opera House on the square. All saloons closed down in 1880 after Piatt County became the first county in Illinois to stop sales of liquor of less than one gallon. Only druggists and physicians were allowed a license to sell liquor.

A multitude of new brick buildings around the courthouse replaced many destroyed by large fires in 1875, 1887, and 1888. In 1885, for protection against the constant threat of fire, the Huffman Brothers installed a 57-foot well for downtown merchants. In 1891, a well was dug for the entire city, three sides of the square were paved with stone, and electric light poles lined the square.

Starting in 1878, the newspapers began printing a Letter List noting the addressees of mail not yet picked up from the post office. Rural mail service commenced at the end of the century.

In 1884, Judge Harvey E. Huston invented and manufactured a Telerema telephone that was sold throughout the United States until 1888 when Bell Telephone Company surged in popularity. William F. Lodge installed private telephone lines to his family members and businesses, finally organizing the Piatt County Telephone Company in 1899.

As Monticello expanded, additional schools were built at the north and south ends of town and a third courthouse replaced the second one. Samuel Allerton (a cattle baron, area landowner, and third-richest man in Chicago) and his wife, Agnes, helped provide for the new library—which was named after her. Lyda Coleman, the first librarian, served the public from 1897 until 1912.

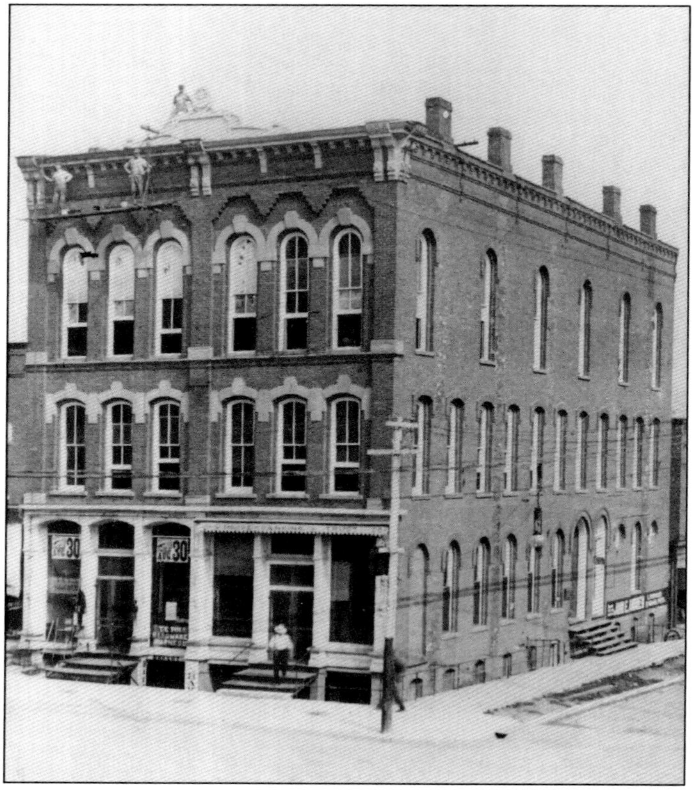

Workmen stand atop the Rhoades Opera House, completed in 1873 at 100 West Washington Street, site of the first dwelling built after the town was platted. The opera house offered seating for 500 people on the top floor. In 1897, it was converted into a roller-skating rink. The downstairs east half held the H.V. Moore Banking and Trust Company. The *Monticello Bulletin* newspaper offices occupied the basement. (PCHGS.)

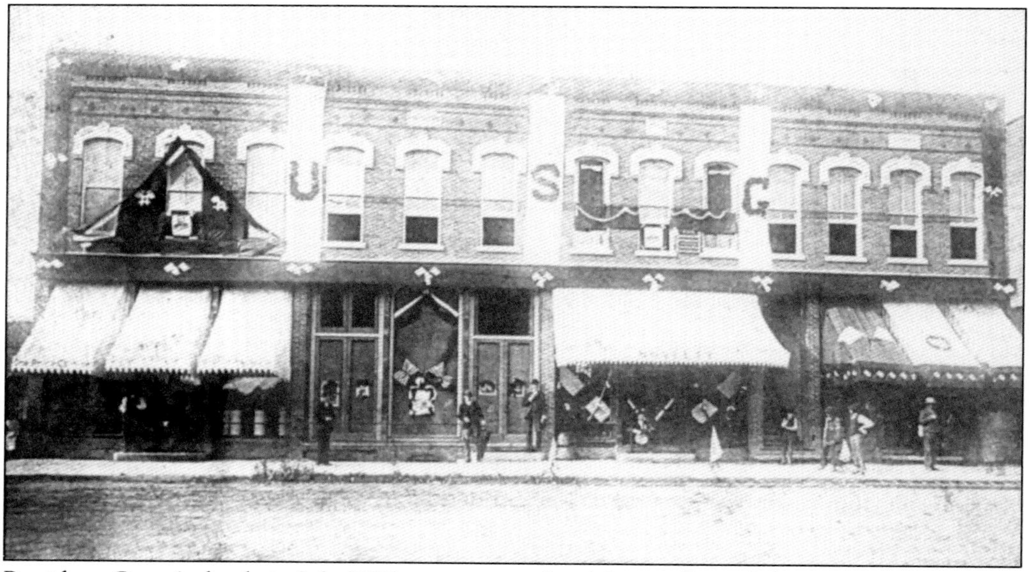

President Grant's death in July 1885 was mourned in Monticello with bunting hanging down from windows on Washington Street across from the courthouse. The letters *U*, *S*, and G were sewn onto three strips suspended from a piece of bunting running the length of the building. Additional dark bunting and crossed American flags added to the town's homage to the former president. (APL.)

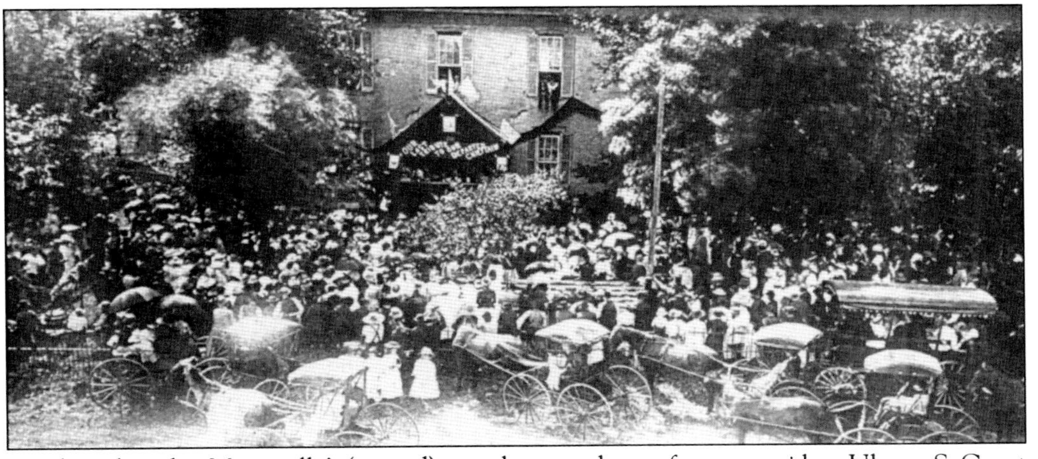

People gathered at Monticello's (second) courthouse to honor former president Ulysses S. Grant with a public display of affection. In this 1885 photograph, citizens gather on foot and in carriages, trying to protect themselves from the hot sun with umbrellas. The banner above the doorway reads, "Our Last Tribute to our Fallen Chieftain." (APL.)

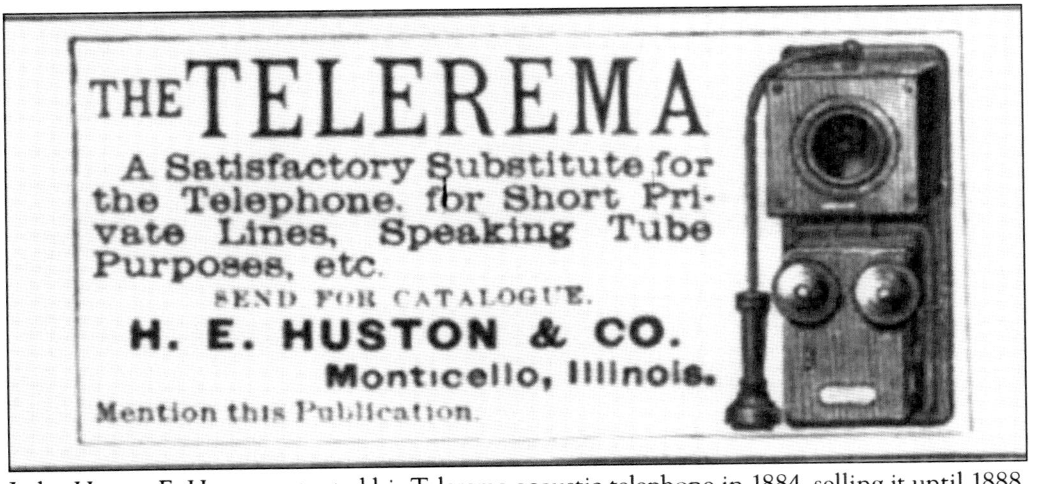

Judge Harvey E. Huston patented his Telerema acoustic telephone in 1884, selling it until 1888, when Alexander Graham Bell's telephone gained a greater foothold among users. Huston also received a patent in 1883 for a mechanical telephone. Huston was married to Susan Stickel (daughter of Daniel Stickel, the owner of the first store in Monticello). Huston died in 1895 in Chicago. (PCHGS.)

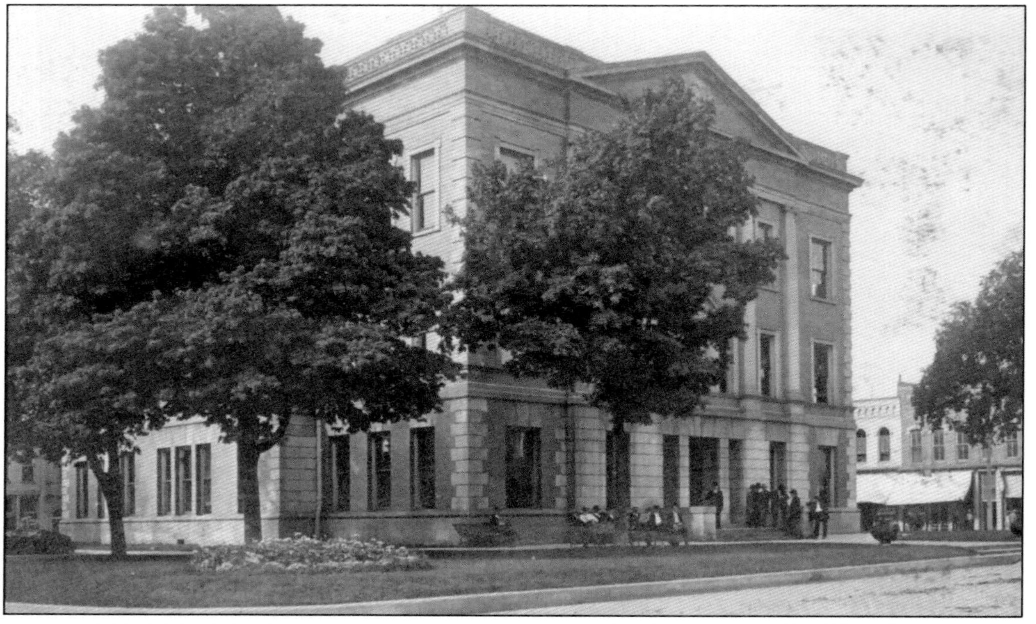

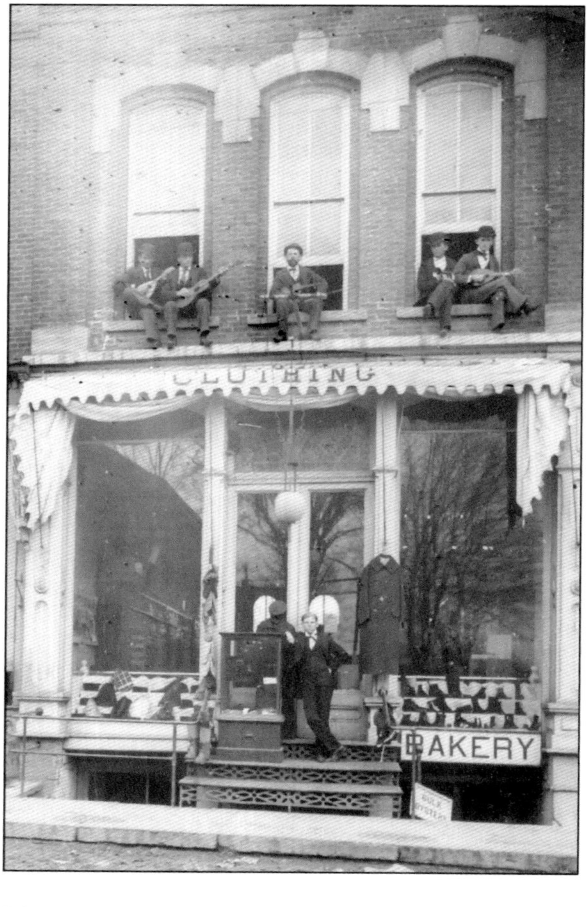

On September 22, 1903, after the third courthouse's foundation was laid, an audience of 6,000 watched the building's cornerstone be placed in position. Architect Joseph Royer of Urbana completed construction of the building in 1904. Steam heating came under the street through pipes from the jail. A group called the "Liars Club" met each afternoon on six courthouse benches, purchased from A.B. Zybell and marked with "L.C." (APL.)

Nathan E. Rhoades and Son Clothing store is seen in 1896 at 102 West Washington Street (where First Mid-Illinois Bank is now located) with five men and their musical instruments sitting in the second floor windows. The men in the windows are, from left to right, William Griffith, John Clark, Persie Jones, unidentified, and Frank Miner. Sherman Metz stands in the doorway. A bakery operated out of the basement. (APL.)

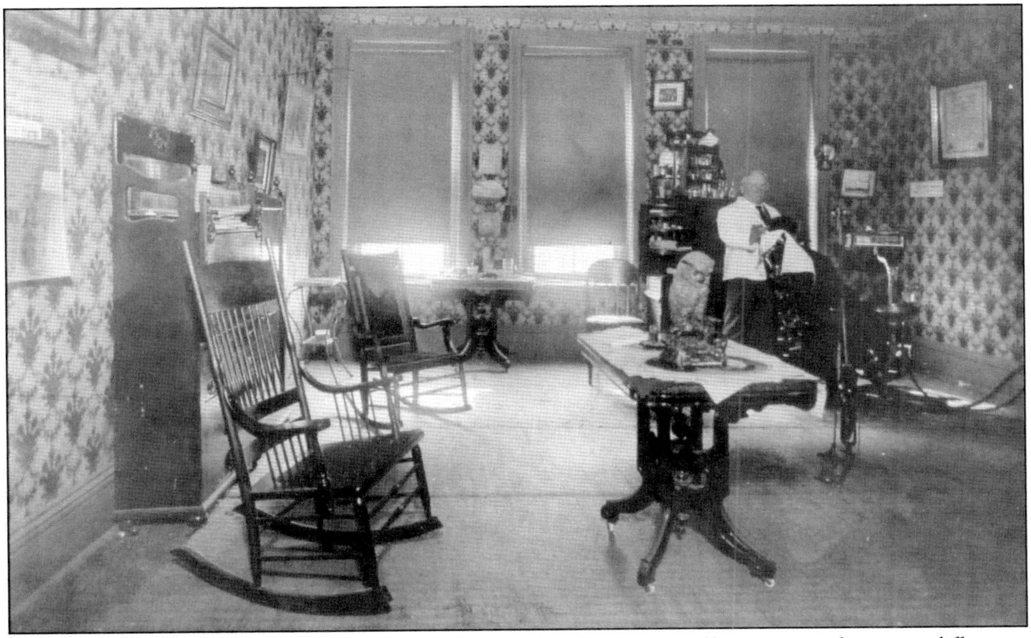

From 1900 until his death in 1914, Dr. William L. Lord's dentist office was on the second floor at 104 West Washington Street. He was one of two sons of Philander A. Lord, who, for a number of years, ran the Boom Store at the corner of West Washington and Market Streets. (APL.)

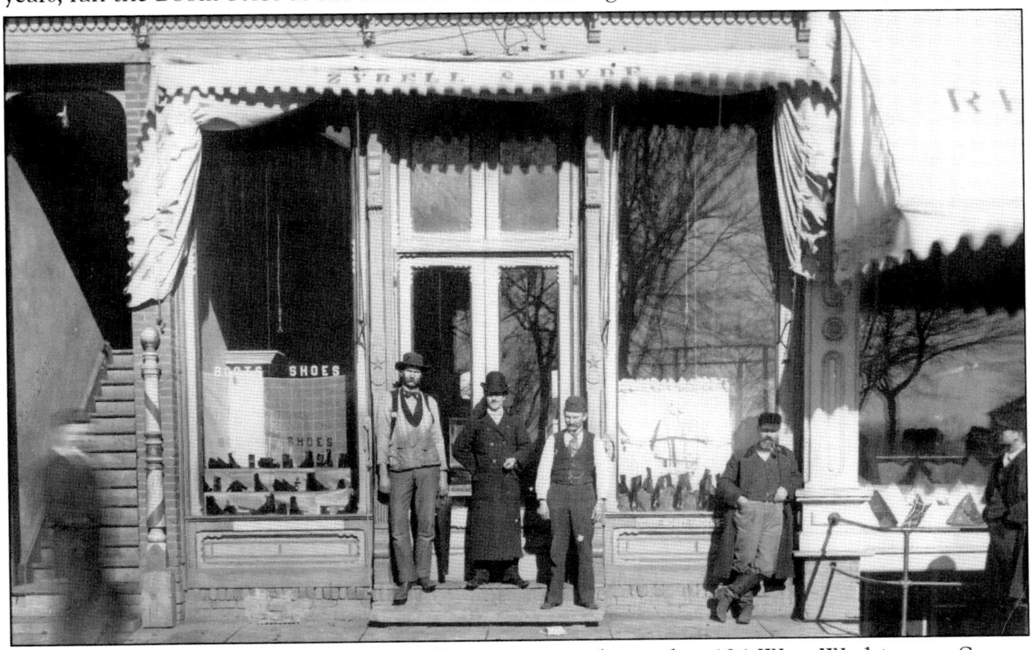

Around 1892, the A.B. Zybell & Hyde Shoe store was located at 104 West Washington Street. August Zybell was born in 1832 in Prussia. As a boy, he herded sheep and geese for Otto von Bismarck. He arrived in Monticello in 1858 and ran his business until 1894. Pictured, from left to right, are unidentified, James Buchanan, unidentified, Zybell's son Robert, Abraham Honselman (Ann Honselman's son), and unidentified. (PCGHS.)

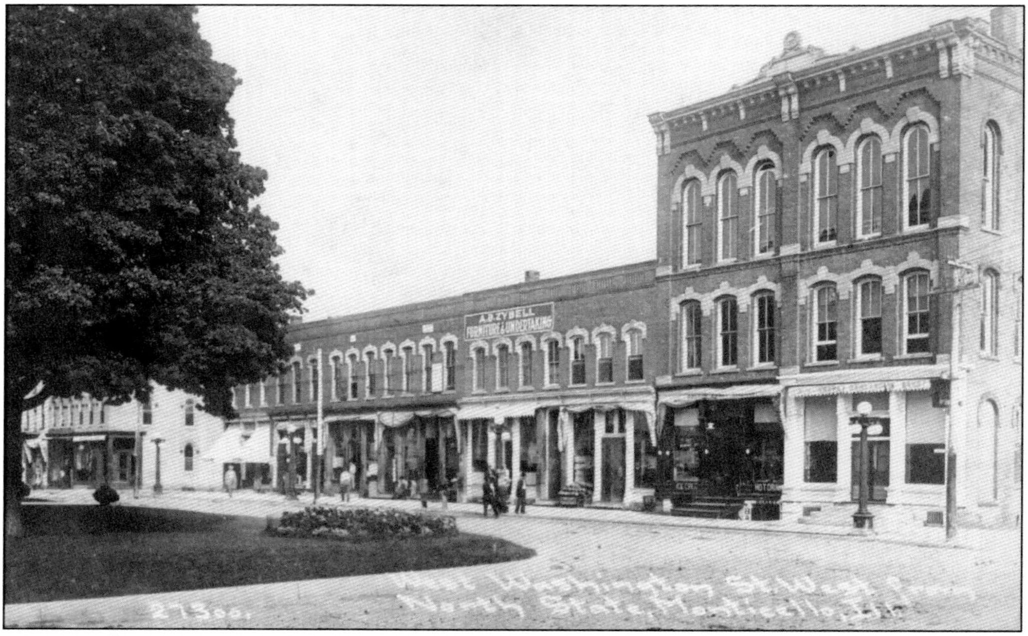

West Washington Street is seen across from the courthouse, with State Street running at the bottom of the photograph. The Moore State Bank replaced the building on the right. Albert B. Zybell (son of the shoe store owner) first operated his furniture and undertaking business at 106 West Washington Street before constructing a building at 112 North State Street that he connected to his other storefront. (APL-SR.)

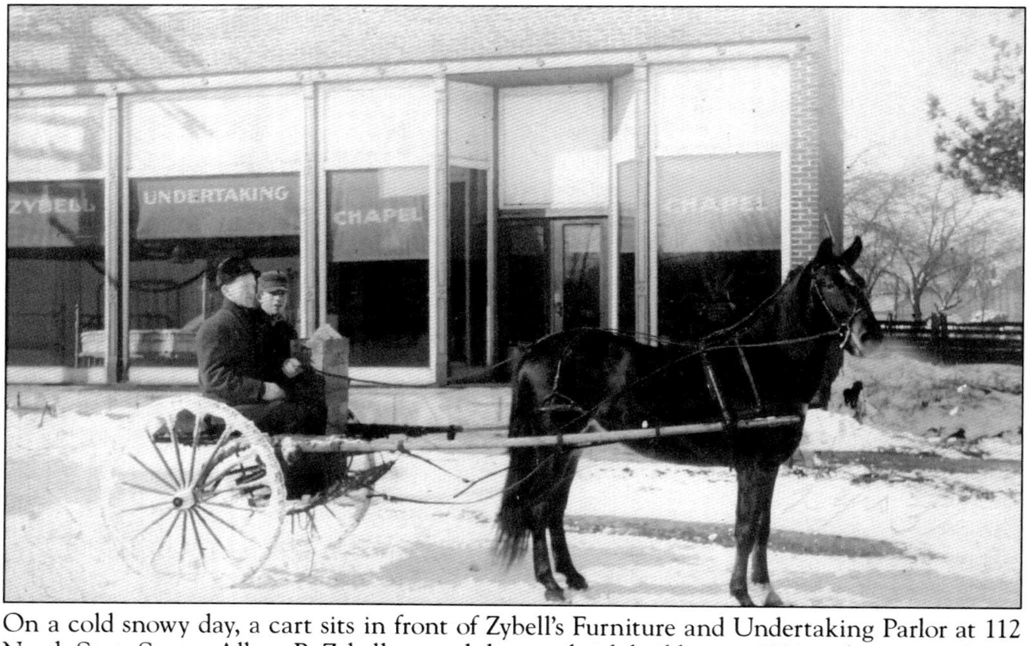

On a cold snowy day, a cart sits in front of Zybell's Furniture and Undertaking Parlor at 112 North State Street. Albert B. Zybell erected the new brick building in 1904 and connected it to his building at 106 West Washington Street. He operated his business until 1924. J.R. Heath and Son purchased the building in 1945. It burned down in 1960. (RS.)

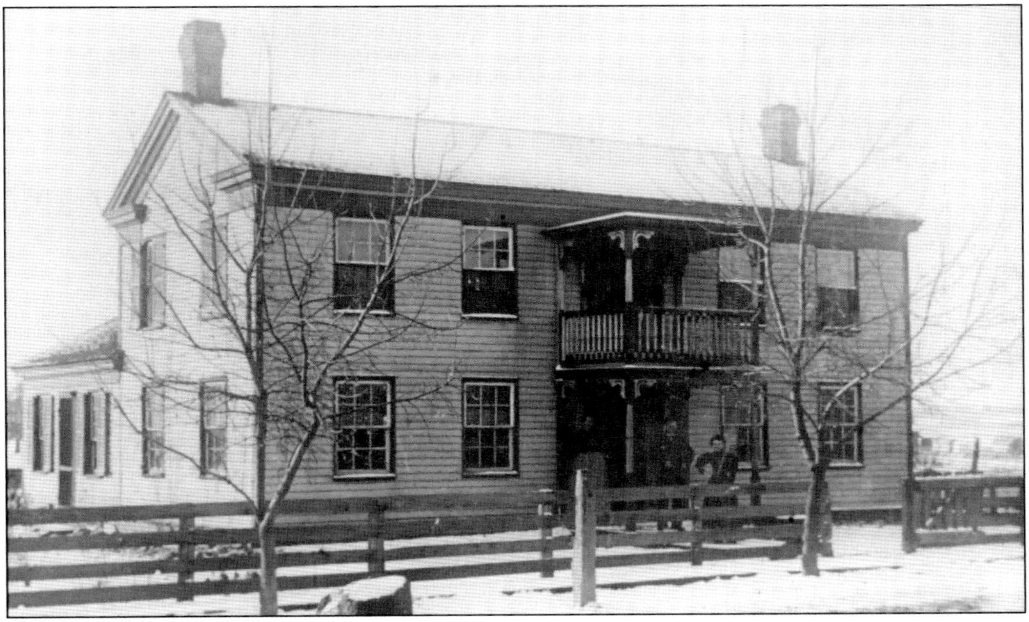

This frame house originally sat at the northeast corner of State and Main Streets. Dr. William B. Noecker sold it in 1880 to John and Matilda Clearwater Griffith, who moved it to its present site at 603 East Center Street. In 1972, it became an antique store, but it is a home once again. (PCHGS.)

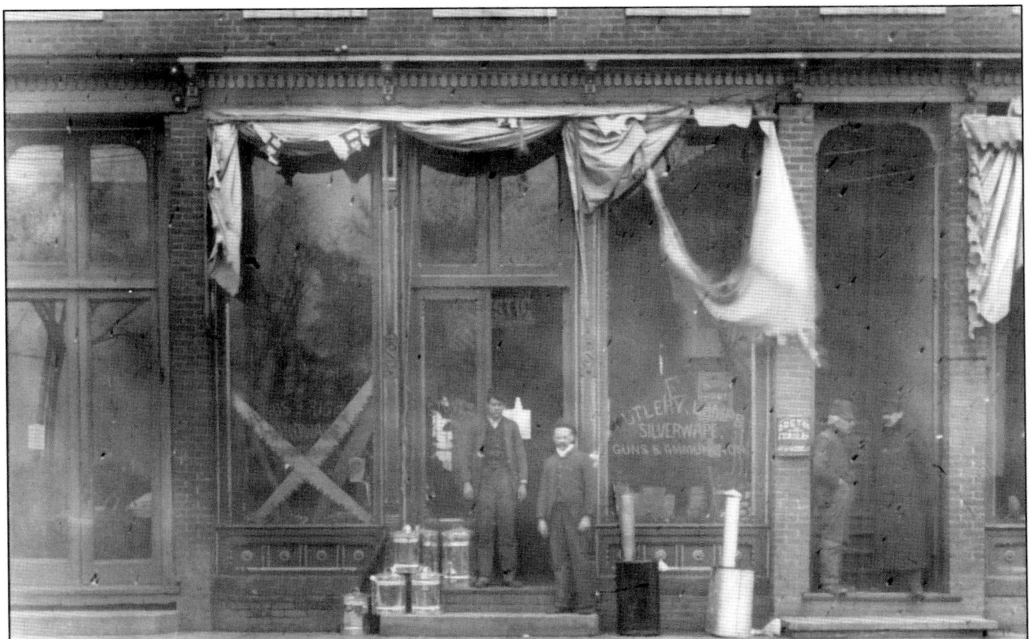

Henry Payne Harris arrived in Monticello in 1889 and partnered with W.S. Ridgely in a hardware store. In 1897, Harris became the sole proprietor of the Harris Hardware Store located at 110 West Washington Street. Crisscrossed saws appear in the left window, and cutlery, silverware, guns, and ammunition are advertised in the right window. The men pictured are, from left to right, Herbert Walsh, William Ridgley, and two unidentified. (PCHGS.)

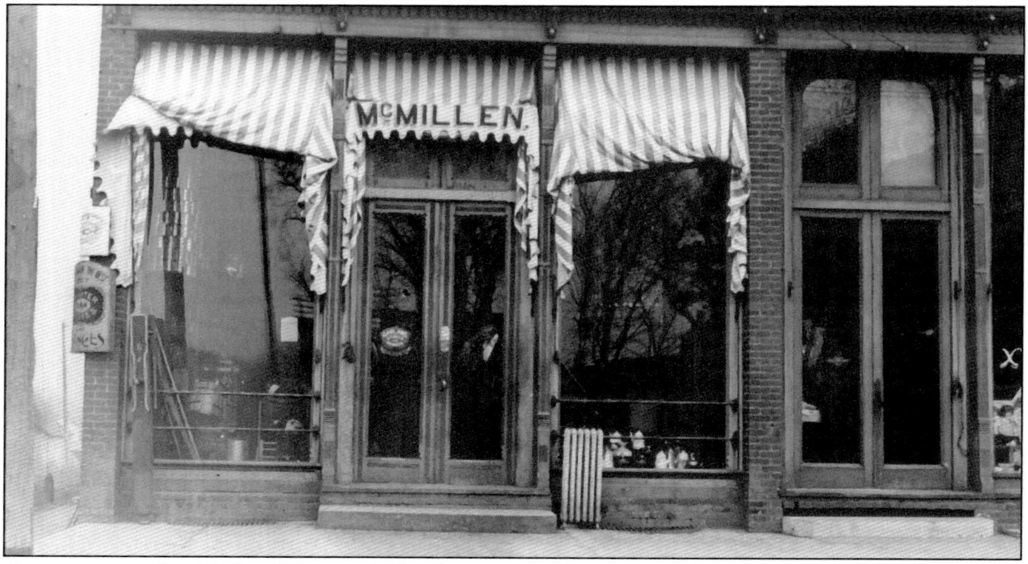

Two men peer from behind doors of Charles Coe's and George McMillen's hardware store, located at 114 West Washington Street. Daniel Stickel, one of the first merchants in town, ran a hardware store at the same location around 1866. Other hardware or grocery stores followed. This structure was built for the *Piatt County Herald* in 1884. Later, it was occupied by Frank Mailander's clothing store and Raycraft Drugs. (PCHGS.)

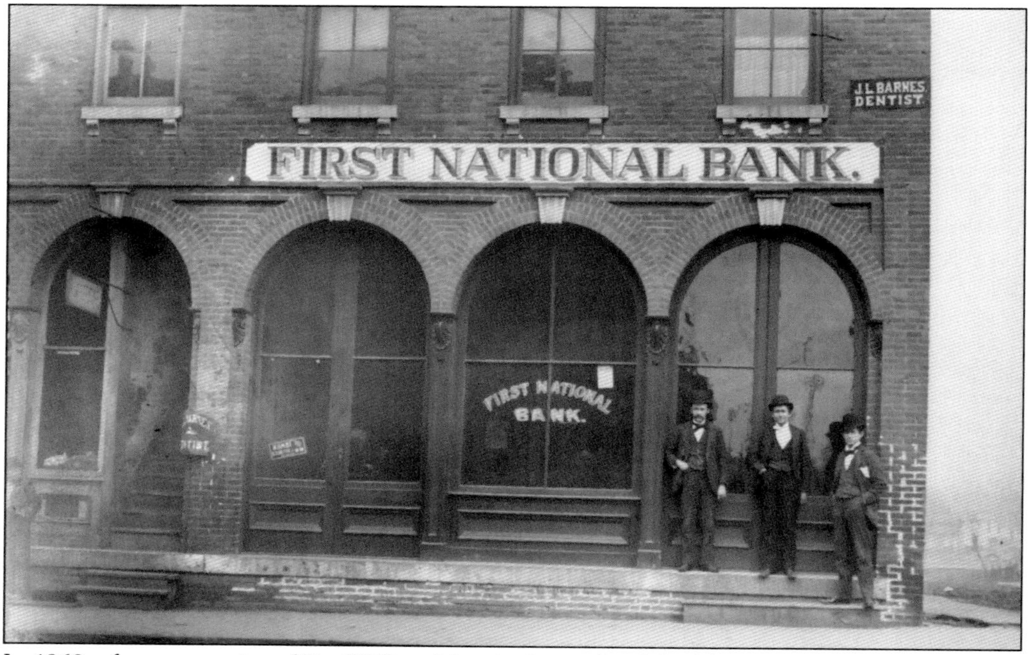

In 1868, after two stories of Dr. William Noecker's new brick building at 200 West Washington Street were already occupied, the structure collapsed. Noecker rebuilt it immediately. There, in 1883, he established the First National Bank. The men in the 1896 photograph are, from left to right, George Noecker, Otis Moore, and William Dighton (bank president in 1921). A dentist, Dr. J.L. Barnes, had offices above the bank. (PCHGS.)

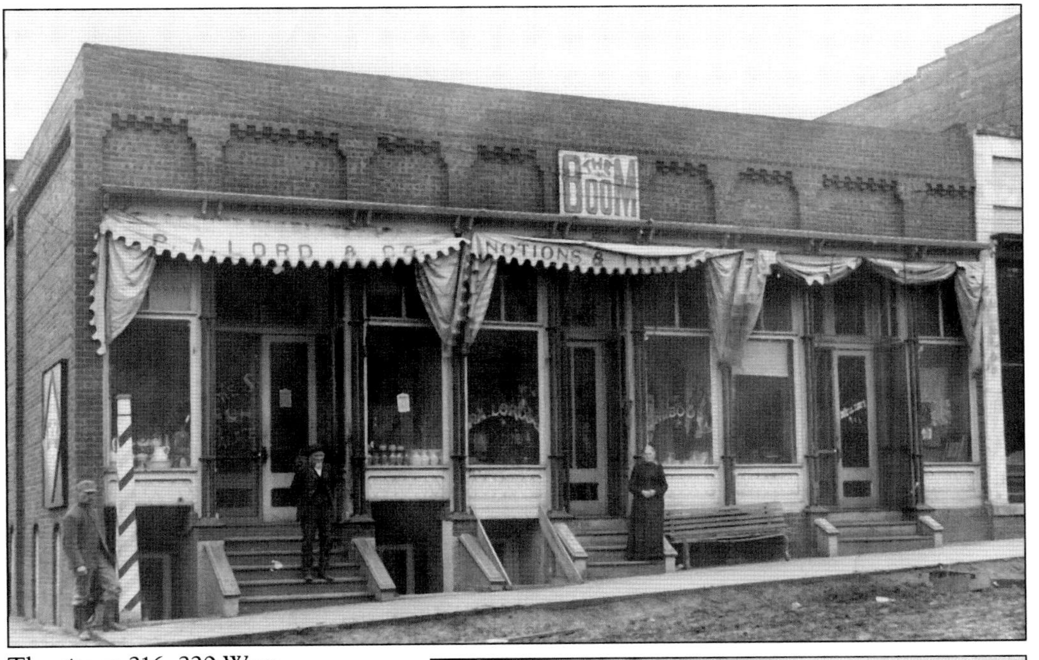

The site at 216–220 West Washington Street was originally home to an old log blockhouse and stockade. The current structure was erected in 1888 on three lots. Mr. and Mrs. Philander A. Lord stand in front of their mercantile and grocery business in this 1893 photograph. The banner reads "The Boom" for the Boom Store. They operated the store from 1890 until 1902. (PCHGS.)

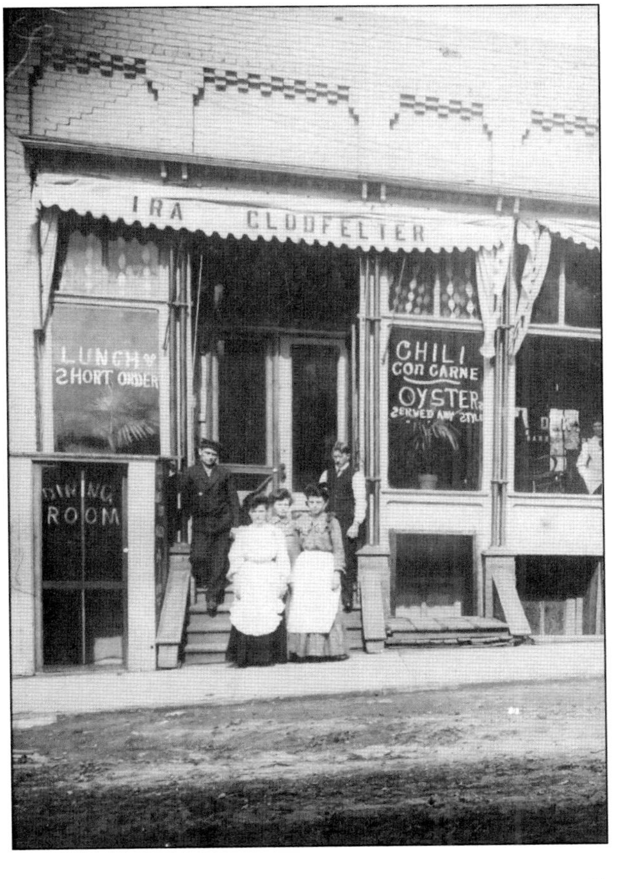

After managing Hotel Sackriter for nine years, Ira Clodfelter then took over the property known as the Boom Store at 218–220 West Washington Street and ran his Corner Restaurant for 22 years until he sold it in 1912. He died in 1928 in an interurban train wreck. Other Clodfelter family members—Howard, Ella, and James—continued to run restaurants on the square over the years. (APL.)

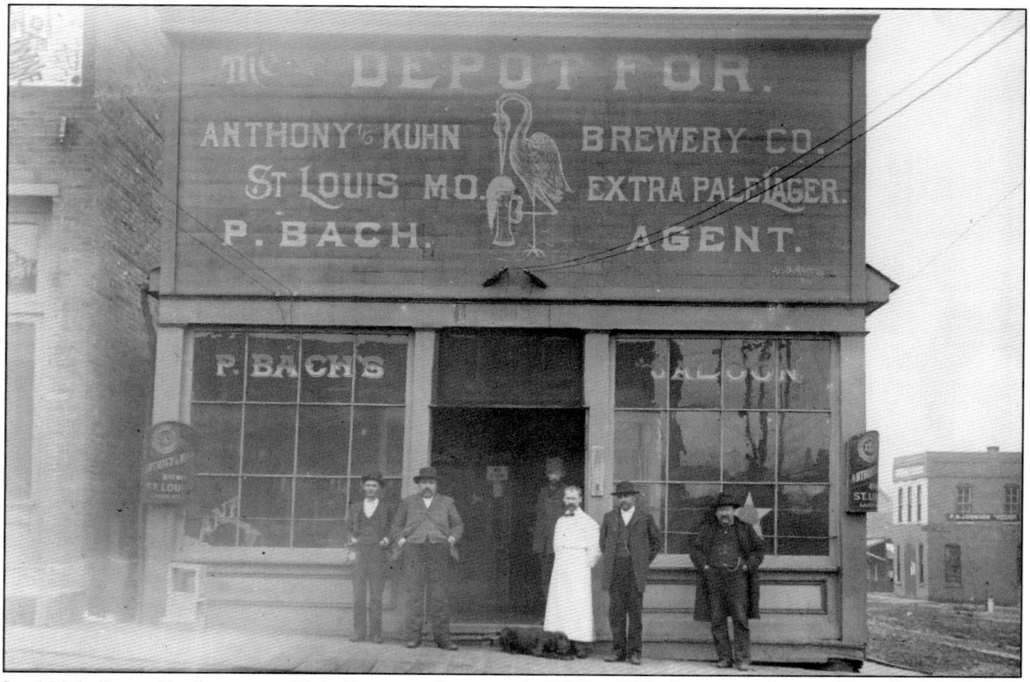

In 1896, Peter Bach opened his Depot saloon at 219 West Washington Street (on the southeast corner of Market and Washington Streets), selling Extra Pale Lager from the Anthony Kuhn Brewery Co. of St. Louis. Dutch Norfolk (left) and Peter Bach stand to the left of the doorway. William Fisher (third from right), Peter Bach Jr. (second from right), and Walter Johnson stand to the right. The site has housed mostly restaurants or taverns since 1896. (PCHGS.)

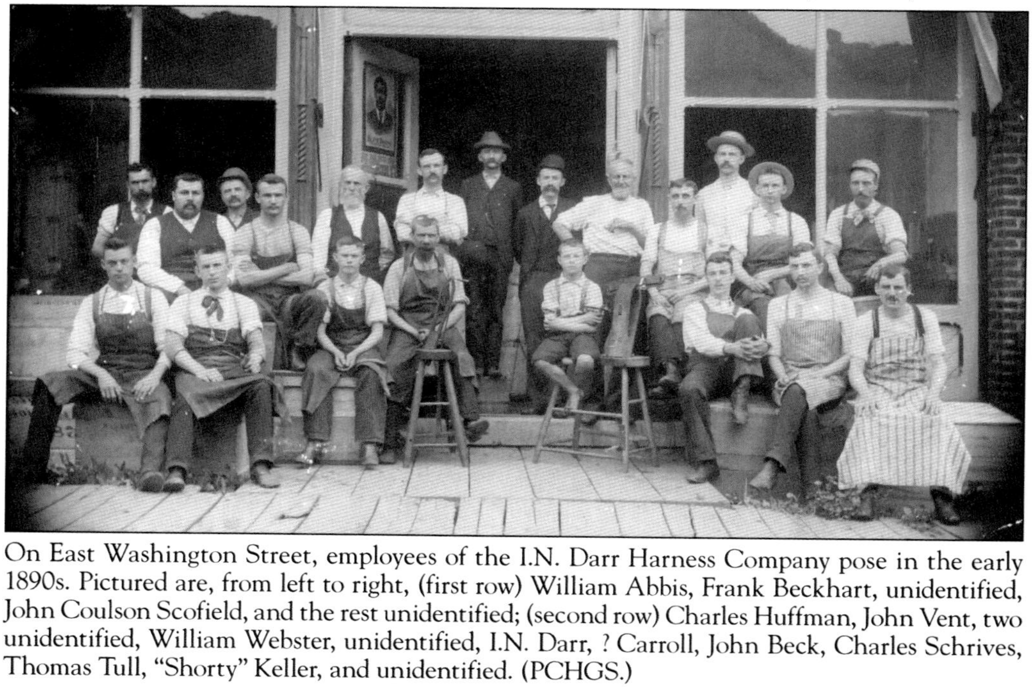

On East Washington Street, employees of the I.N. Darr Harness Company pose in the early 1890s. Pictured are, from left to right, (first row) William Abbis, Frank Beckhart, unidentified, John Coulson Scofield, and the rest unidentified; (second row) Charles Huffman, John Vent, two unidentified, William Webster, unidentified, I.N. Darr, ? Carroll, John Beck, Charles Schrives, Thomas Tull, "Shorty" Keller, and unidentified. (PCHGS.)

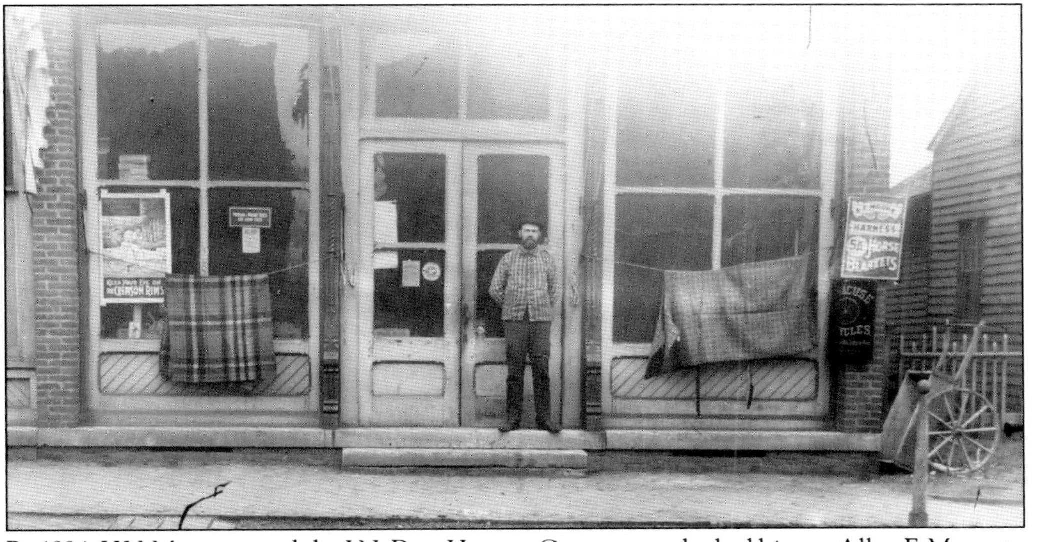

By 1894, H.V. Moore owned the I.N. Darr Harness Company and asked his son Allen F. Moore to manage it for him. Eventually, Allen owned the business. The sign on the right reads "A.F. Moore Harness." The man in the photograph has been listed as either Thomas Tull or Fred Schenck. Tull also owned a harness and hardware business in town. (PCHGS.)

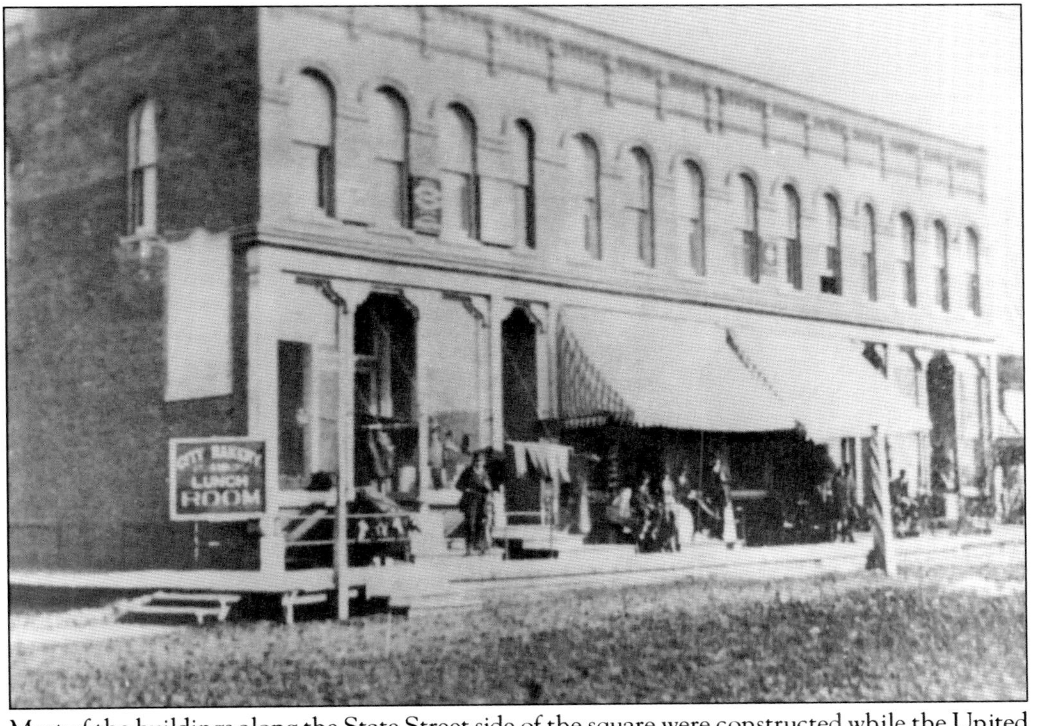

Most of the buildings along the State Street side of the square were constructed while the United States recovered from the 1873 depression. In 1875, Devore and Miller erected several brick office buildings there. The area was called the Union Block. A two-story building, nicknamed "Old Romeo," used for the Masonic hall, was located on the block but was relocated around town several times. (PCHGS.)

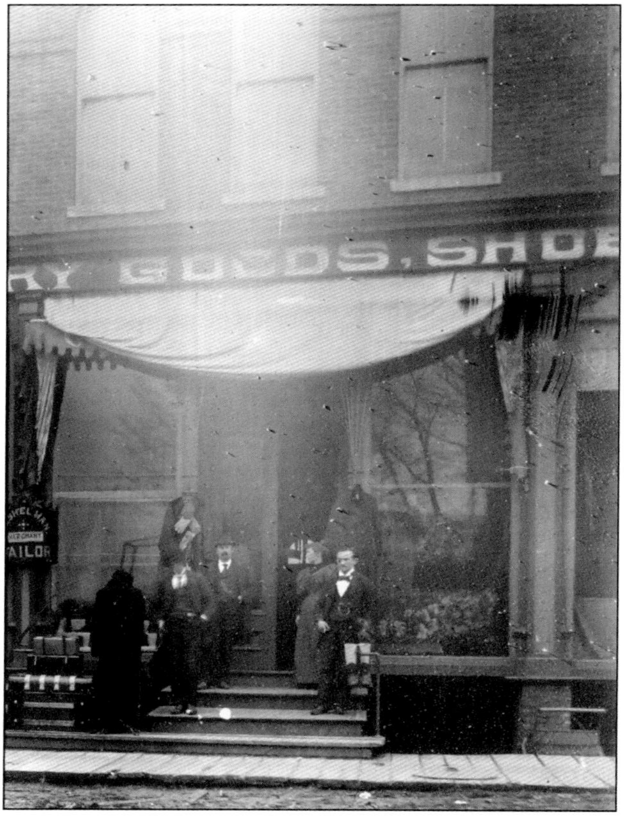

From 1879 until approximately 1885, J.W. Race Dry Goods was located at 103–105 South State Street. The company changed its name to the Race-Handlin Company in 1892. In 1894, when J.N. Dighton erected a new two-story building covering four lots at the northeast corner of Washington and State Streets, Race-Handlin took over three of those lots for its business. (PCHGS.)

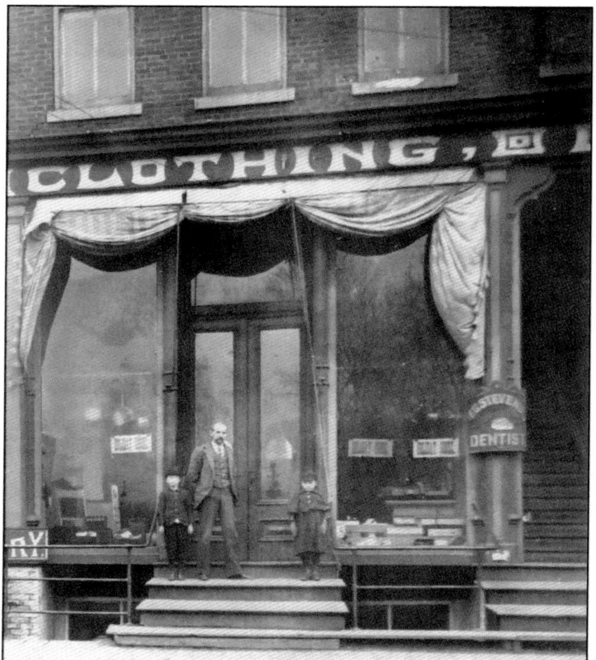

Horace Meacham stands in front of a store near 101 South State Street in the Union Block in the early 1900s. Signs for "Holiday Goods" appear in the windows. A dentist, Dr. F.G. Stevens, had offices upstairs. Business such as George McMillen's Hardware, William Eshelman Tailor, Dresback Bakery, Stamets Inn, Hemphill's Café, and others were located there over the years. (PCHGS.)

Located at 109 South State Street, Rocksy's Lunch Room & Confectionery sold lemonade, fruits, tobacco, and cigars in the early 1900s. The men in the photograph are, from left to right, William Fisher, Ira Snyder, Elmer Walsh, Wirt Rock, and Irvin Martin. Other, later businesses included Jones and Litters Meat Market, Kash-Karry Market, and Oehmke's Pure Food Market. (PCHGS.)

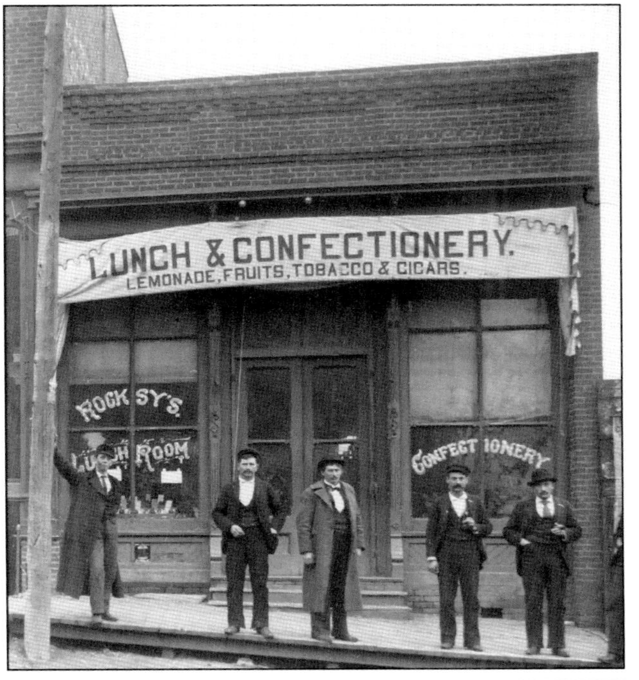

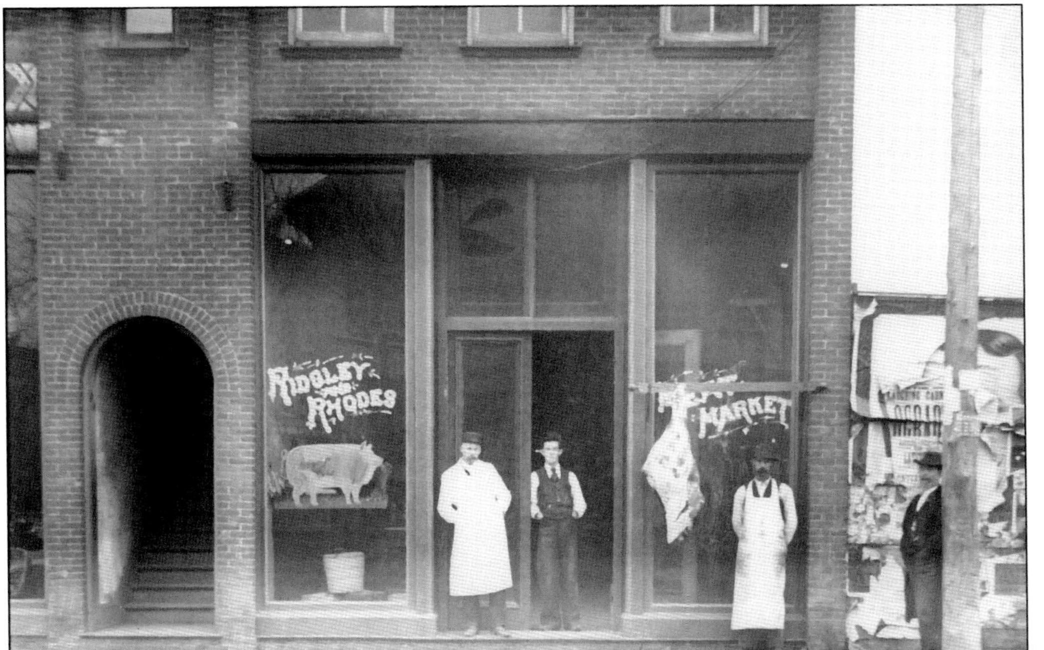

Ridgely and Rhodes Meat Market opened at 102 East Washington Street around 1893 before J.N. Dighton constructed his large building on the northeast corner of State and Washington Streets. From left to right, the men are John Ridgely, Piatt Smith, possibly Rhodes, and Morris McMillen. McMillen ran a bakery immediately west of the butchers. (PCHGS.)

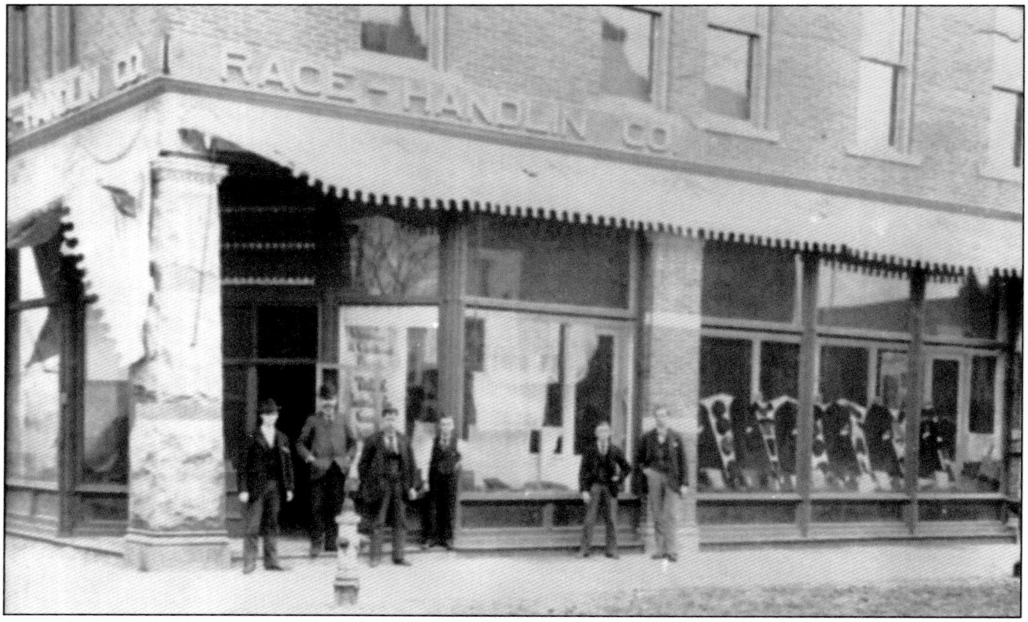

Out of view in this photograph, an iron drinking fountain resembling a long-haired man holding a basket stood near Race-Handlin when the company moved to East Washington Street. People used tin cups attached to the fountain to catch water dribbling out of the statue's mouth. Horses drank from the basket, and dogs slurped from an iron pan at the fountain's feet, sometimes preferring to lap at the fountain's mouth. (APL.)

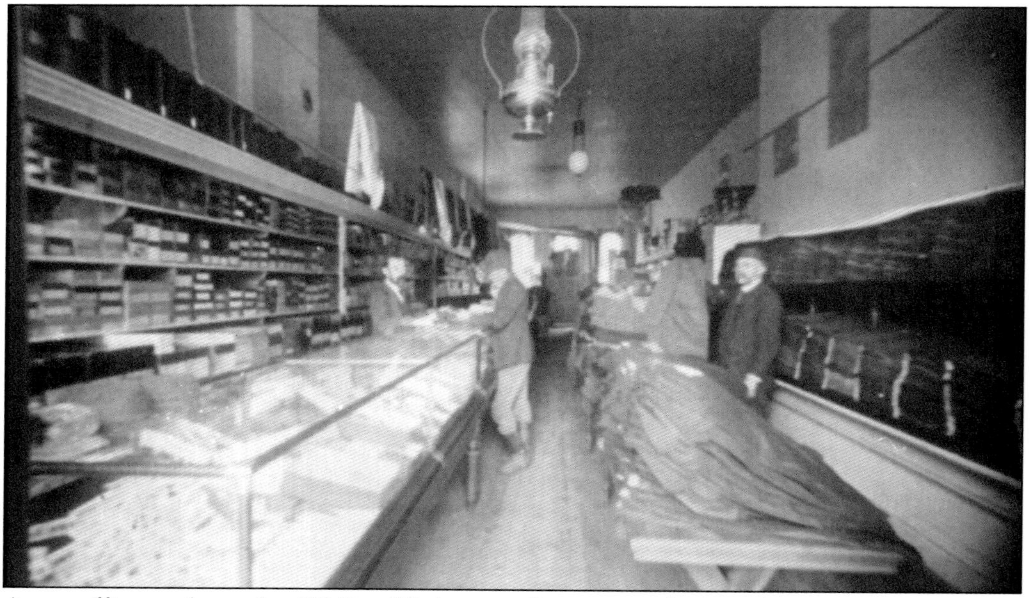

A post office was located at 102 East Washington Street around 1874. After Dighton constructed his buildings in 1882, Race-Handlin took over three of the new spaces. Each boasted a 21-foot frontage and 100-foot depth. Race-Handlin Company was sold around 1910, becoming the H.P. Martin Company. With more ownership changes, it changed names to the M & M 5 Cent to $1.00 Store, Kaiser's, and eventually Stage's. (APL.)

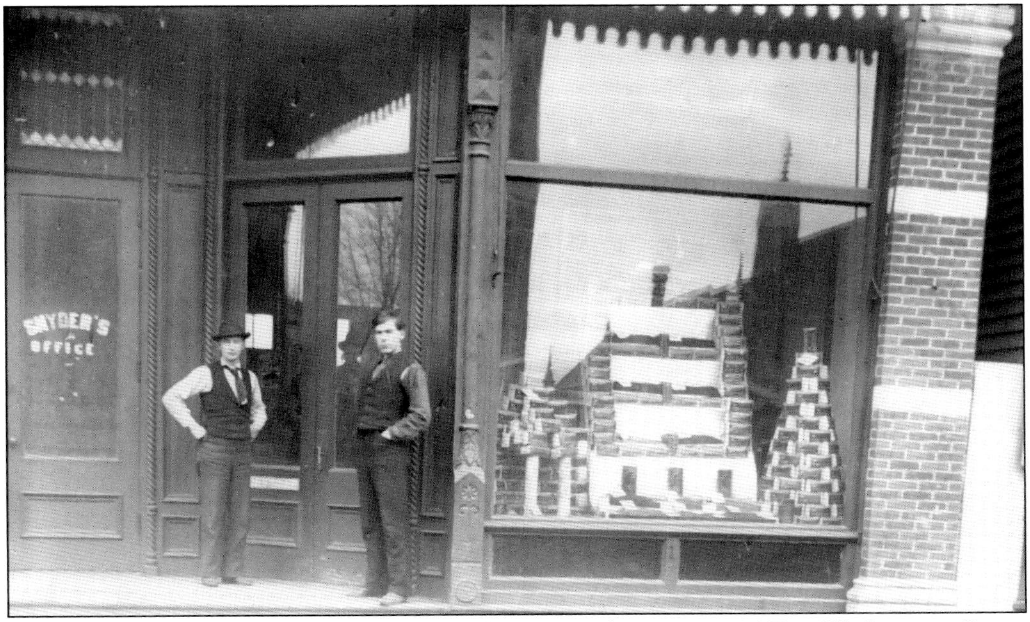

Keith Knott (left) and Charles Hinton stand in front of a store at 106 East Washington Street with bags of coffee displayed in the window. For years, J.N. Dighton had owned the corner lot and the building occupied by T.M. McMillen's bakery. Dighton also owned the next lot, where Ridgely and Rhodes Meat Market operated. (PCHGS.)

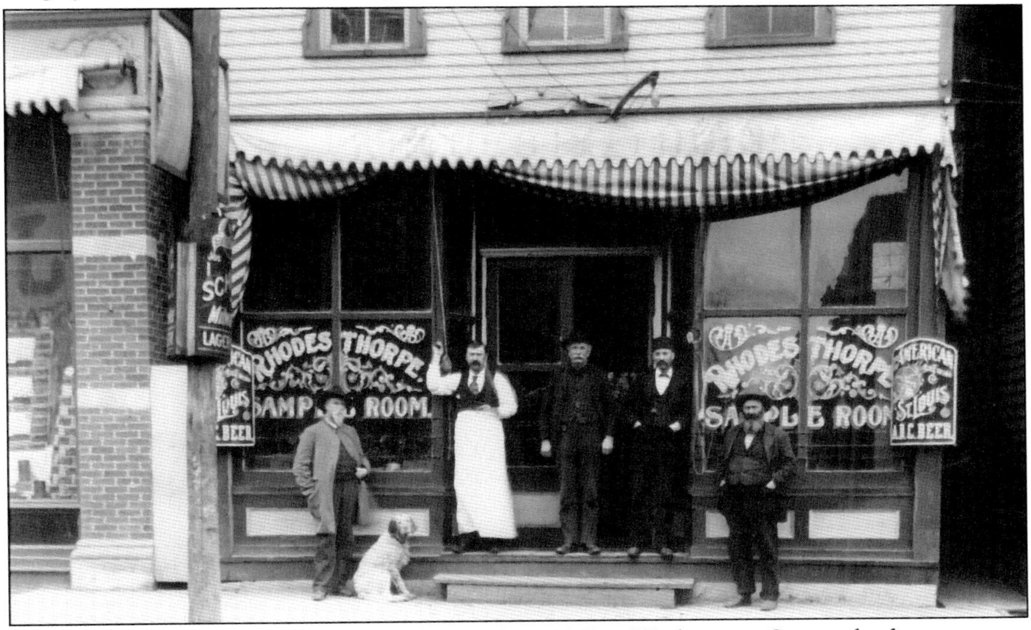

The Rhodes-Thorpe Sample Room was located at 108 East Washington Street, the first structure east of the new Dighton four-lot building at Washington and State Streets. Signs on the left and right advertise American St. Louis A.B.C. Beer. In front of the frame building are, from left to right, John Albert, Pointo (or possibly Pointer) the dog, Edward Thorpe, William Robison, George Rhoades, and William Scott. (APL.)

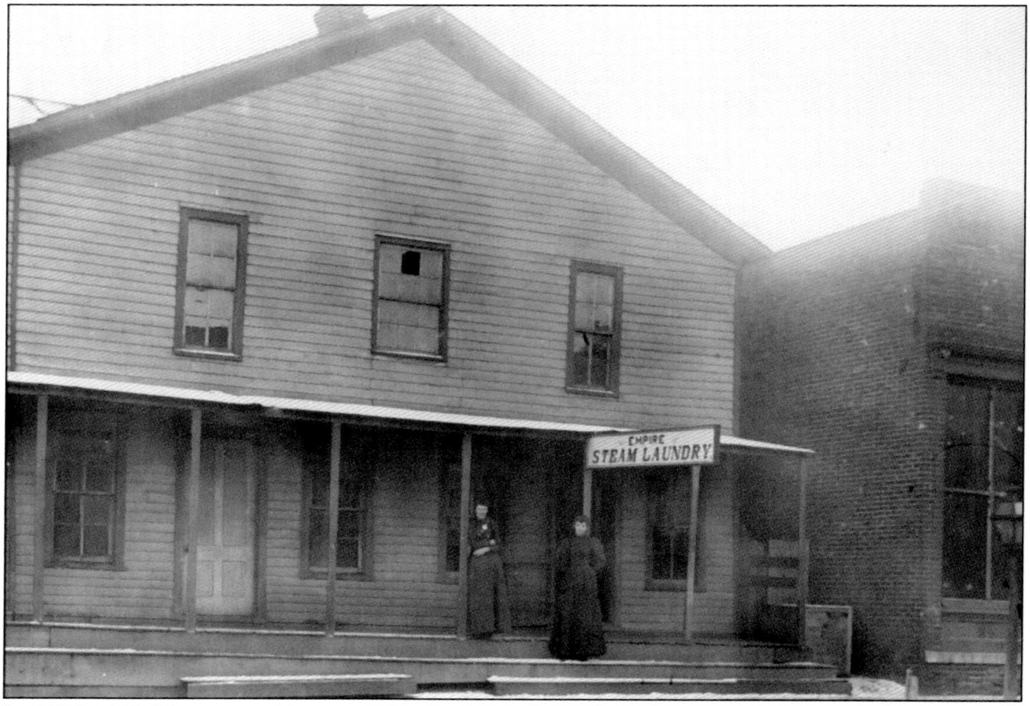

In 1895, Mell Cline moved her new Empire Steam Laundry to 115 East Washington Street, at the corner of Independence Street, near the England Hotel. She employed between six and twelve people. This 1898 photograph shows Cline and her daughter Alma Kreason, who, along with her husband, Benjamin, ran the laundry. The Fireproof Garage, now incorporating Fasprint and other businesses, was later built here. (PCHGS.)

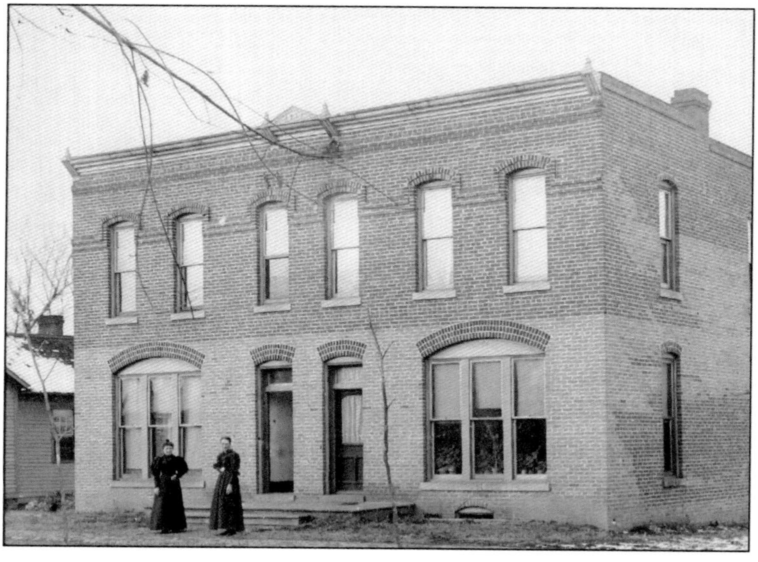

In 1893, Dr. Knott Jr. built a brick duplex, the first such building in Monticello, at 206–208 East Washington Street. Standing in front of the duplex are Mollie Knott (left) and her mother, Mrs. Lyons. Eventually, this structure became known as the Stayton Duplex. It was demolished in 1998 and replaced by a parking lot for the Mackey-Wright funeral home across the street. (PCHGS.)

From 1874 until 1888, the structure at 100 South Charter Street consisted of one story with a front porch. Dr. William B. Caldwell purchased it in 1885 for a drugstore and medical practice, also brewing and bottling a pepsin laxative for his patients. The current brick structure was built in 1888 and became known as the Bender Building. Various drugstores operated there for almost 100 years. (DC.)

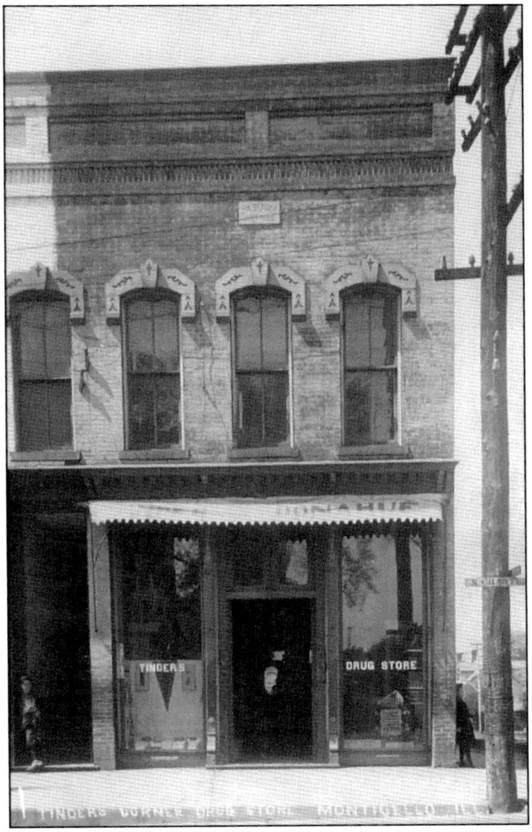

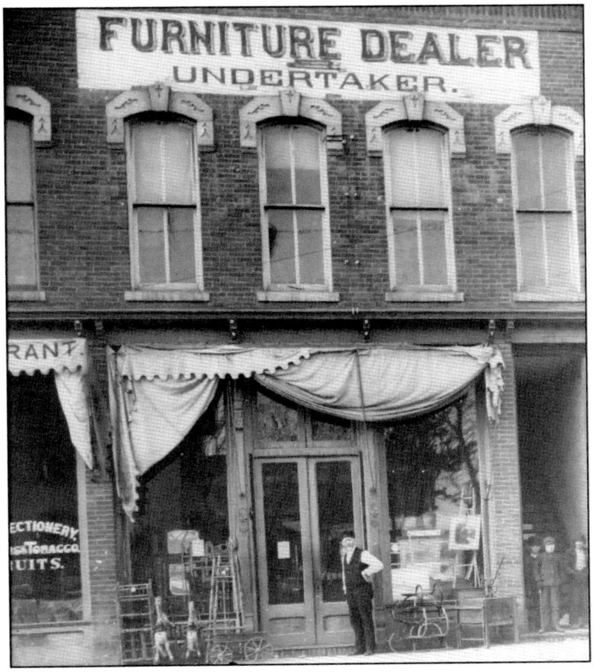

John E. Andrew's combination furniture and undertaking business is seen at 102 South Charter Street. Andrew was elected sheriff in 1882 and also served as mayor for three terms. At various times, this building held a restaurant and a bowling alley, as well as Charles Holderman's cigar factory on the second floor. (PCHGS.)

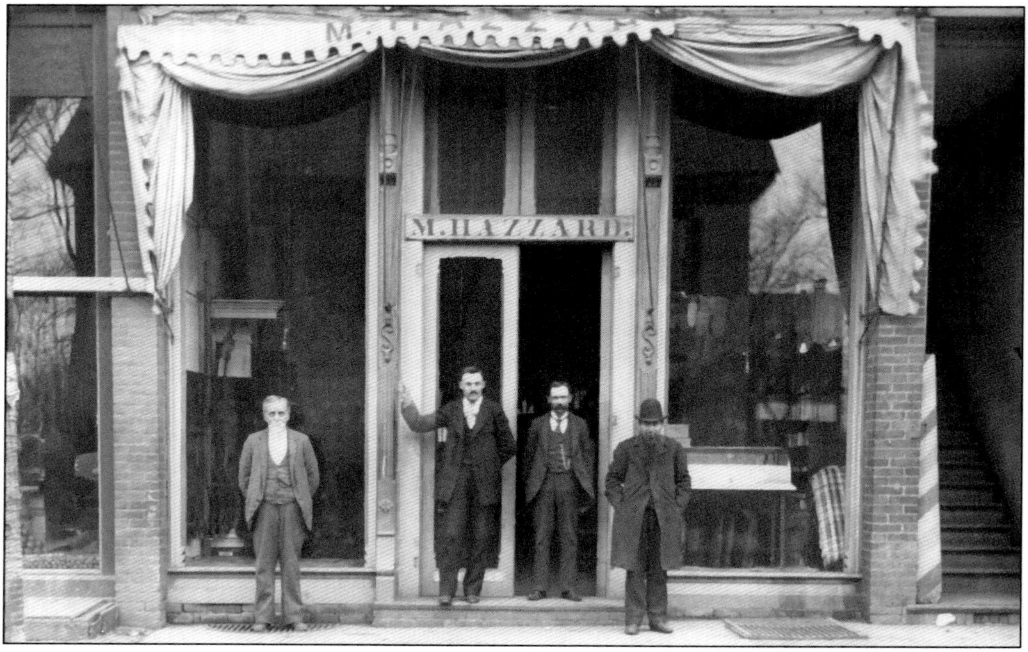

Michael Hazzard operated a grocery and dry goods business at 106 South Charter Street from 1867 until 1904. After a fire consumed the original frame building, he replaced it in 1888 with a brick structure. The men pictured are, from left to right, Eph Garver, William Lowery, Hazzard's son Albert, and owner Michael Hazzard. Michael Hazzard's wife gave birth to quintuplets in September 1880. Unfortunately, the children died within the month. (PCHGS.)

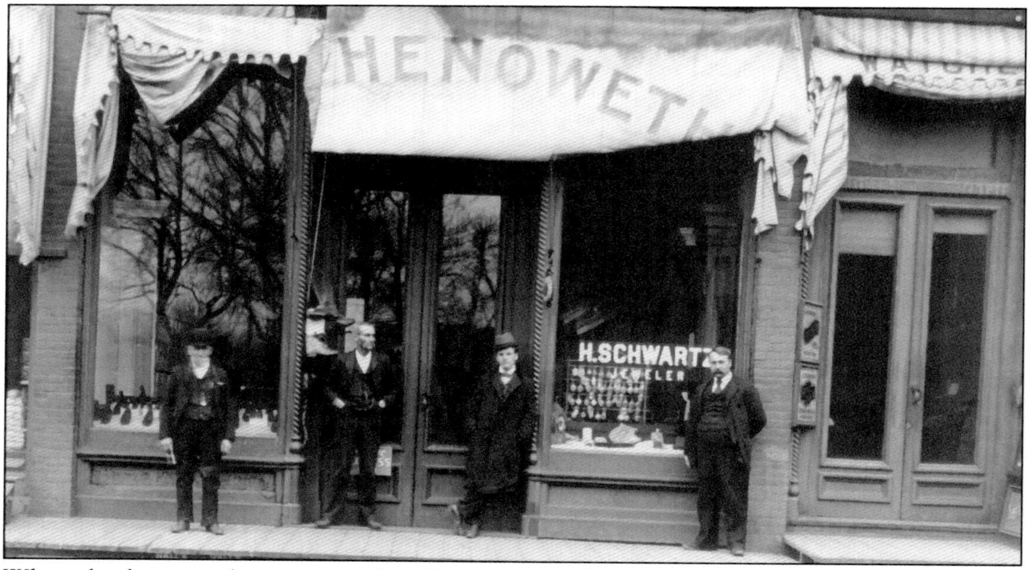

When the first courthouse was replaced, it was moved to the site of 112 South Charter Street. Chenoweth Drug Store eventually took over the spot in the 1890s. Haagen Schwartz ran his jewelry establishment inside the north section of Chenoweth's building. The men pictured are, from left to right, Henry Sackriter, Riley Hyde, unidentified, and Haagen Schwartz. The far right doorway appears to be that of 108 South Charter Street. (APL.)

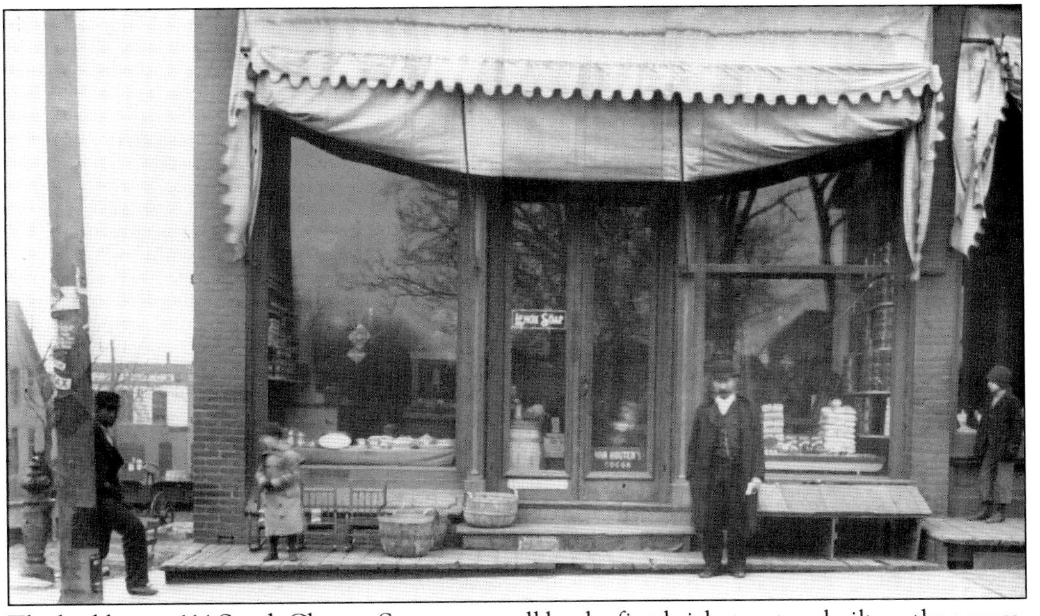

The building at 114 South Charter Street may well be the first brick structure built on the square. It held a millinery store in 1856. It is rumored that it once had two stories, but it is unclear how or when the second story was removed. In 1892, Sackriter's Grocery was housed there. The men are Dane Conley (left) and Eugene Coffin. The children are unidentified. (PCHGS.)

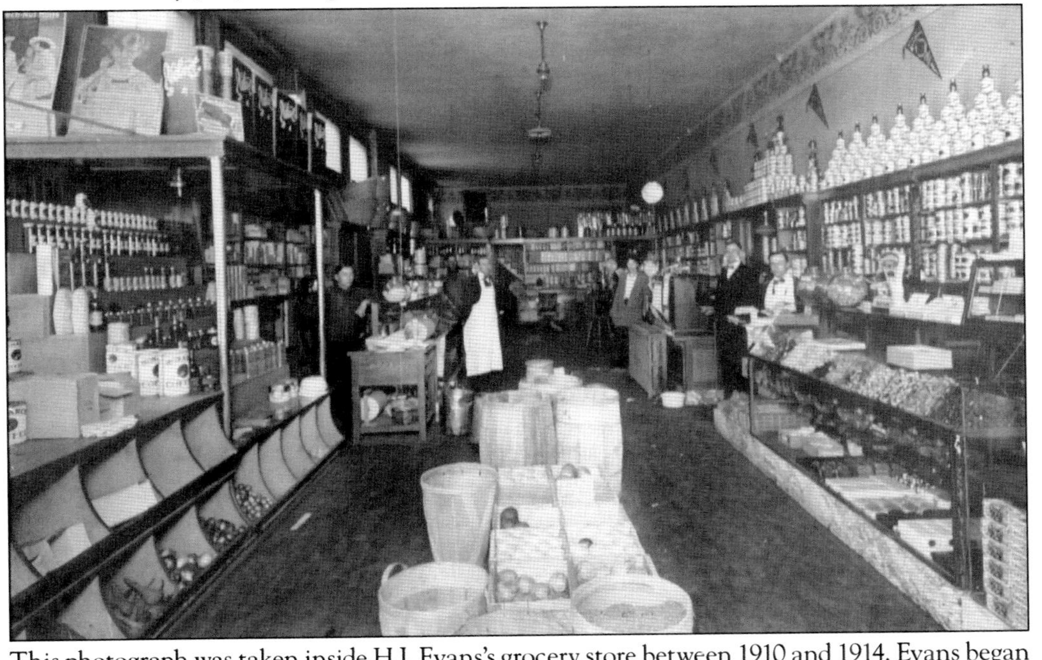

This photograph was taken inside H.J. Evans's grocery store between 1910 and 1914. Evans began working in Sackriter's Grocery in 1889. In 1894, he partnered with A.C. Thompson, H.P. Harris, and W.D. Ridgely to open the Star Grocery. He opened his own store in the Kratz Building at the southwest corner of Main and Charter Streets in 1910. Four years later, it was destroyed by fire. (APL.)

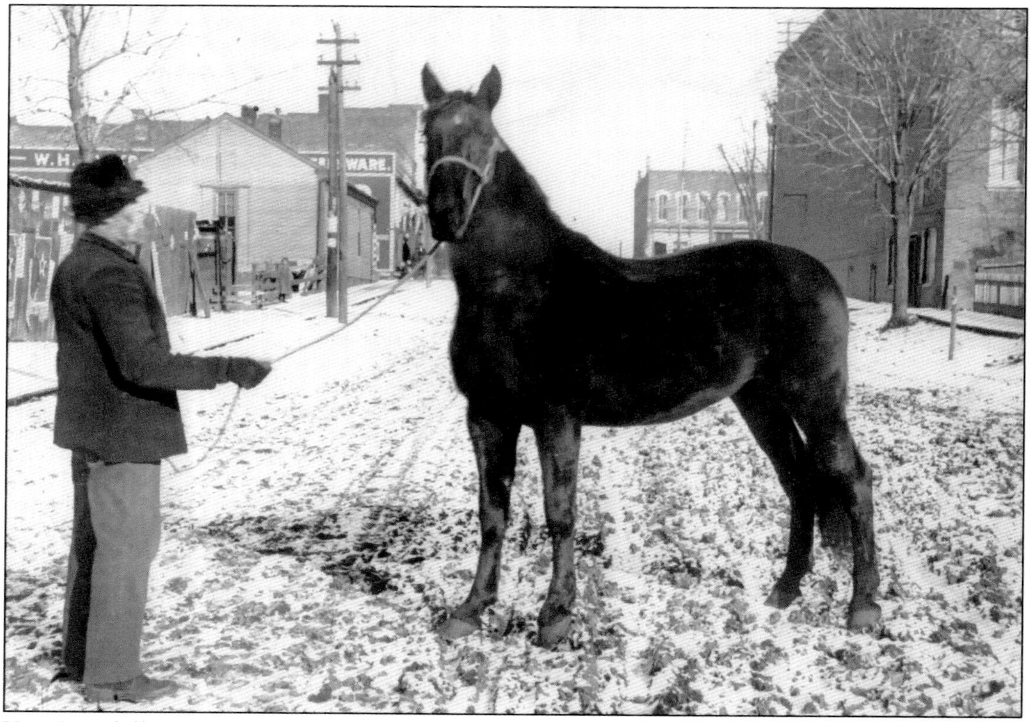

Kap Crandall and a horse stand in Charter Street south of Main Street. The far right structure is the Piatt-Bryden Building, the second building on the square, constructed around 1860 by Jacob Piatt. W.E. Smith Grocery is listed as owner from 1878 until 1898 and, later, H.J. Evans's grocery was there. The block of West Washington Street brick buildings constructed in 1881 appears in the background. (PCHGS.)

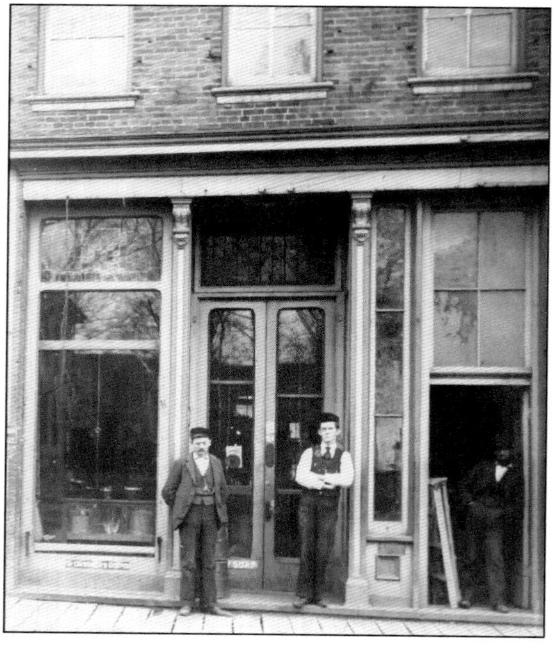

Maurice Lowry (left) and Piatt Smith (center) stand near an unidentified man by 107 West Main Street. The first business noted at this address, around 1873, was Julius Brown Hardware. Later, it was home to J.D. Leiper's Bargain Store. Dr. Frederick W. Keele, a dentist, and Dr. Charles M. Bumstead had offices overhead, and next door at 109 West Main Street, Harry Martin had a cigar factory. (PCHGS.)

Henry Sackriter, a German restaurateur, built the Sackriter Hotel in 1892 at 210 West Main Street next to his home. He connected the two structures with an underground tunnel. Guests paid $2 per day to stay. Some people spent entire winters; one couple lived there for 40 years. Eventually designated a state architectural landmark, the hotel fell into disrepair and was replaced by a parking lot in 1985. (APL.)

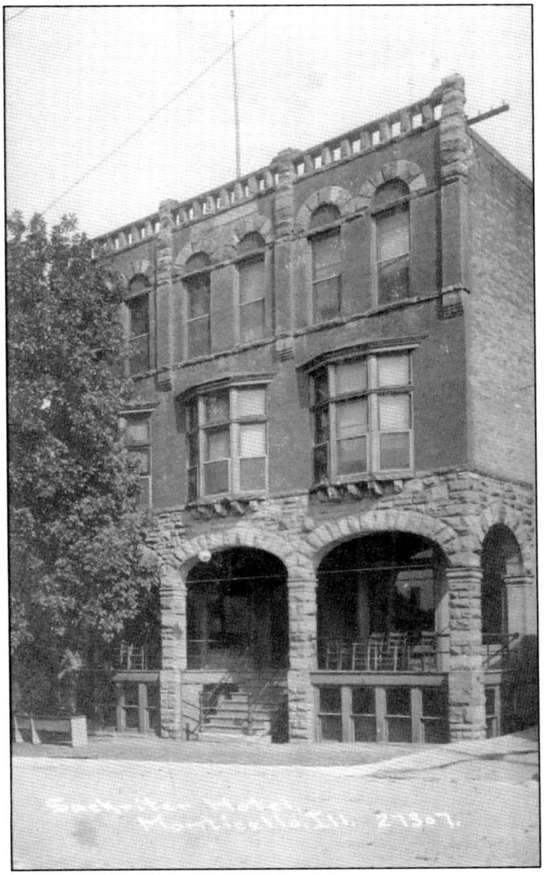

The area across Market Street was known as the Manufacturing District. This 1900 photograph shows Harrington Brothers buggy factory at 424 West Main Street. One of Monticello's first industries, Harrington Brothers opened for business in the 1870s. In addition to regular buggies or road wagons made for the rutty trails, it made special wagons for postal deliveries. The business employed about 20 men. (PCHGS.)

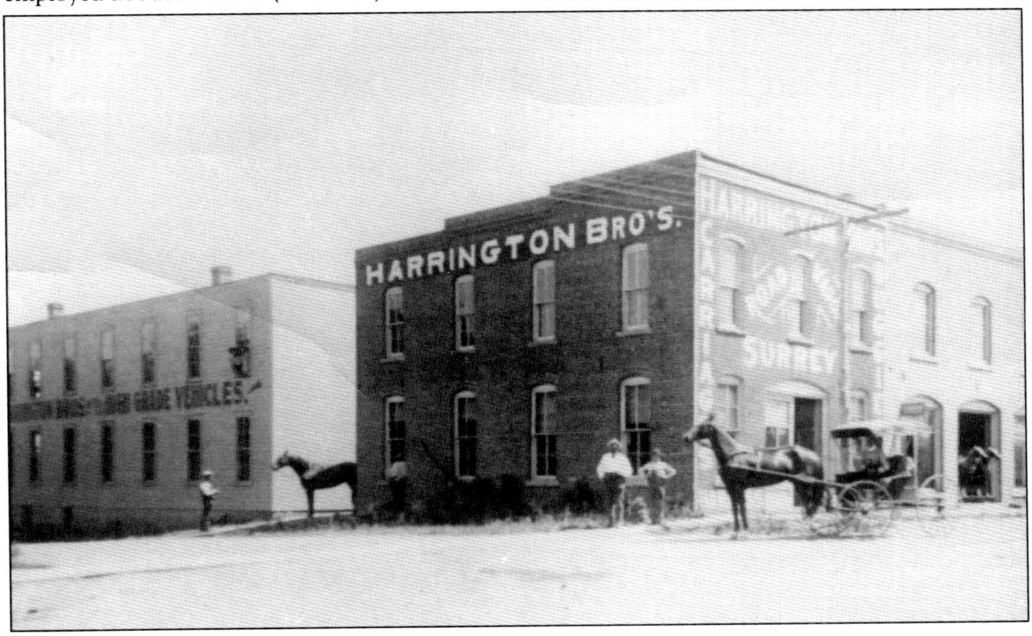

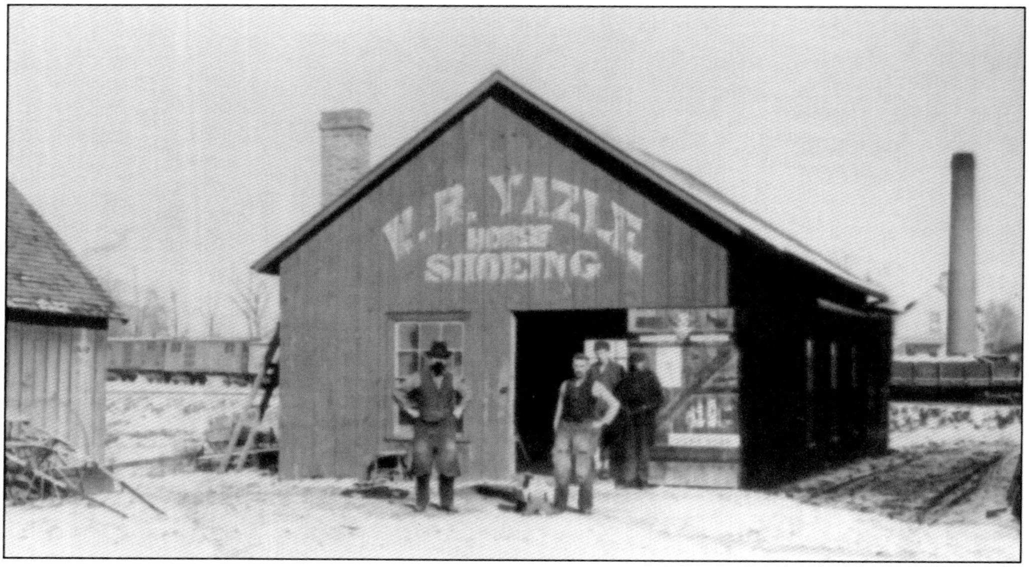

Blacksmith William Yazle's horseshoeing and blacksmith business was located at 224 West Livingston Street, later the Viobin site. Pictured, from left to right, are William Yazle and Benjamin Markel, and two unidentified men. To the east of Yazle's business sat Ball's Grocery and behind, as can be seen in this photograph, ran the Illinois Central Railroad tracks. (PCHGS.)

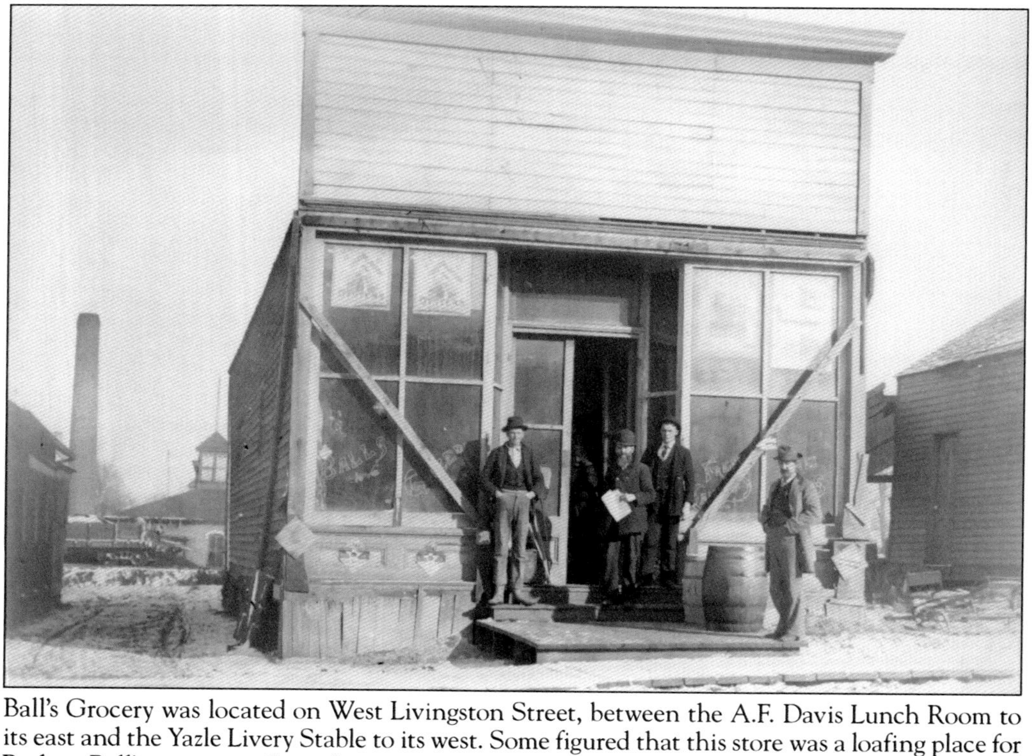

Ball's Grocery was located on West Livingston Street, between the A.F. Davis Lunch Room to its east and the Yazle Livery Stable to its west. Some figured that this store was a loafing place for Rodney Ball's customers. Signs for oysters appear at the top of the left windows. Pictured, from left to right, are Tod Dillen, Thomas Ball Sr., Monroe McShurley, and Robert Griffith. (PCHGS.)

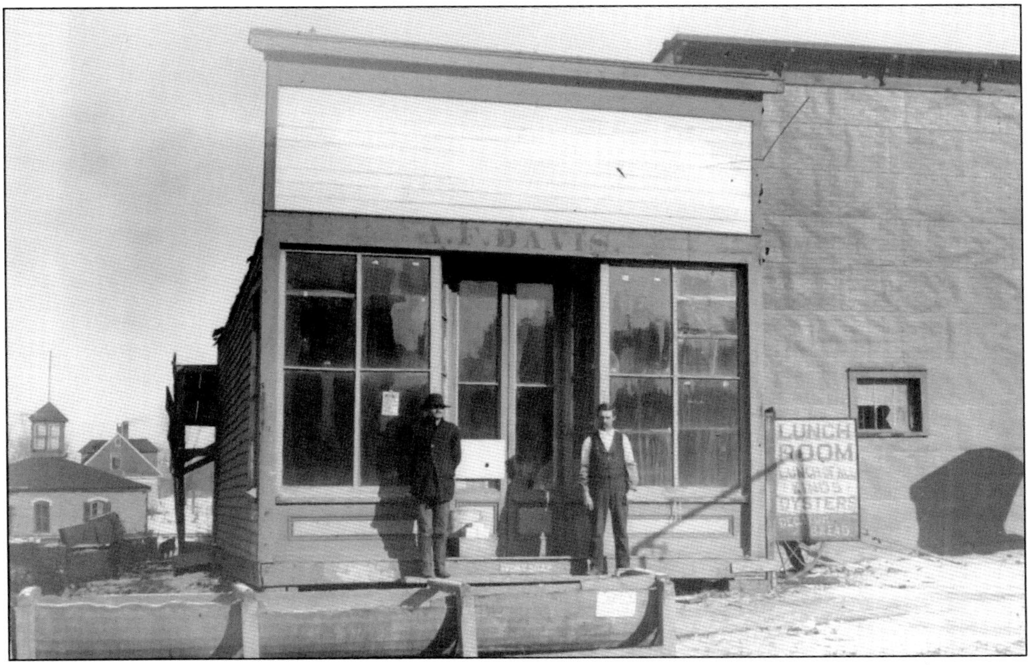

The A.F. Davis Lunch Room was located at 226 West Livingston Street in 1896, near the corner of Market and Livingston Streets where the Viobin office now sits. One of the men is Frank Bush. The sign to the left announces that the restaurant offers lunches of all kinds, including oysters, a very popular treat at the time. (PCHGS.)

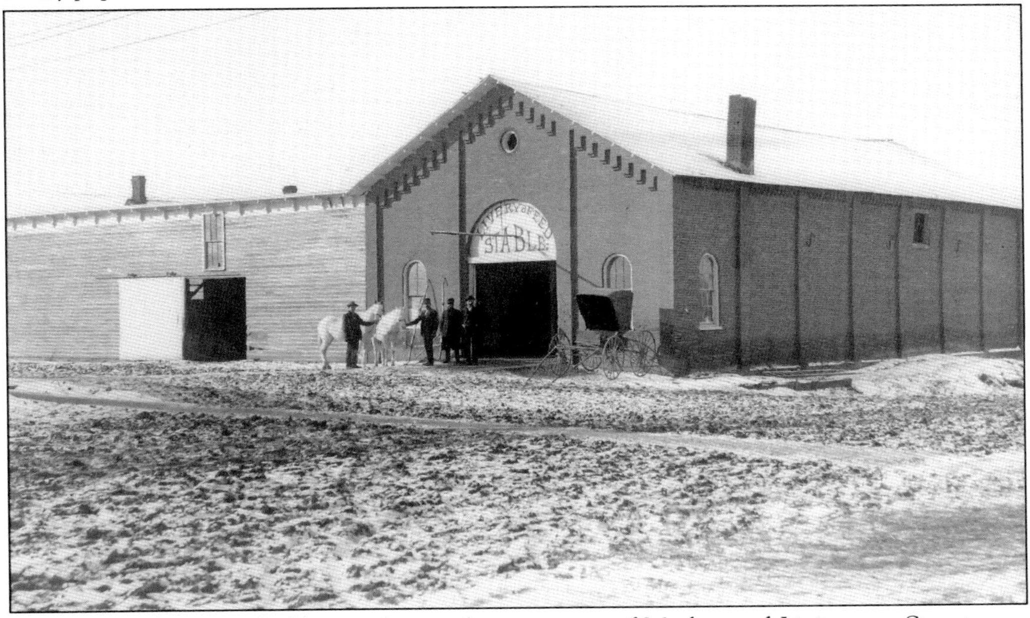

The McIntosh Livery Stables on the southwest corner of Market and Livingston Streets was established in 1899 and comfortably housed 300 head of stock. With the advent of the automobile, the business became unprofitable and McIntosh sold it to Allen F. Moore, who then leased it to the Deep Rock Gas Station in 1923. (PCHGS.)

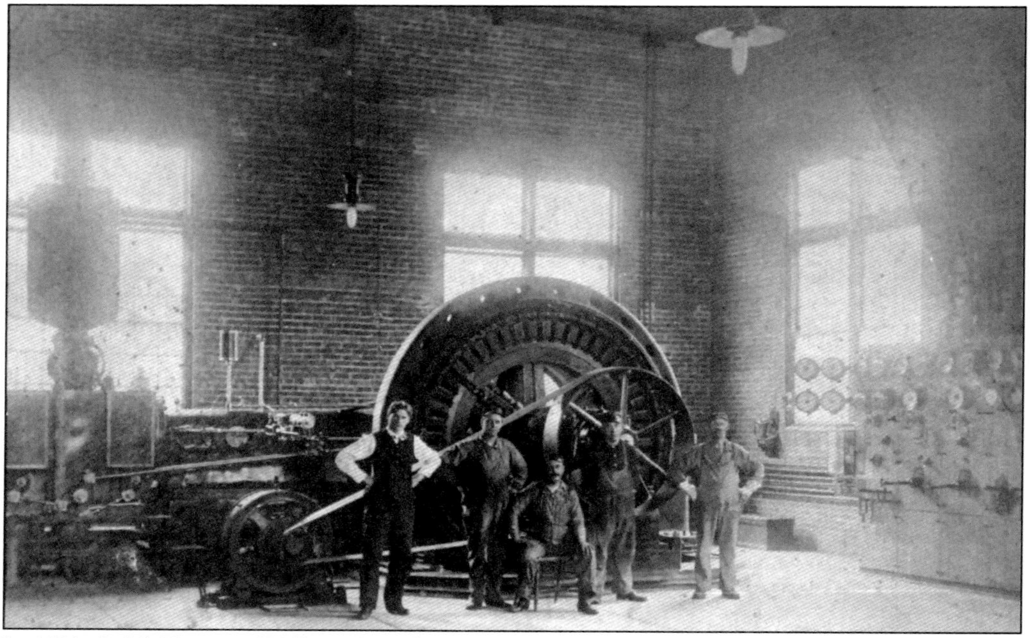

In 1891, Caleb Tatman, William F. Lodge, and James P. Lodge organized the Monticello Electric Light Company. They erected a power plant in 1892 at 301–303 North Market Street. Although installed, electric meters did not determine customers' bills. Rather, the company charged by the number of bulbs in a building. In 1913, Illinois Traction System (the Interurban) bought the utility company. (PCHGS.)

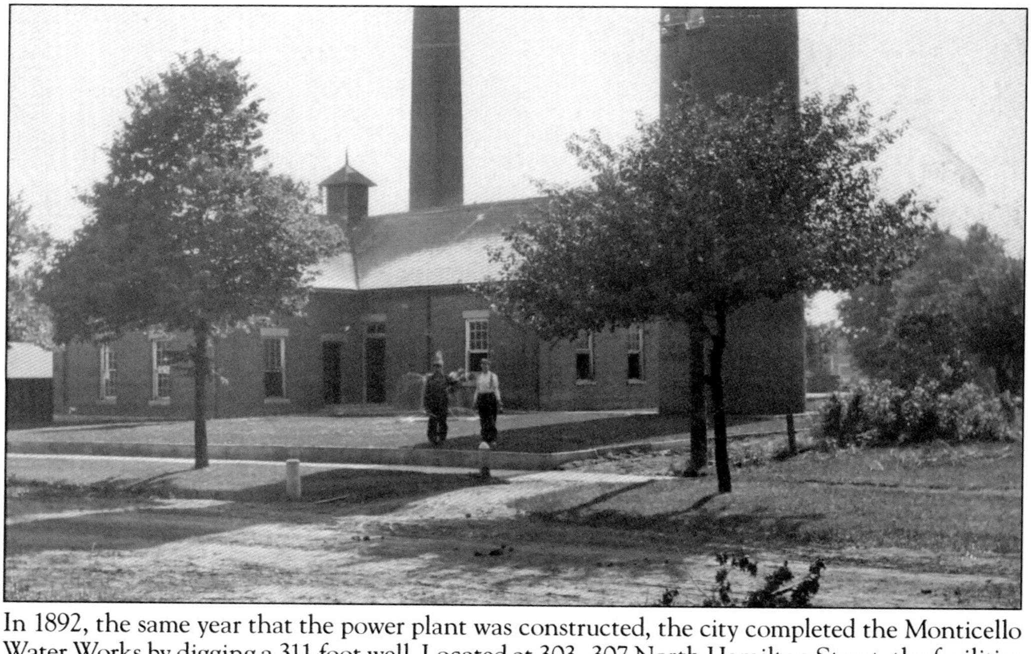

In 1892, the same year that the power plant was constructed, the city completed the Monticello Water Works by digging a 311-foot well. Located at 303–307 North Hamilton Street, the facilities ran on steam produced by two coal-burning boilers. The two men are C. Starkey (left) and engineer Jack Bell. (PCHGS.)

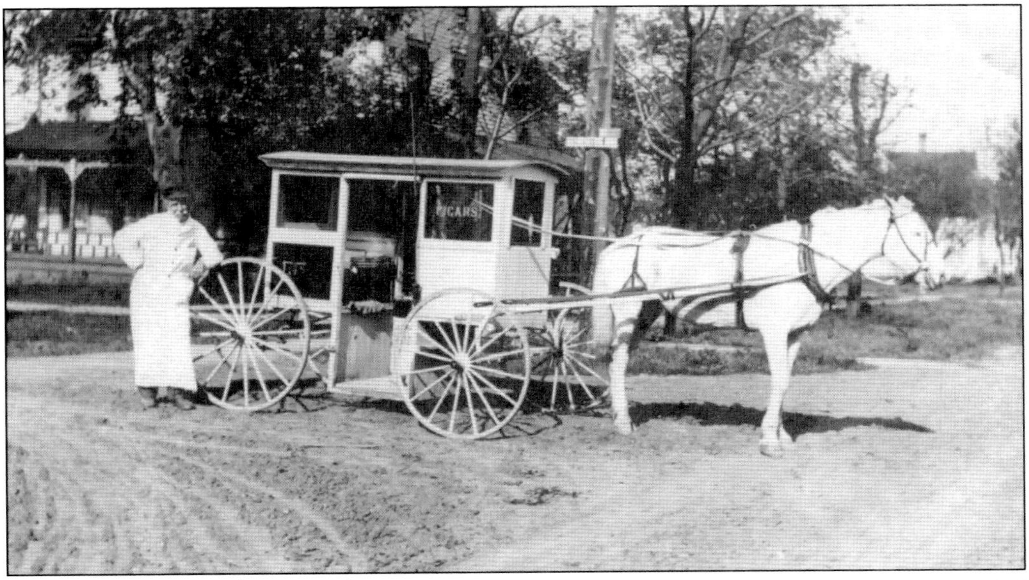

George Johnson stands next to his delivery cart at the corner of South State and Bond Streets. "Cigars" is painted on the cart's window. Son of the first postmaster, Jonathan Johnson, George was born in 1844 and died in 1922. He participated in Sherman's Civil War March to the Sea and spent three months as an inmate in notorious Andersonville Prison. (PCHGS.)

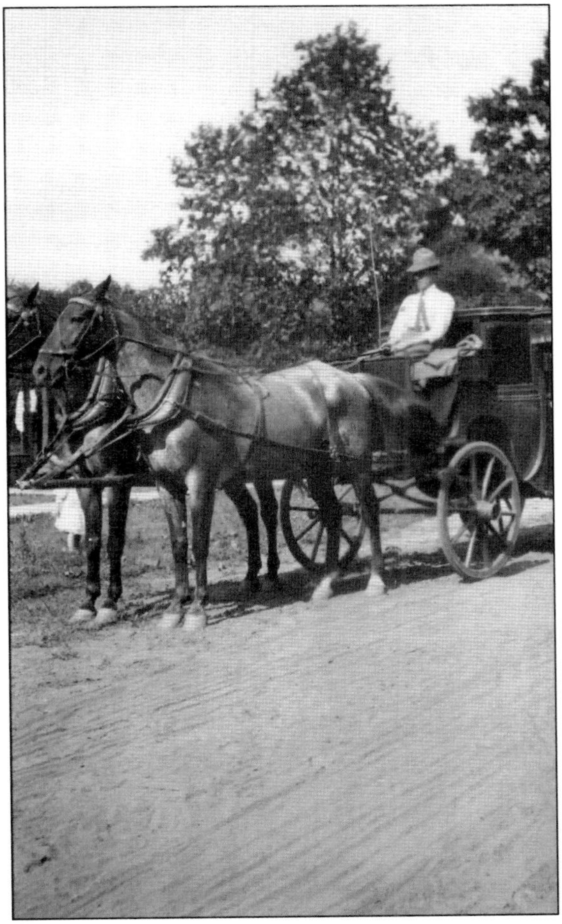

Son of Henry and Emily Saint, Walter Saint was born in 1875 and died in 1909. He operated the Walter Saint Taxi Service in Monticello long before the Interurban train served Monticello. Other forms of transportation included a hack line (stagecoach) between Monticello and Bement run by William Motherspaw. (PCHGS.)

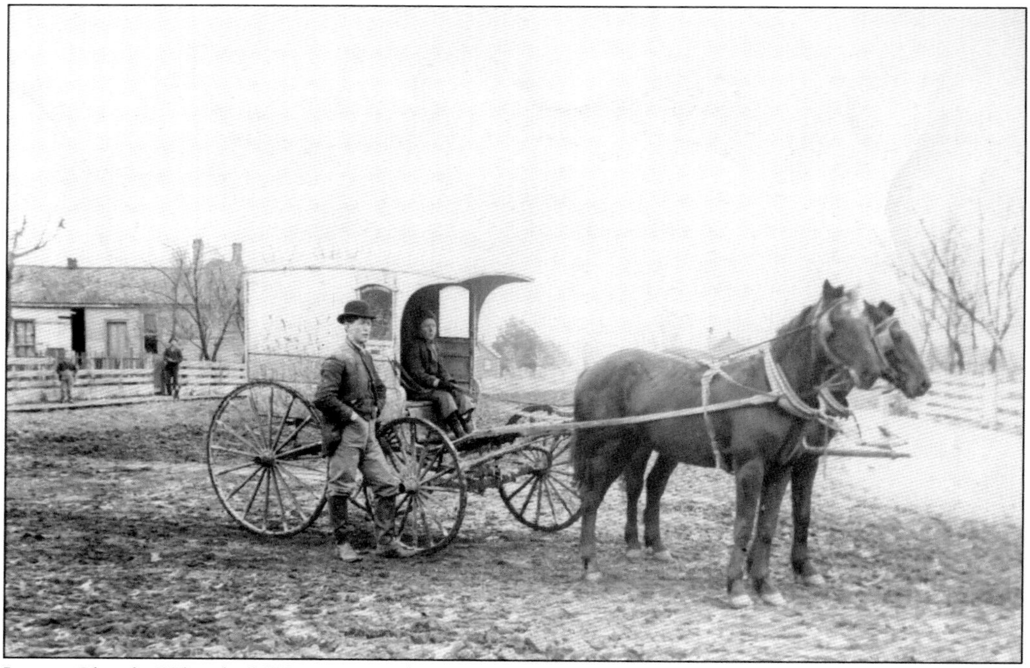

James Claude "Shocky" Weaver stands next to the delivery wagon for Star Grocery, located at 113 West Main Street. In 1899, when the Pepsin Syrup Company began, Weaver was the sole employee. He boiled up the medicine, then bottled, crated, and carted it to the train depot. When Allen Moore bought into the company, Weaver became laboratory superintendent. He died in 1943. (PCHGS.)

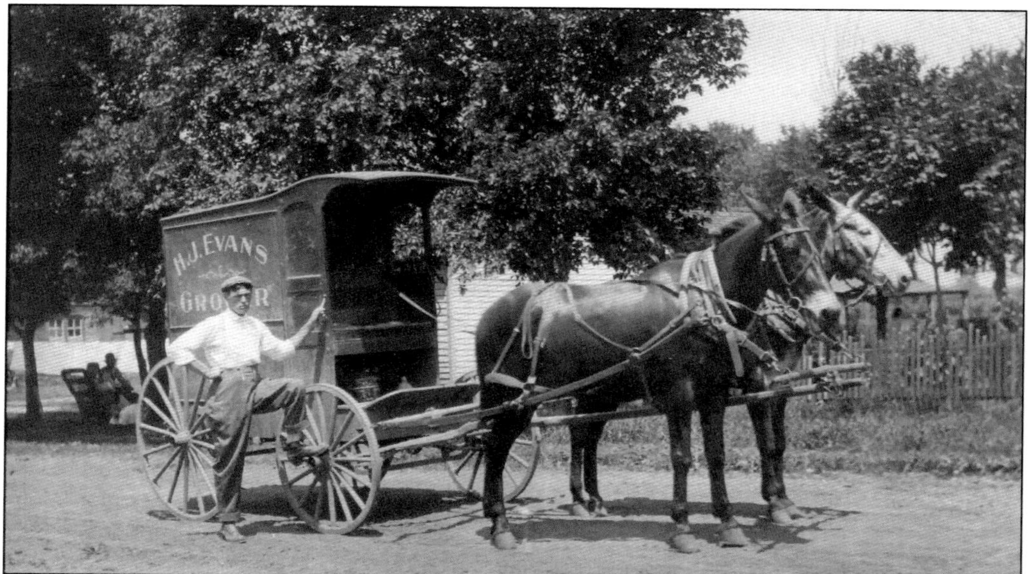

A group of men sits in chairs in the left background while Trent Miner poses with a team of grey mules on his journey around Monticello, delivering groceries for H.J. Evans Grocery Store. Miner drove the wagon for a number of years until a group of stores decided to have the same wagons deliver all supplies. (PCHGS.)

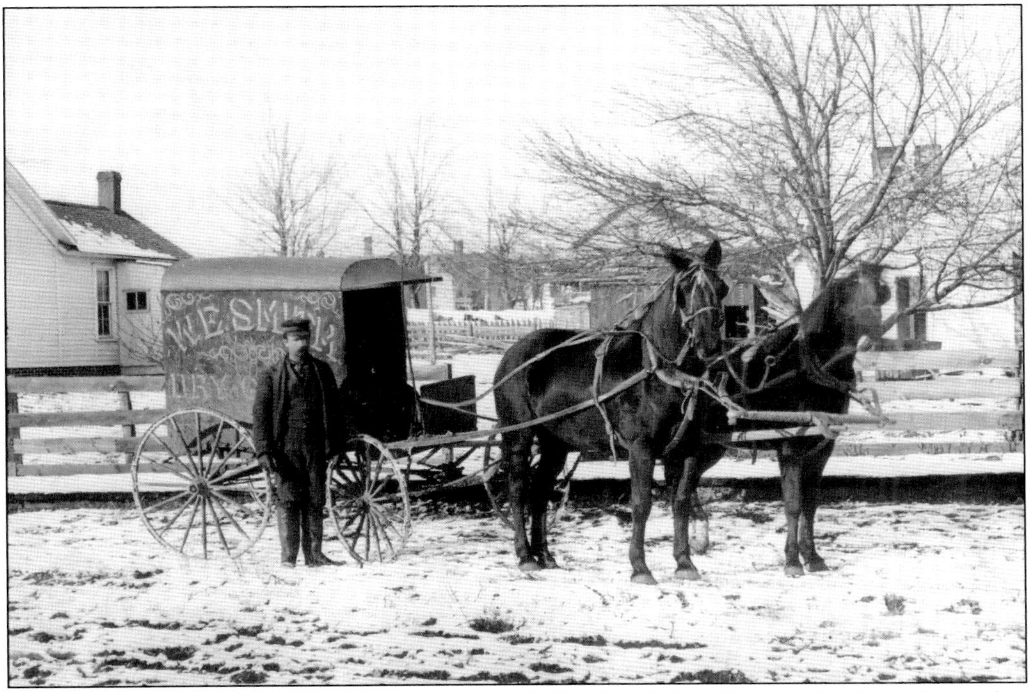

Tug Wilson stands next to the delivery wagon of W.E. Smith Dry Goods, which was located at 109–111 West Main Street. One of the oldest stores in town, Smith Dry Goods opened in 1878, moving 20 years later to the Main Street address. The store closed in 1923 after a downturn in the mercantile business. It is now home to Monticello Drugs. (PCHGS.)

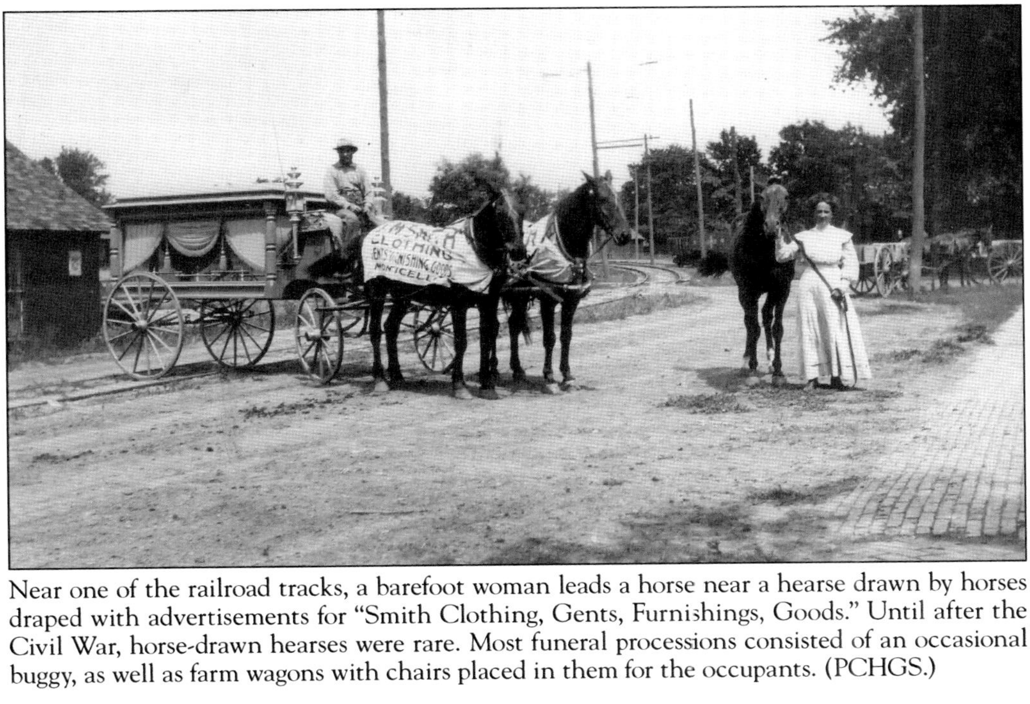

Near one of the railroad tracks, a barefoot woman leads a horse near a hearse drawn by horses draped with advertisements for "Smith Clothing, Gents, Furnishings, Goods." Until after the Civil War, horse-drawn hearses were rare. Most funeral processions consisted of an occasional buggy, as well as farm wagons with chairs placed in them for the occupants. (PCHGS.)

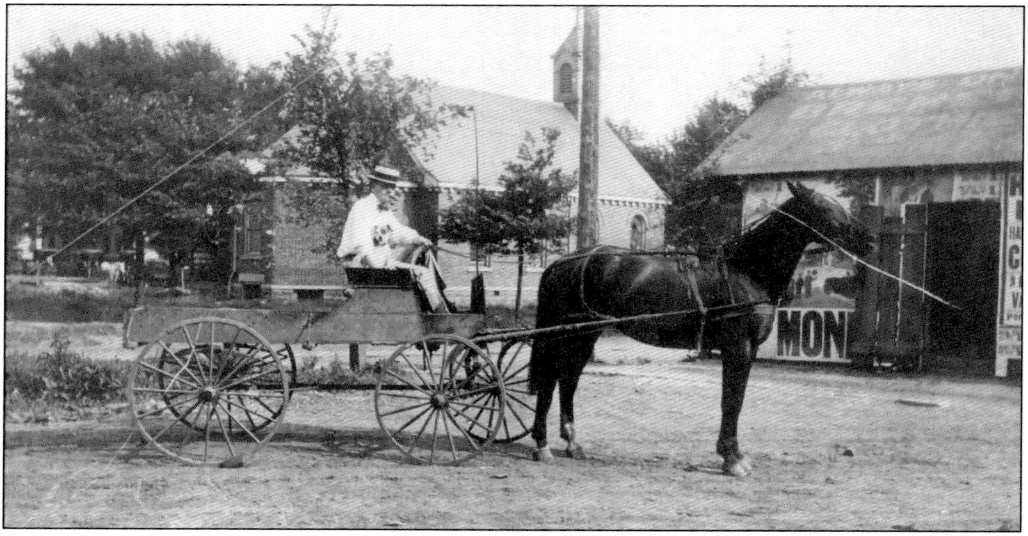

Gummy the dog sits on a wagon with an unidentified man delivering supplies from Walter N. Lux Grocers (located at 105 West Main Street). St. Philomena Catholic Church appears in the background, with an empty lot behind it. The wagon is standing on an empty lot where the current Dairy Queen was later built. (PCHGS.)

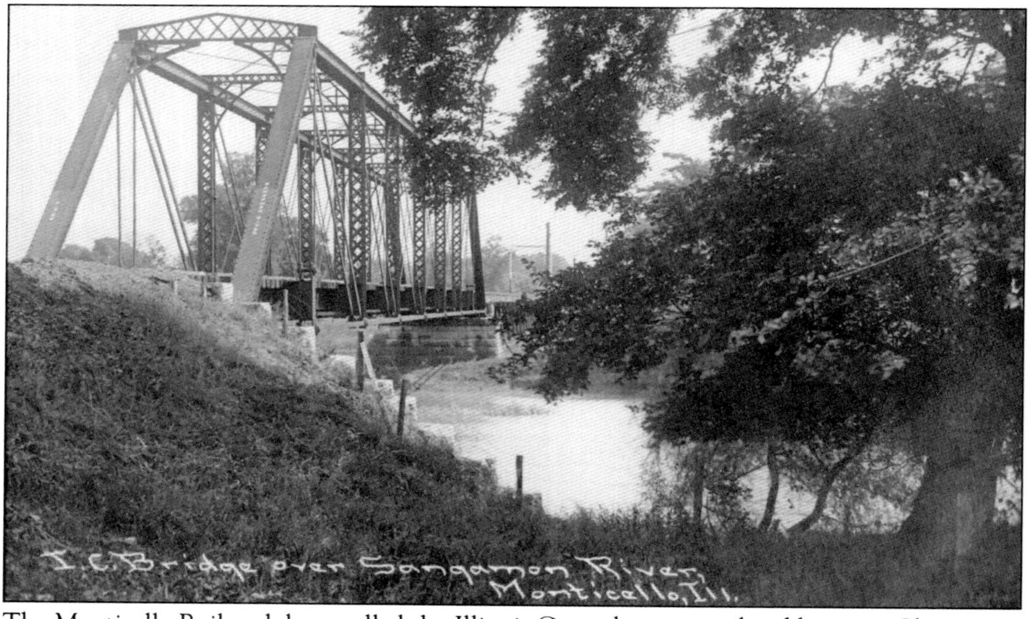

The Monticello Railroad, later called the Illinois Central, was completed between Champaign and Decatur in 1870. This c. 1900 photograph shows the Illinois Central Bridge spanning the Sangamon River. In Monticello's early days, a ferry transported people across the river. Abraham Lincoln was one of those many people who used the service. A new concrete bridge was built in 1949. (APL-SR.)

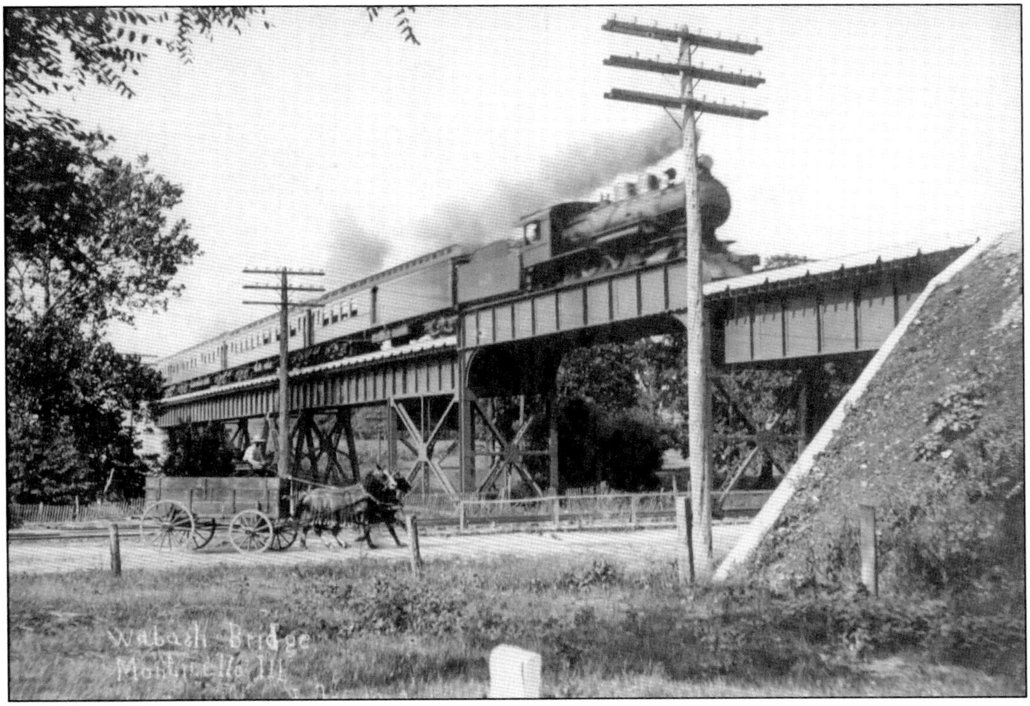

The Wabash Railroad was completed around 1855. A steel trestle was built over Bridge Street after 1899. Graves were moved from the old cemetery during the process. The line was straightened in 1903 to allow for faster speeds. The man in the wagon is Jacob Rudisill. (PCHGS.)

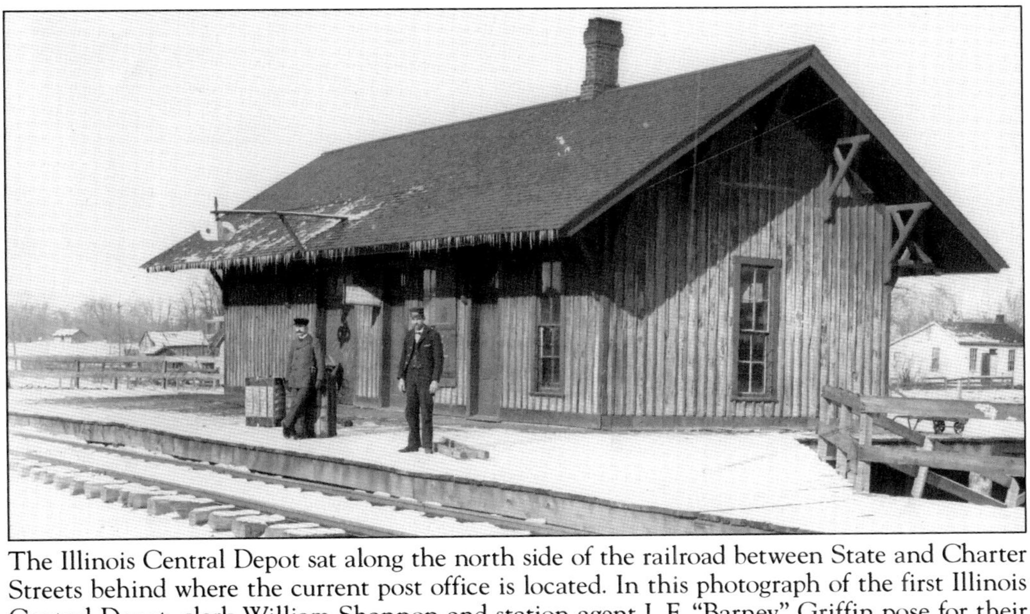
The Illinois Central Depot sat along the north side of the railroad between State and Charter Streets behind where the current post office is located. In this photograph of the first Illinois Central Depot, clerk William Shannon and station agent L.F. "Barney" Griffin pose for their photograph on a sunny winter day. (PCHGS.)

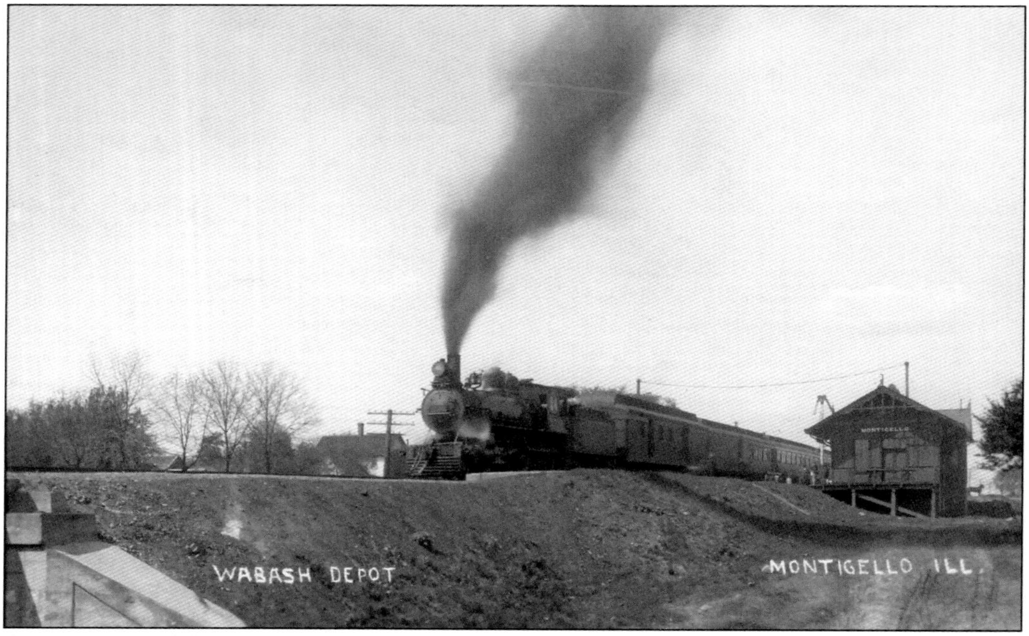

Construction of the first Wabash Depot (on the site of the current parking lot next to 315 West Washington Street) was completed in September 1895. It burned down in February 1899 but was rebuilt within six months, this time with a brick foundation and a slate roof. In 1904, after the Marion Street viaduct was completed, the depot was moved near the grain office. It was relocated near Allerton Public Library in May 1987. (APL.)

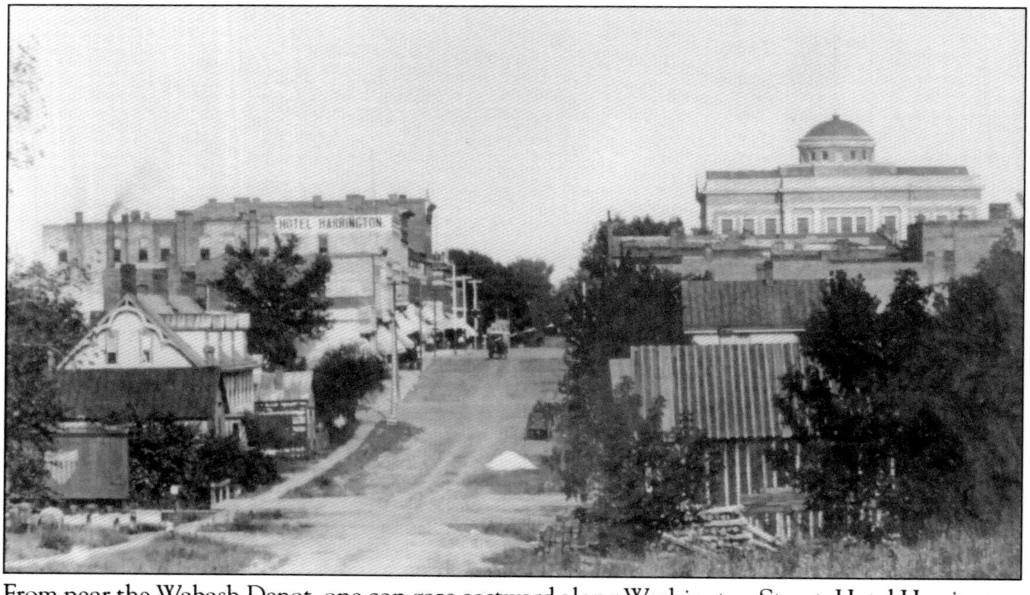

From near the Wabash Depot, one can gaze eastward along Washington Street. Hotel Harrington is emblazoned across the side of one of the buildings. The photograph would have been taken any time after 1903, when Frank and H.C. Harrington opened Hotel Harrington at 204 West Washington Street. It became Kroell's European Hotel in 1904. A wagon can be seen opposite the hotel; another is at the corner. (RS.)

Samuel Allerton, a Chicago agriculture, meatpacking, and banking tycoon with land holdings from New Jersey to Nebraska, helped start the First National Bank of Chicago and Chicago Union Stockyards. With property and family in Monticello, he and his wife, Agnes, donated furnishings and books to the new Allerton Public Library. He planted 5,000 fruit trees along what is now Allerton Road to benefit Monticello residents. (APL.)

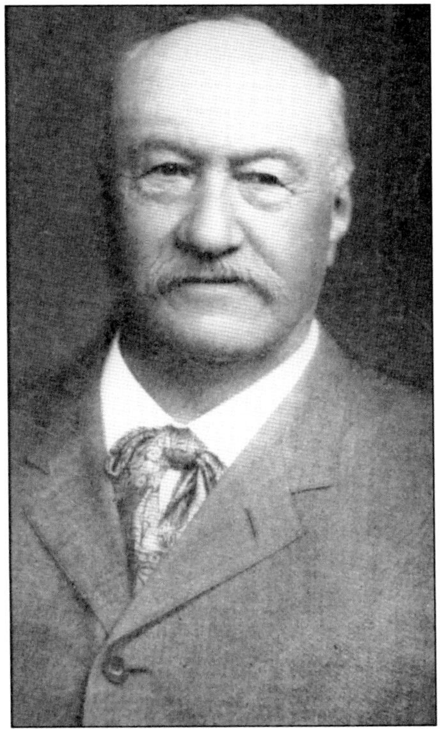

In 1895, Samuel Allerton proposed that if Monticello would erect a library building, his wife would donate the furnishings. The combination two-room library and 800-seat opera house at State and Livingston Streets was completed in 1897. Eugene Debs spoke at the opera house on November 25, 1925. The building's tower was removed in 1904 because of loose bricks. Eventually, the stone balconies were also removed. (APL.)

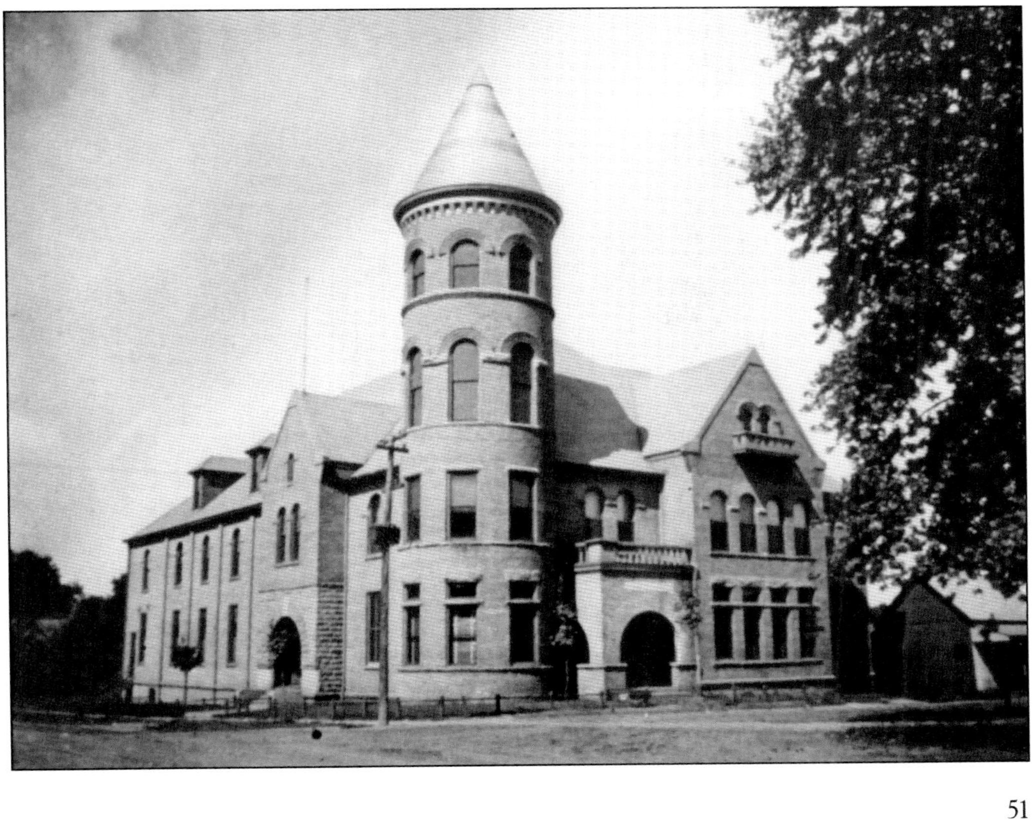

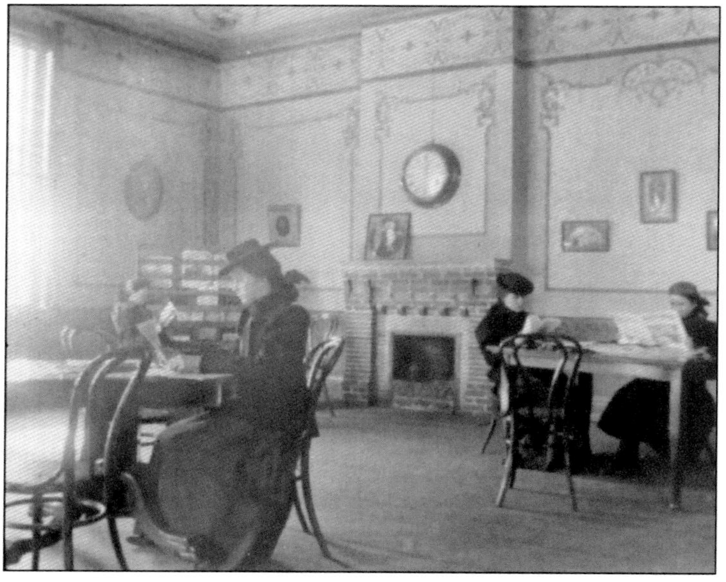

The library was named after Samuel Allerton's wife, Agnes, who donated furniture, shelving, decorations, and 2,500 books, including 300 reference books. After 1948, the opera house ceded its space to allow for the library's expansion. The two original library rooms are now the Garden Room and the archive-research area. The fireplace was removed from the Garden Room when the elevator was installed in 2004. (APL.)

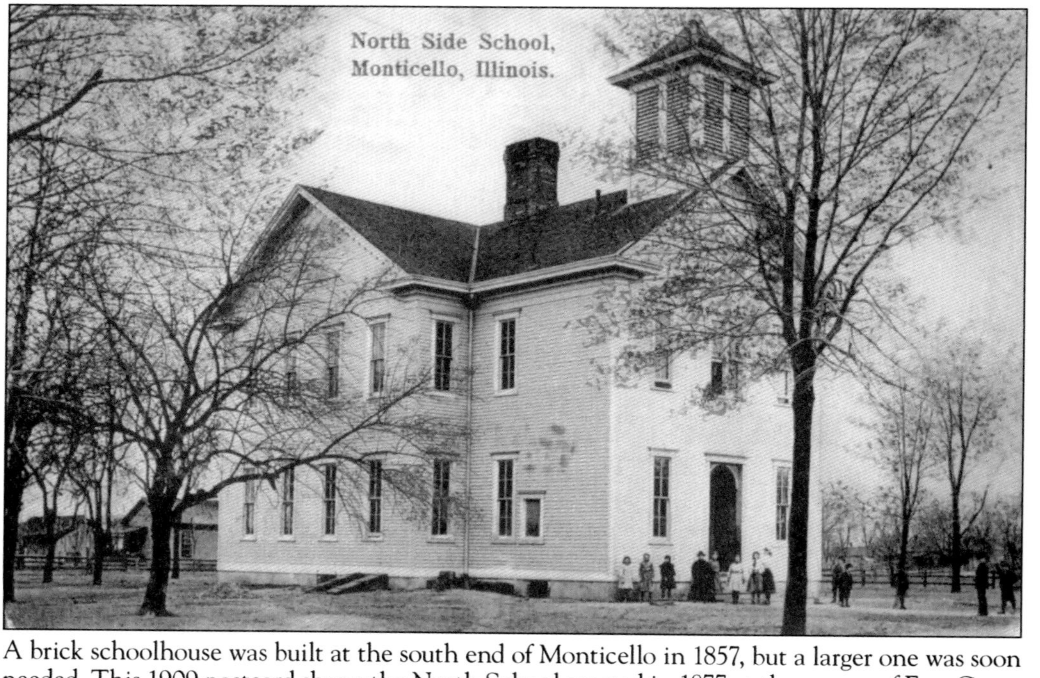

A brick schoolhouse was built at the south end of Monticello in 1857, but a larger one was soon needed. This 1909 postcard shows the North School erected in 1877 at the corner of East Grant and Union Streets. The school, which cost $3,900 to build, had four rooms but by 1903 had used only three of them for teaching. (PCHGS.)

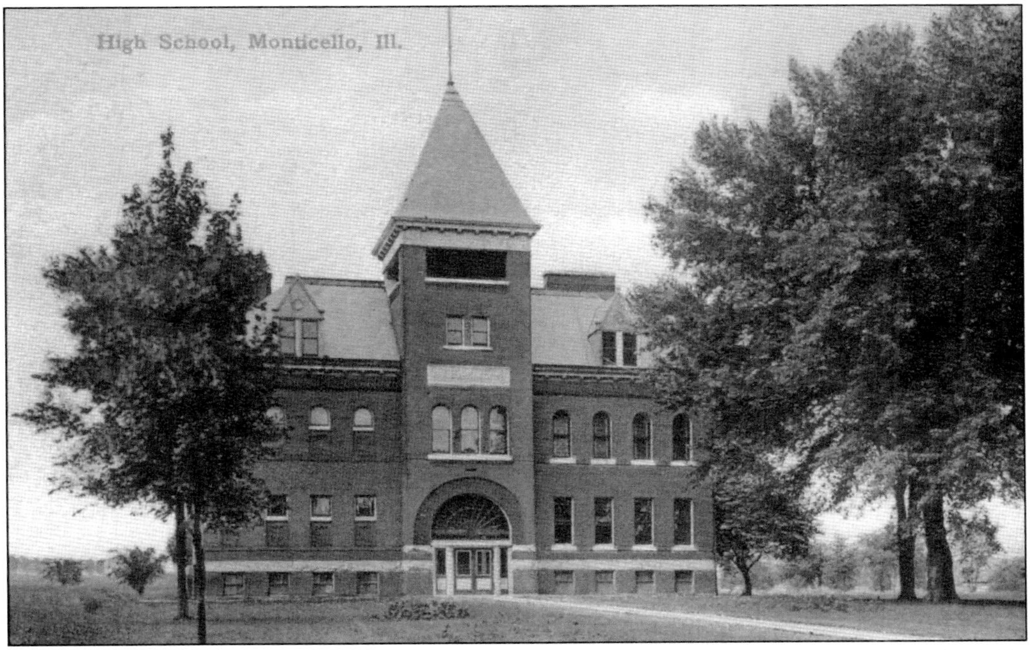

Constructed at the south end of Monticello in 1894, Washington School replaced the 1857 schoolhouse. It retained the designation of South School for decades. Encompassing 14,700 square feet and 10 rooms, it was Monticello's high school until replaced in 1922. Buffalo Bill Cody performed with his Wild West Show during the spring of 1905 and rode his white horse around the schoolyard (APL.)

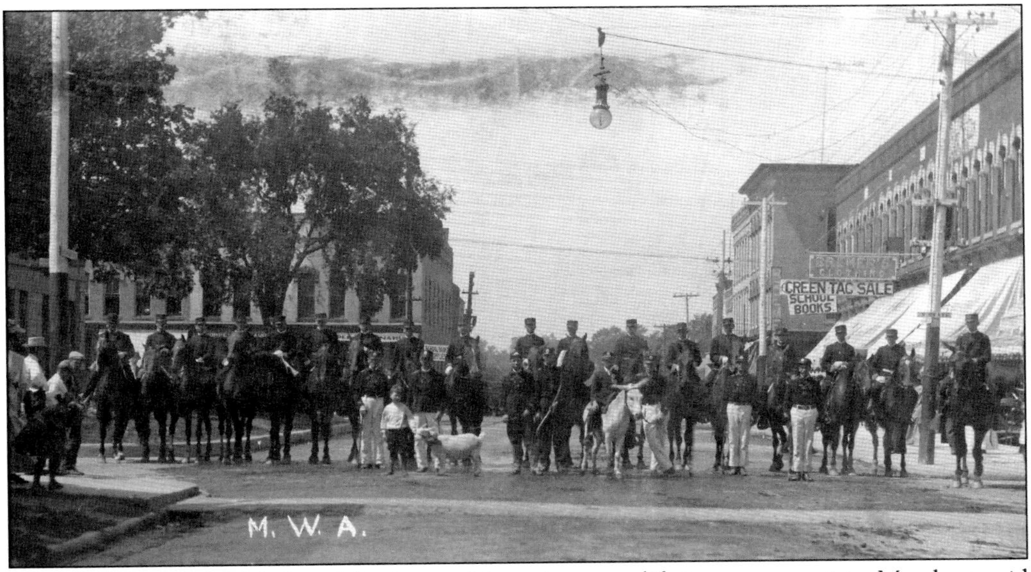

Founded in 1883, the Modern Woodmen of America was a life insurance society. Members paid into a mortality fund to give to families of members who died. Nationwide drill teams performed in events until the late 1930s. Monticello's Camp 346 was established in May 1887 with 22 members. It disbanded in 1937 with 145 members. (PCHGS-FP.)

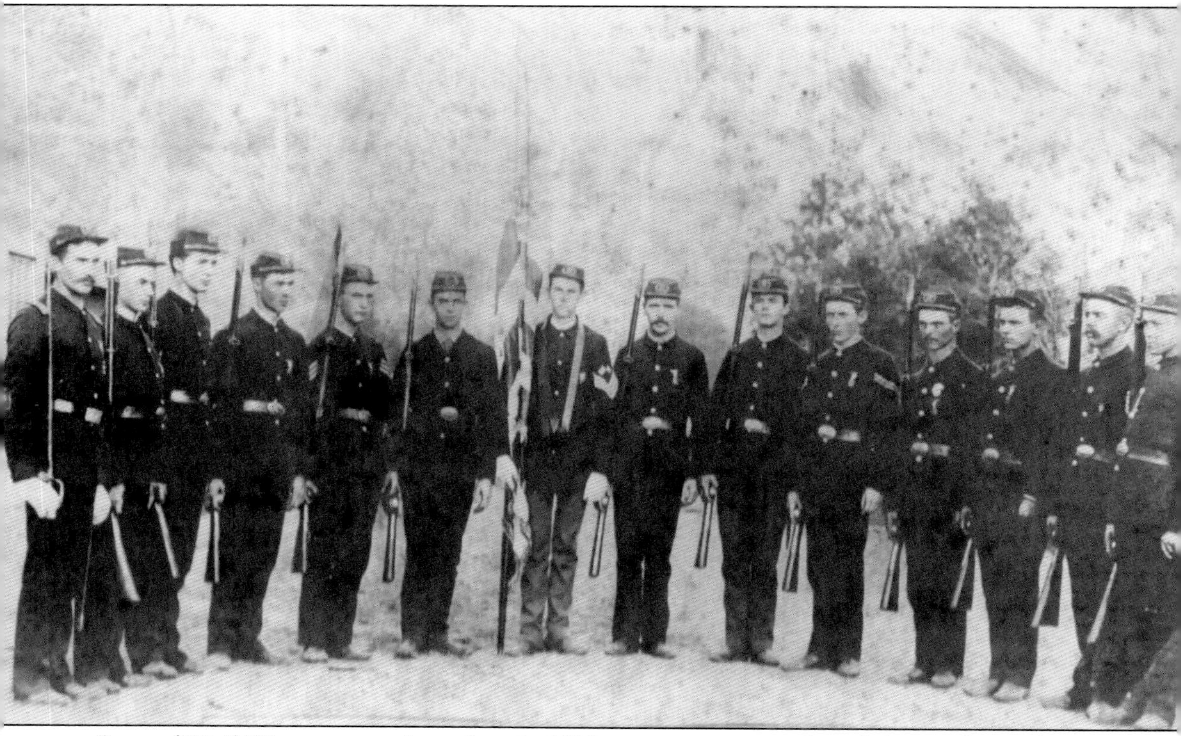

Sons of Civil War veterans dressed up in 1890 to commemorate their fathers' roles in the war. Pictured, from left to right, are Henry Ward, F.E. Davis, Frank Brown, Edward Williams, Clyde Ryder, H.F. McMillen, Louis Lee, Edward Hazzard, Elmer Williams, Harry Martin, Frank Bush, W.T. Wildman, George Keith, and Emmett Malatt. (PCHGS.)

Three

MONEY, MILLIONAIRES, AND MANSIONS 1880s–1920s

The patent medicine business kicked off in Monticello in 1885 when Dr. William Burr Caldwell purchased the Hamilton and Company Drug Store at 100 South Charter Street. Soon, Caldwell was dispensing a laxative containing senna, salicylate, pepsin, and peppermint oil to patients in his backroom. In 1886, he sold the store to Charles Armstrong and Charles Ridgely and began focusing on his medical practice. Dr. Caldwell permitted Ridgely and his new partner, John Bell, to sell his "syrup of pepsin."

Bell sold out to attorney Harry Crea, who then created the Pepsin Syrup Company. Allen Moore and Asler Thompson eventually bought out Crea's interest. As sales climbed, John Hott joined as a partner and funding source, and the business moved to 400 West Washington Street. The company was sold several times until 1985 when the Monticello plant was closed. After falling into disrepair, the buildings were demolished in October 2003.

Additional local patent medicines included Konjola and Joemax products put out by Raycraft Drugs, plus businesses such as Dr. J.D. Knott's Eupepsia Chemical Company, the Pinus Medicine Company, and the Pine Balm Company. The Geno Remedy Company made medicines for chicken indigestion, and the Williams Turkey Tonic Company focused on turkey bowels. The government later investigated several companies for misrepresentation or for violating the Federal Caustic Poison Act by including boric acid, hydrochloric acid, strychnine, or Epsom salt.

While most residents lived in small frame houses, the entrepreneurs who grew rich during the boom years built large houses, many on Charter or State Street, the latter nicknamed "Millionaires Row." As one person recalled, "Before 1930, there were two kinds of people in Monticello . . . Those on North State Street and all the rest of us." At one time, at least seven millionaires lived on the street.

The wealthiest residents had names such as Allerton, Moore, Kirby, Dighton, Hott, and England. Years later, Donn Piatt (chauffeur at one time to John Kirby) said, "When I was a kid growing up here, we had five chauffeur-driven limousines. They lived a lifestyle that has never been repeated."

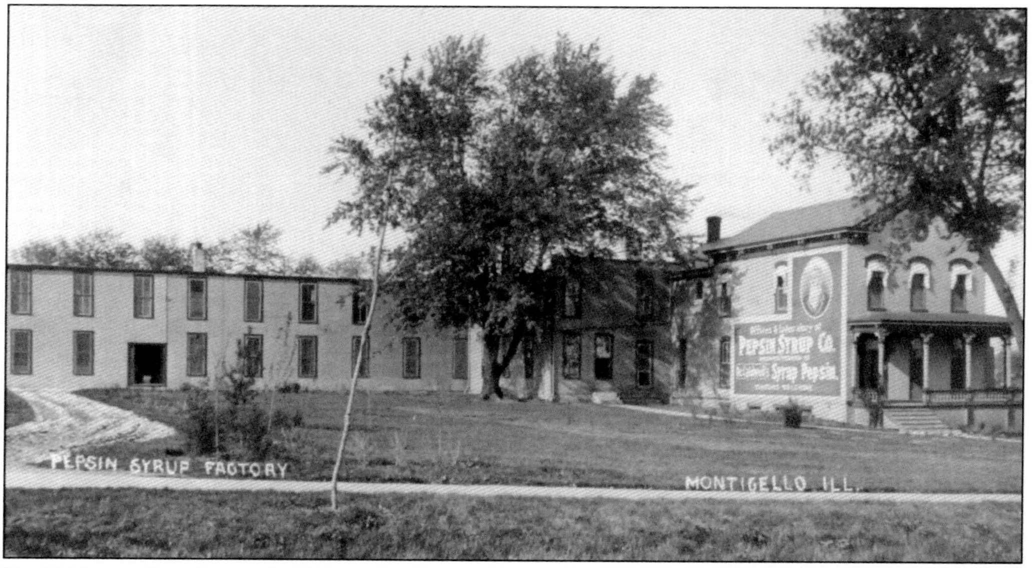

By 1903, needing larger facilities, the Pepsin Syrup Company bought 180 feet of property west of the Wabash Railroad, including Daniel Stickel's two-story brick house. After renovations and additions, the new factory served the company's purposes until another addition, this time with four floors, was added to the northeast corner in 1914. Monticelloans called the area "Pepsin Hill." (RS.)

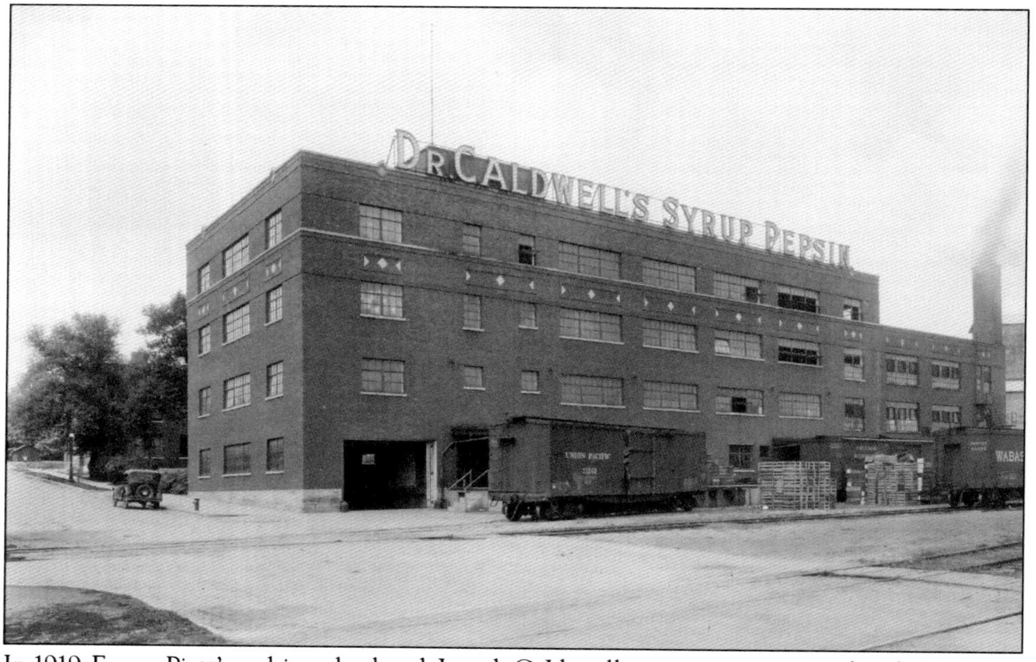

In 1919, Emma Piatt's architect husband, Joseph C. Llewellyn, was commissioned to design a new four-story building, which William F. Lodge constructed for $100,000. With 150 employees and a growing customer list, Pepsin added two more buildings in 1924. Purchased in 1984, Pepsin Syrup was finally closed in 1985. After years of deterioration, the factory was demolished in October 2003. (PCHGS.)

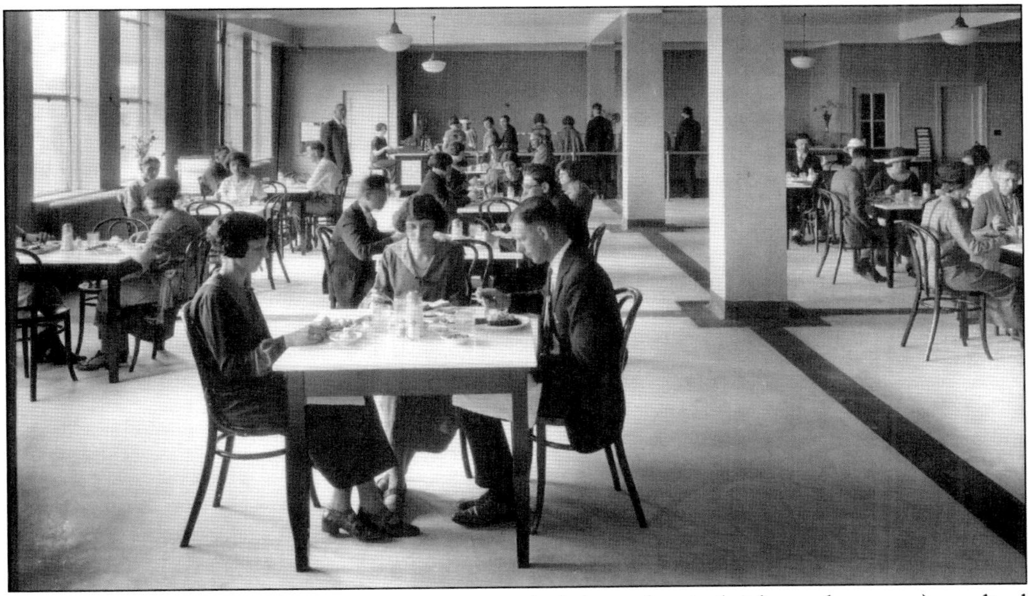

The 1924 Pepsin Syrup Company expansion included a cafeteria (with meals at cost), medical facilities, a swimming pool, a balconied gymnasium with marble-lined showers and locker rooms for men and women, a game room, and a women's recreation lounge. Workers' hours shrank from 54 to 44 hours per week. (PCHGS.)

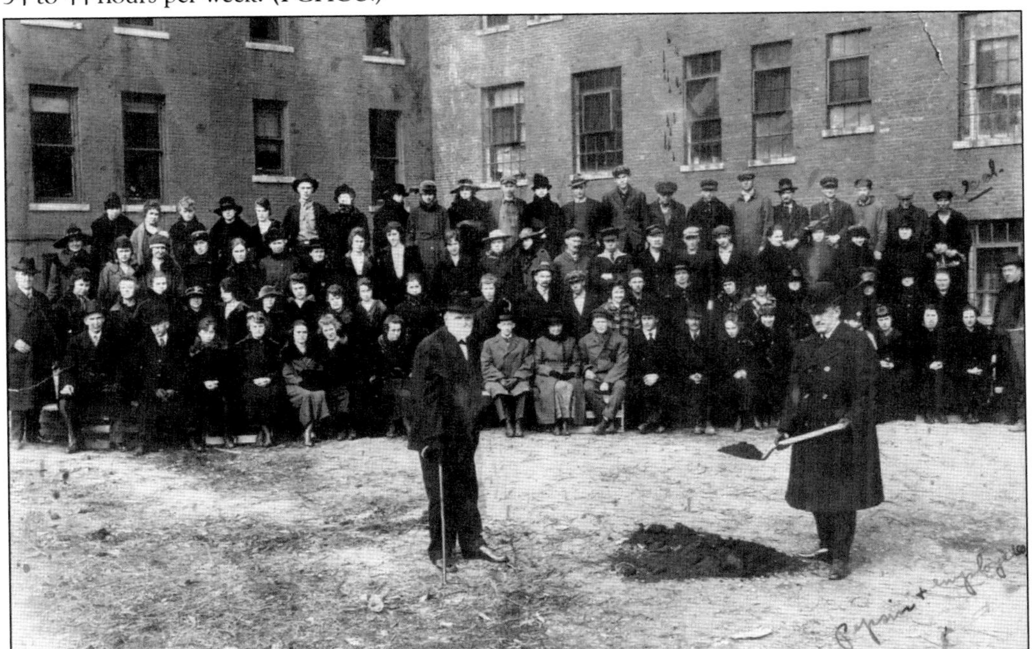

Employees stand outside the Pepsin Syrup Company in 1918. In 1925, the company sold for $5 million to Household Products Company, a division of Sterling Drugs Company. Sterling Drugs's products included Fletcher's Castoria, Campho-Phenique, and Bayer Aspirin. The original Pepsin Syrup Company was renamed Dr. W.B. Caldwell Company in 1934, with subsequent name changes as years passed. (PCHGS.)

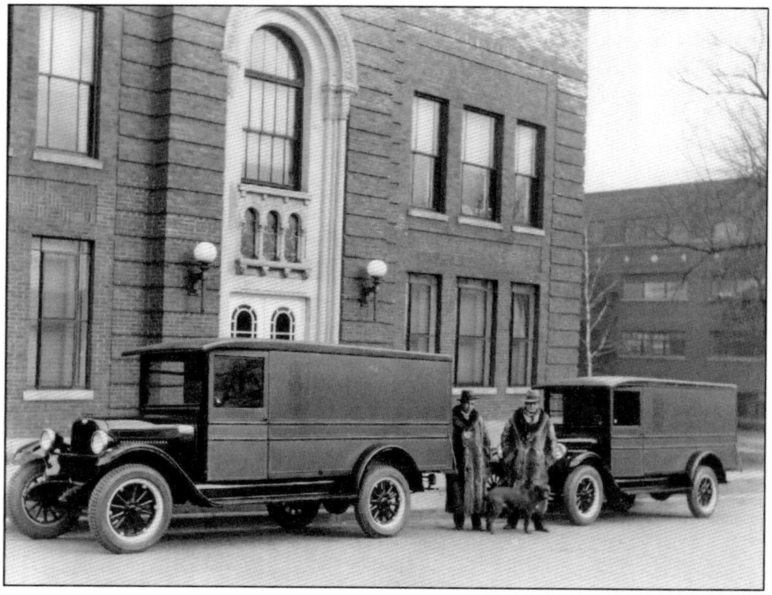

Raccoon coats are most closely associated with male college students of the 1920s and reached the height of the craze around 1928, prior to the Great Depression. The men are unidentified, but it is believed that they are company managers Maxwell Hott (left) and Donn Piatt. The vehicles are marked, "Dr. Caldwell's Syrup Pepsin, The Family Laxative." (PCHGS.)

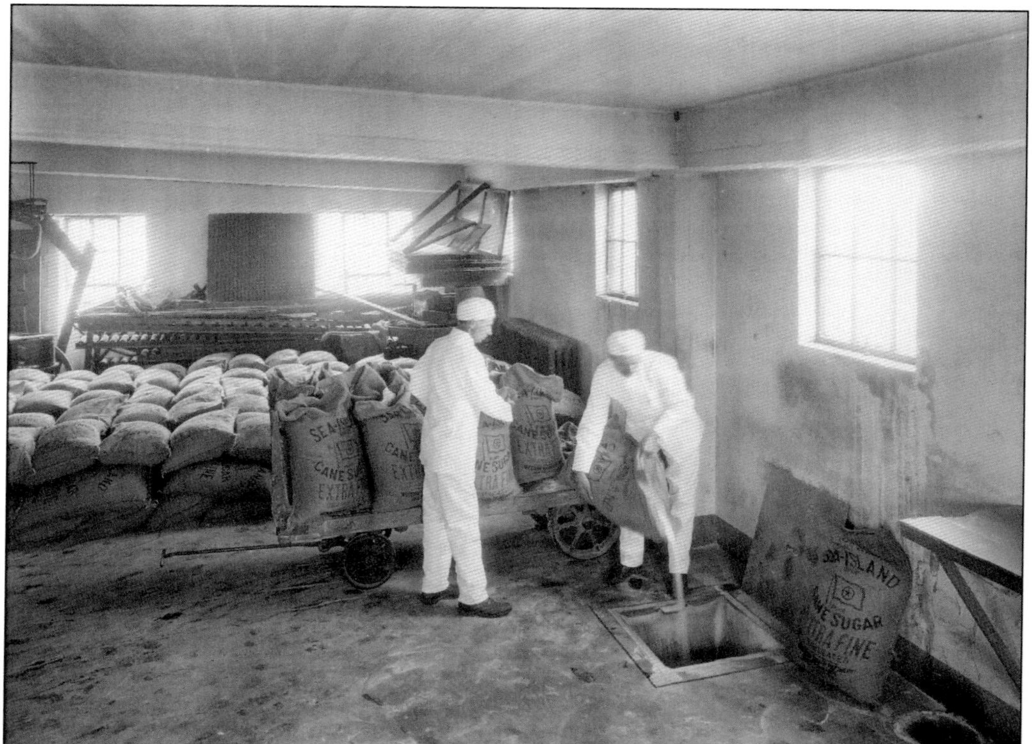

Pepsin Syrup Company employees pour the contents of twenty 100-pound bags of pure cane sugar—one of the laxative's main components—into a hopper connected to a tank on the floor below, where the rest of the ingredients were combined. A motor spun the mixture to immediately dissolve the sugar. (PCHGS.)

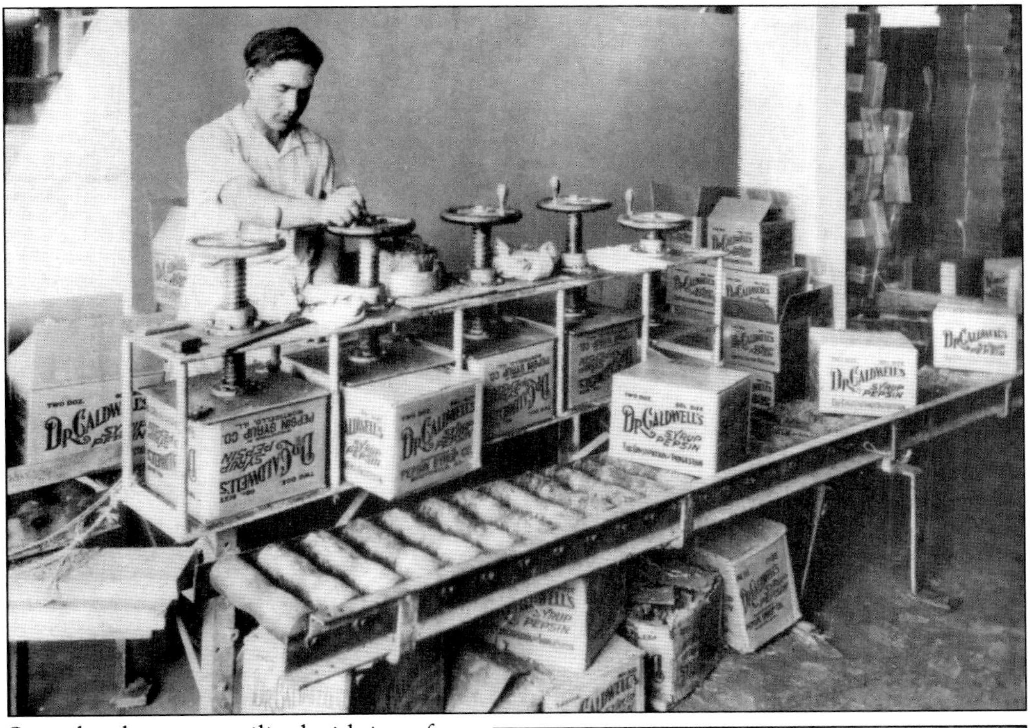

Syrup bottles were sterilized with jets of scalding water, then filled with syrup. Filled cases traveled on an inclined conveyor belt to an employee who glued the flaps and sealed the cartons before the boxes continued to the next station. Thousands of cases of the syrup were stored in a warehouse, ready for immediate shipment. The company sold between 10 and 11 million bottles of the brew in 1923. (PCHGS.)

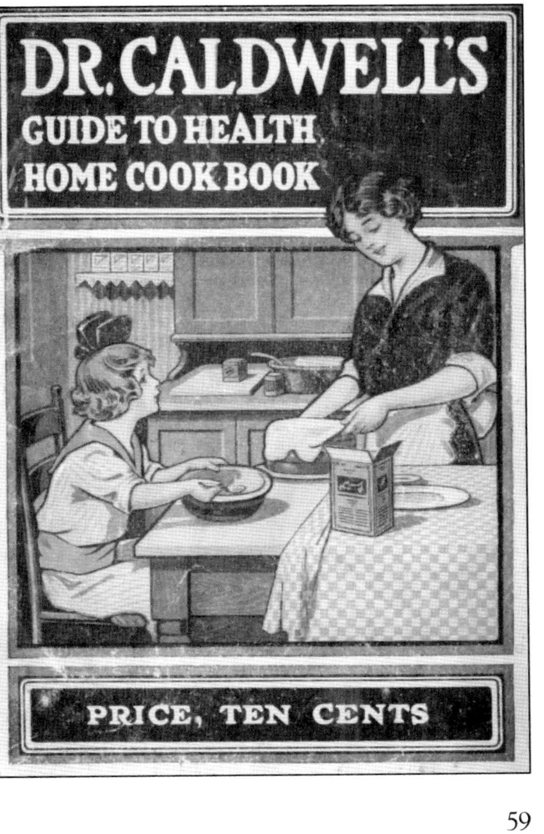

A majority of pages in the 1910 *Dr. Caldwell's Guide to Health Home Cookbook* from the Pepsin Syrup Company display a person's photograph, name, and testimonial, interspersed with recipes and health concerns alleviated after using the product. For cirrhosis of the liver, the company claims that the use of the syrup "will enable the patient to build up his body and resist the disease, thereby in the end curing it." (MH.)

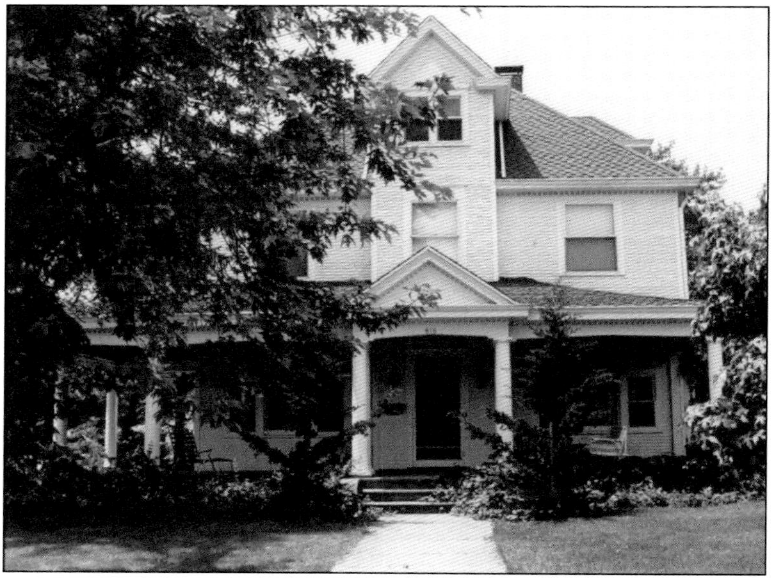

W.C. Handlin is believed to be the first owner of the house at 816 South Charter Street. Later owners were Elim and Mary Hawbaker. They married in 1909 and bought the house in 1920. Hawbaker served as county judge for eight years. A carriage barn built around 1902 sits at the back end of the property where current owners operate an antique store. (APL.)

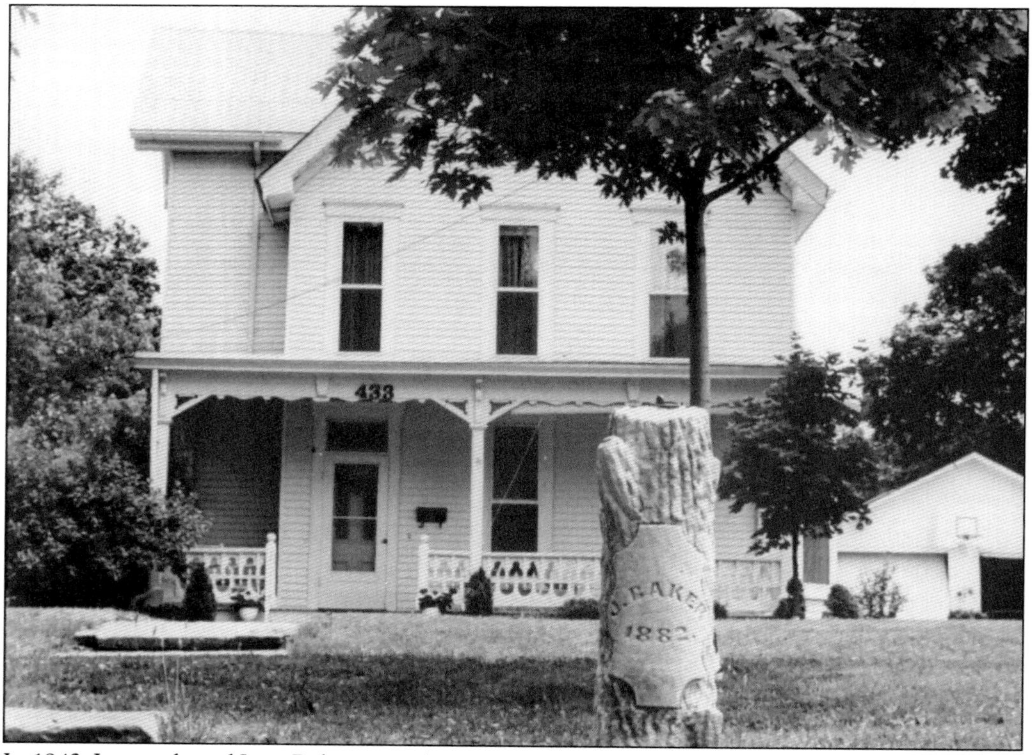

In 1843, Jeremiah and Jane Baker moved to Monticello from Ohio and became large landowners. The Queen Anne house at 433 South Charter Street was built for them with a railing identical to the one across the street at number 412. It was known to have the first bathtub in town. The limestone slab sidewalk is historic, as is its limestone carriage post carved with "1882" and "J. Baker." (APL.)

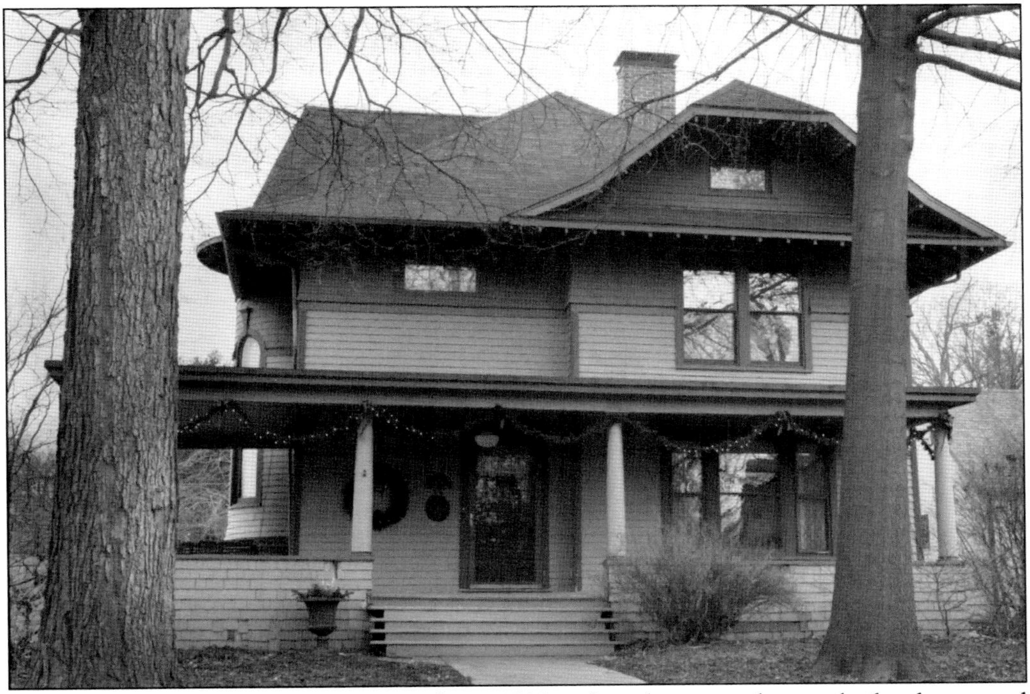

Dr. William Matson moved to Monticello in 1898 and, within several years, built a house and carriage barn at 407 South Charter Street. He sold his medical practice and the property to Dr. Brent Barker in 1907. The Craftsman touches were added in 1915 after a fire destroyed the roof. Members of the Barker family continued to live there until Dr. Barker's daughter's death in 1977. (APL.)

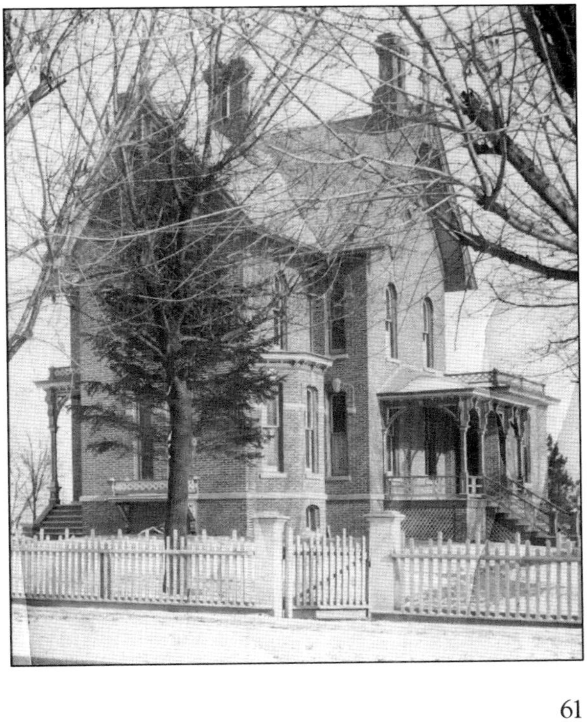

Around 1873, Preston Huston, bank partner to Moore and Dighton, built a Victorian Gothic Revival house at 915 North State Street (the original address was 913). With 11-foot ceilings and double front doors to accommodate hoopskirts, it was also the first house with electricity, running water, and central heating. Later, it was home for Charles Nelson Thompson, and then his daughter, Jessie, and her husband, William Dighton. (APL.)

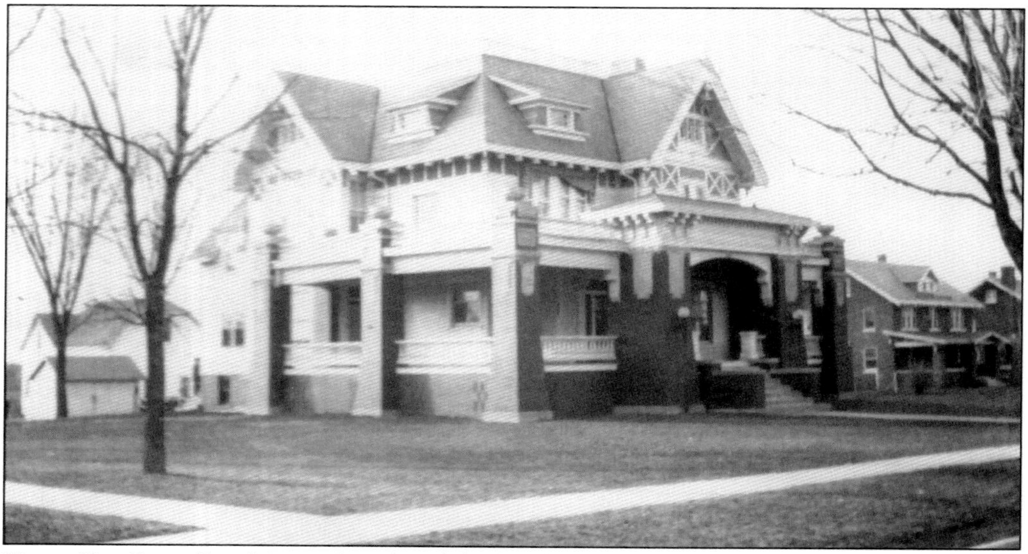

Henry Van Rensallaer Moore, founder of the first bank in Piatt County, owned the farmhouse at 1004 North State Street. Built around 1875, it was remodeled with a front extension in 1917. Owner N.E. Hutson made changes in 1939, and his architect grandson Kennedy Hutson added another extension in the 2000s. Styles now blend Queen Anne, Italianate, and Georgian architectures. (SR.)

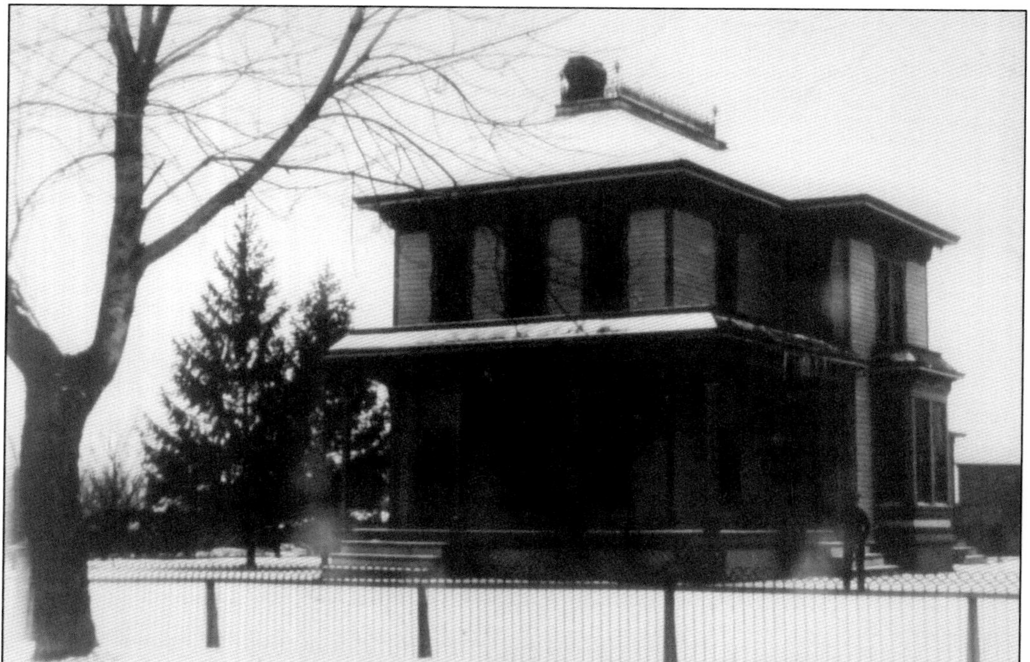

The Ryder house at 802 North State Street started out as an Italianate-style frame house with a widow's walk on top. Later residents included H.P. Martin (owner of a department store on the square) and Bradford Moore, son of Allen F. Moore. During a significant remodeling, wings and porches were added, with porticos supporting the porches. (APL.)

One of the oldest houses on North Charter Street, the home at number 844 charms everyone with its light pink color. It has been claimed that the white wrought-iron fence was added in the 1960s by Elmer Priebe, a former chauffeur and farm manager for Robert Allerton. The house is listed by the Historical Preservation Board as having historical and architectural significance. (APL.)

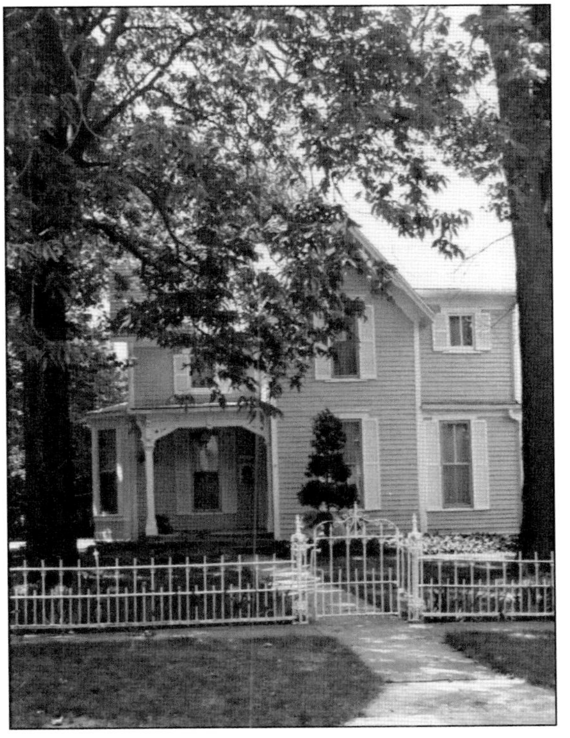

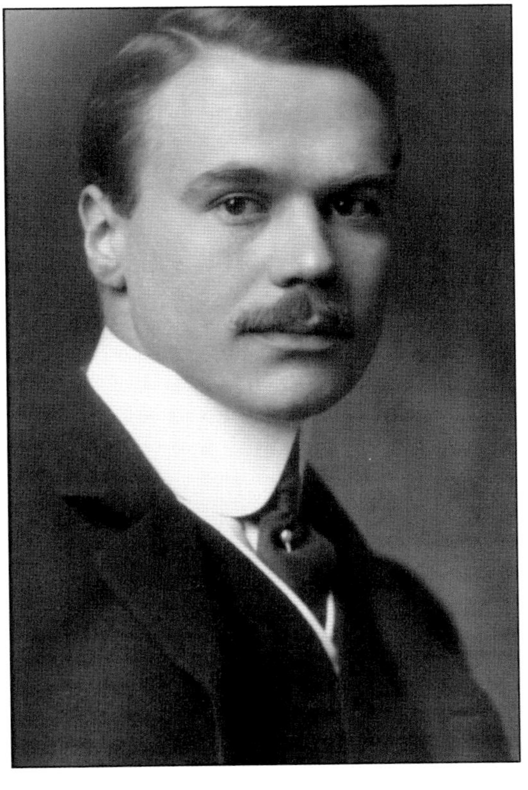

Born in 1873, Robert Allerton was the son of Samuel Allerton, Chicago's third-wealthiest resident. In 1906, the *Chicago Tribune* named Robert the "Richest Bachelor in Chicago." He built a magnificent mansion outside Monticello on family land and filled the estate with sculpture. Rich, artistic, and nearly deaf from a childhood illness, he loved the beauty of central Illinois but not the cold winters. (JG.)

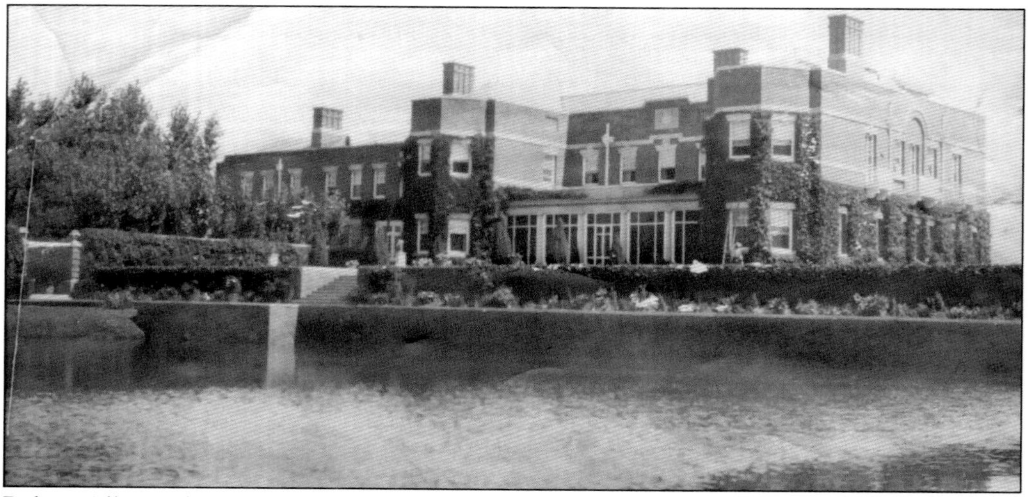

Robert Allerton began construction of his mansion in 1899 a few miles outside the city limits. After the interior was completed, he furnished it with antiques and artwork from around the world. In this old photograph, one can see the parapet that runs around the roofline. By 1908, after several years of rain and ice seeping inside, the parapet was removed and the roof was modified (see next photograph). (JG.)

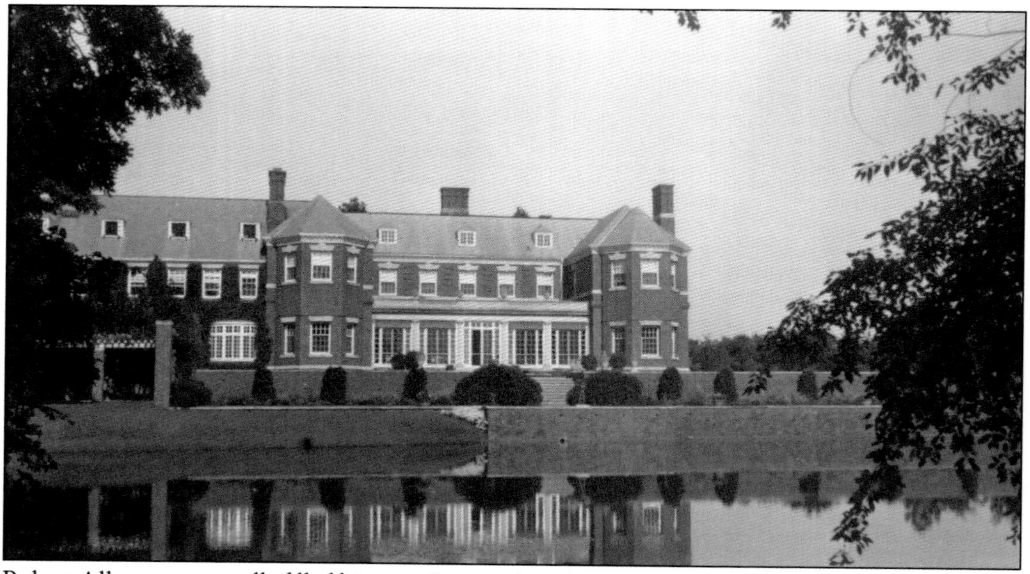

Robert Allerton eventually filled his estate's grounds with statuary and gardens, moving the sculpture around as he experimented with his landscaping visions. Allerton donated 5,500 acres of his total 12,000-acre estate to the University of Illinois in 1946. Now called Allerton Park and Retreat Center, it is a favorite among residents and visitors, especially to see the fall colors. (JG.)

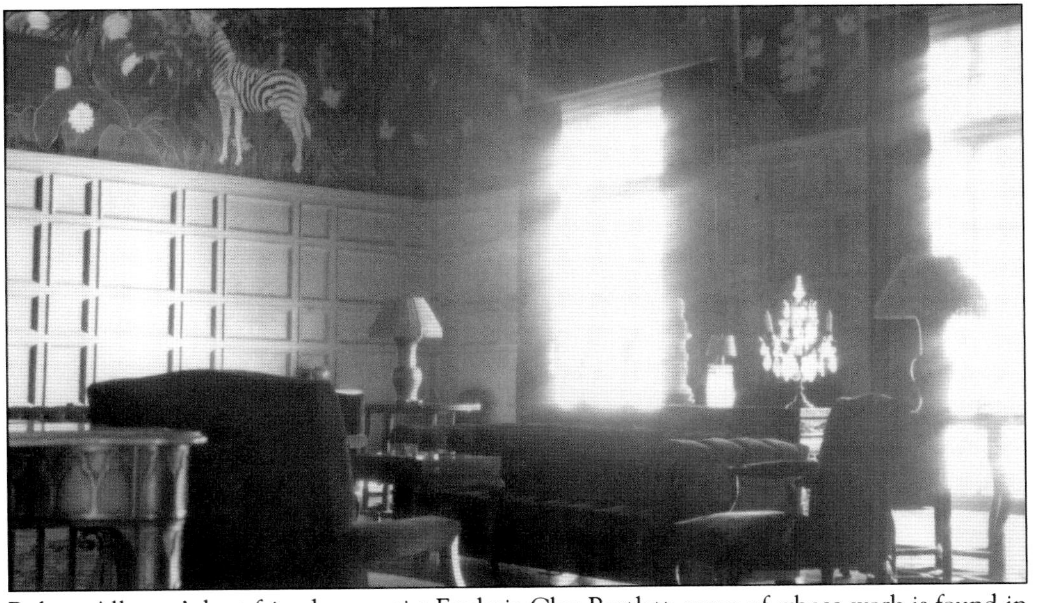

Robert Allerton's best friend was artist Frederic Clay Bartlett, some of whose work is found in the Chicago area. In 1927, after the death of his second wife, Bartlett designed and painted a jungle mural for Allerton surrounding the top of the music room (now one of the mansion's libraries). Eventually, Allerton removed parts of the mural and covered the rest with whitewash and bookcases. (JG.)

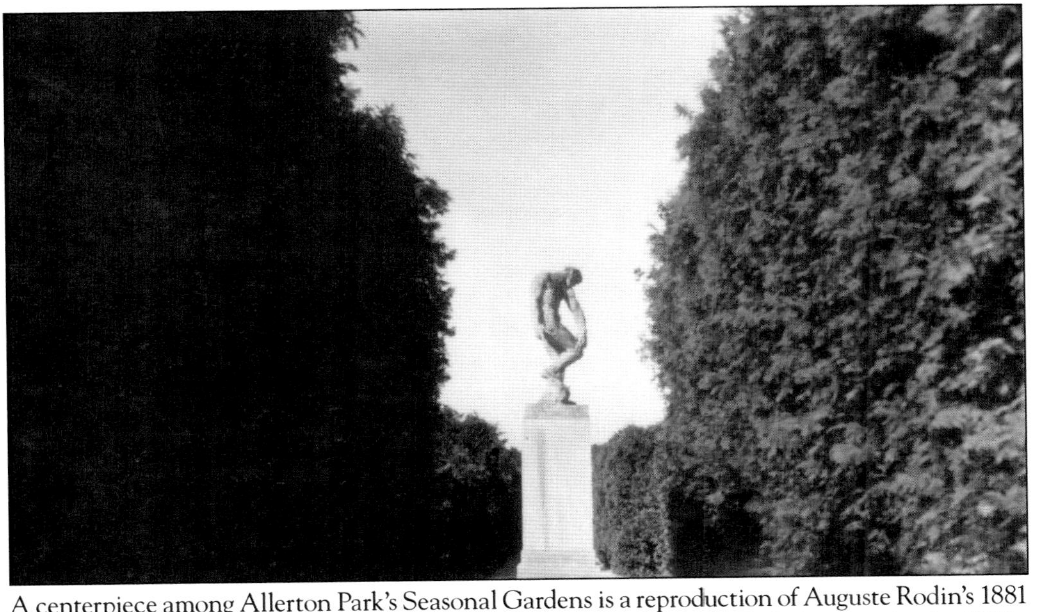

A centerpiece among Allerton Park's Seasonal Gardens is a reproduction of Auguste Rodin's 1881 sculpture *Adam*. Robert Allerton acquired the bronze casting from Rodin's estate in the 1920s. He commissioned a stone reproduction for his estate before giving the original sculpture to the Art Institute of Chicago in 1924. After the reproduction was damaged beyond repair in 1975, another replica was commissioned. (JG.)

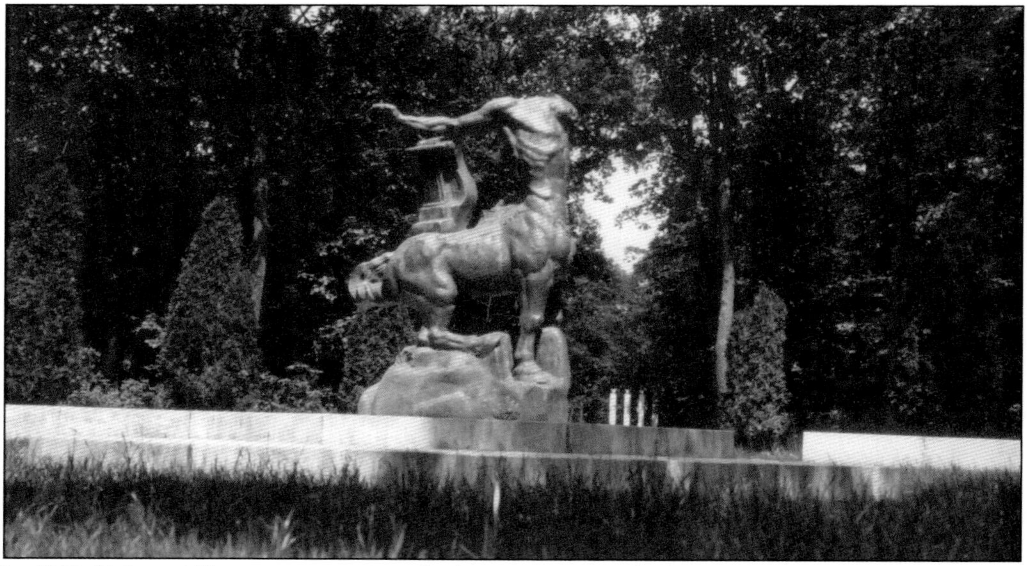

In 1929, Robert Allerton commissioned a bronze casting of *The Death of the Last Centaur* from Émile-Antoine Bourdelle, a student of Rodin and one of Rodin's favorite artists. The piece is a favorite among hikers heading from the Sunken Garden to Carl Milles's *Sun Singer,* which sits at the farthest reaches of the park. (JG.)

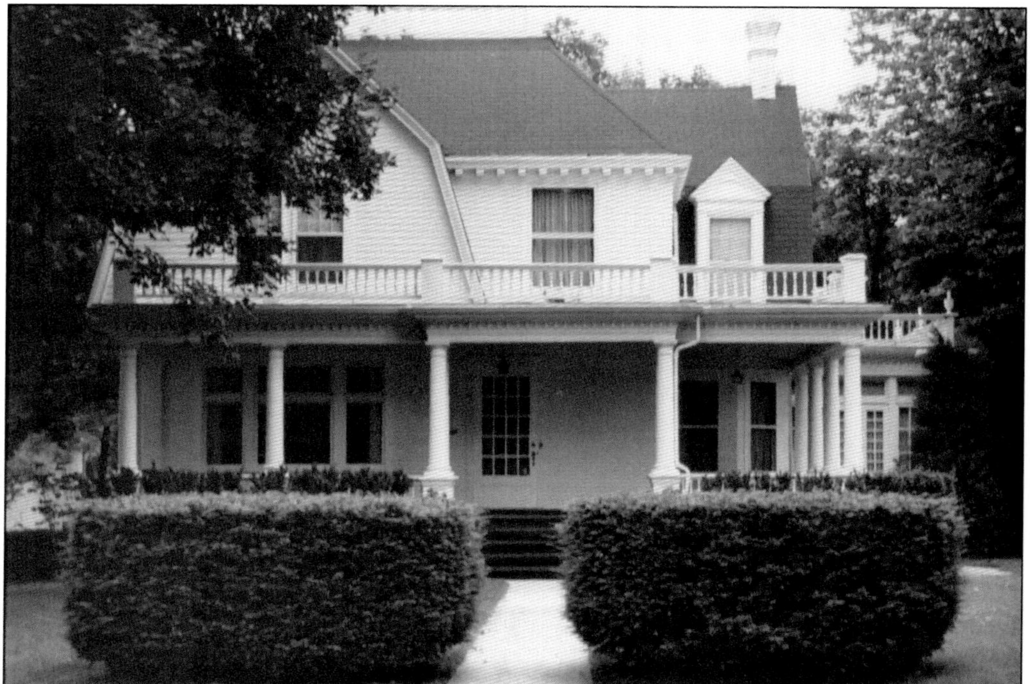

This Queen Anne house at 707 North State Street was built in 1898 on James Piatt land for Sarah Dighton, the widowed mother of William and Mary Dighton Burgess. Sarah's son William Dighton eventually lived across the street at 712 North State Street. Her daughter Mary lived next door at number 719. Sarah died in 1918. (APL.)

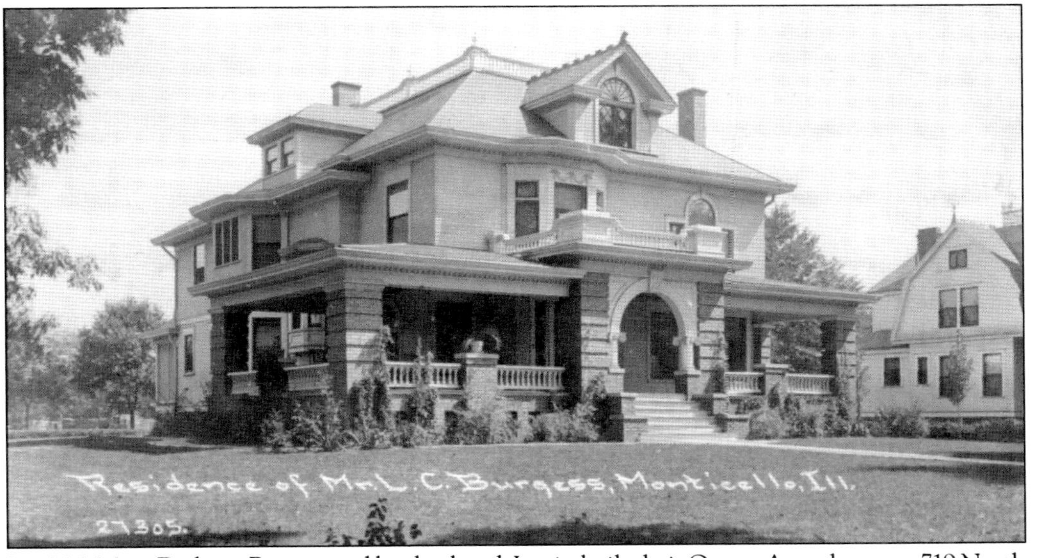

In 1906, Mary Dighton Burgess and her husband, Louis, built their Queen Anne house at 719 North State Street, next door to her mother, Sarah Dighton. In addition to a sidewalk connecting the two backdoors, the Burgess house included heart-shaped lavatories, a central vacuum system, an ice door on the side porch, and a basement ballroom. The carriage house was added in 1980. (SR.)

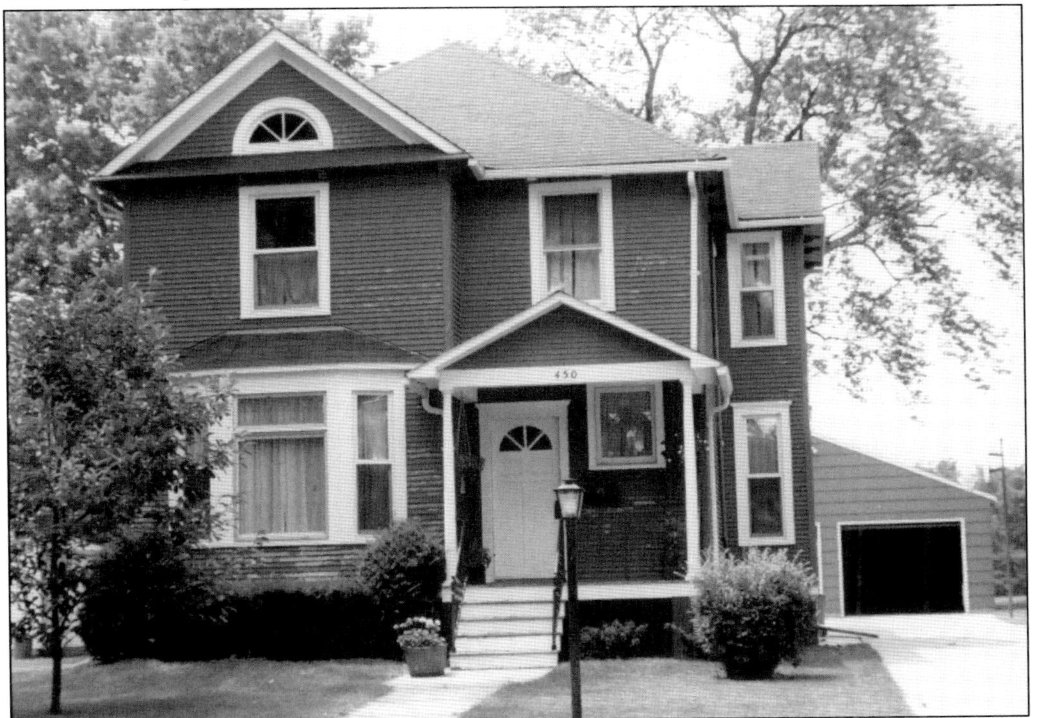

William Piatt built the house at 450 Elm Boulevard in 1901 for his daughter Elizabeth Jemima "Mima" and her husband, William E. Smith. Eventually, their son and Piatt County treasurer William Piatt Smith, his wife, Gertrude, and their son Gordon lived there. Subsequent owners included Ralph W. Bear and Phillip Blankenburg. (APL.)

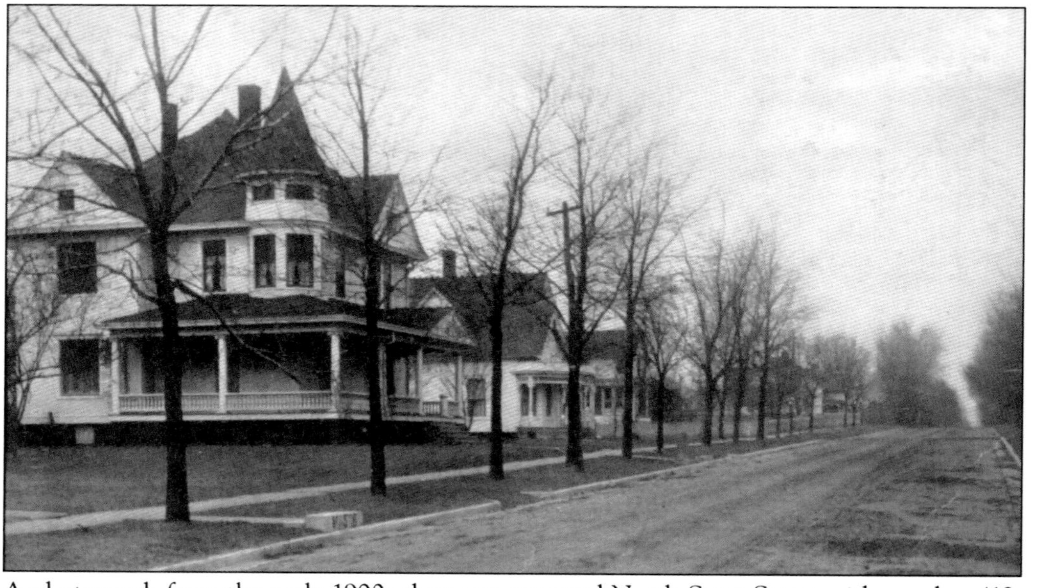

A photograph from the early 1900s shows an unpaved North State Street with number 412, prominent in left foreground, with its round tower. The Queen Anne house was built in 1902 for a member of the Ridgely family. Later owners included Allen M. Moore, Olen Woolington, and John Hott. The house faces State Street, and its brick carriage house faces Charter Street. (SR.)

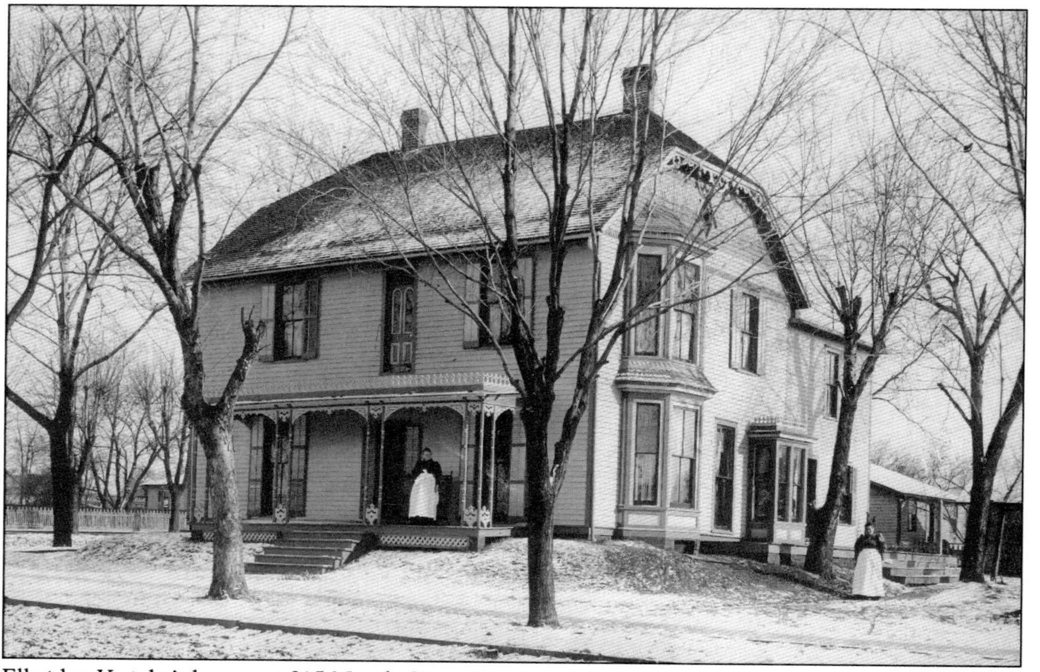

Elbridge Knight's house at 315 North State Street, on the southeast corner of State and Center Streets, is pictured with Hannah Fleming in the yard and Anna R. Knight on the porch. An apartment building now occupies the lot. Knight arrived in Illinois in 1856 and worked for 40 years as a grain buyer. Later, he and his son operated a hardware business until 1909. Elbridge died in 1914. (APL-HS.)

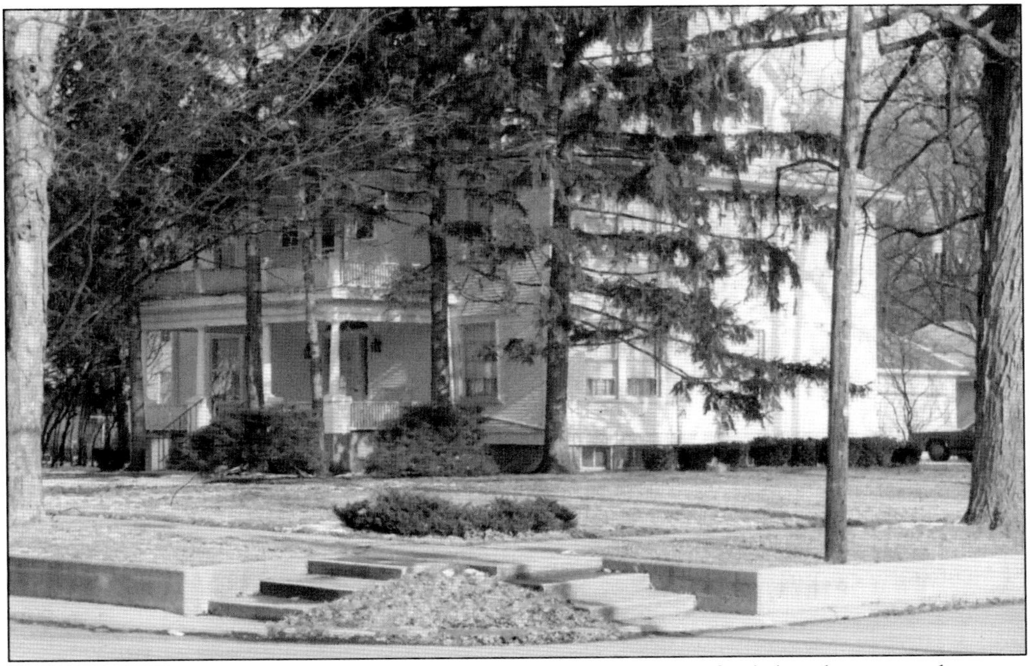

Herbert D. Peters, founder of the *Piatt County Herald* newspaper, built his three-story home at 315 South Buchanan Street in 1906. Nine years later, Harry Kaiser of Kaiser Abstract Company bought the house. Two more generations of Kaisers—his son Herbert and later his grandson Herbert Jr.—lived there. The house was sold in 2012 after the death of Herbert Kaiser Jr. (APL.)

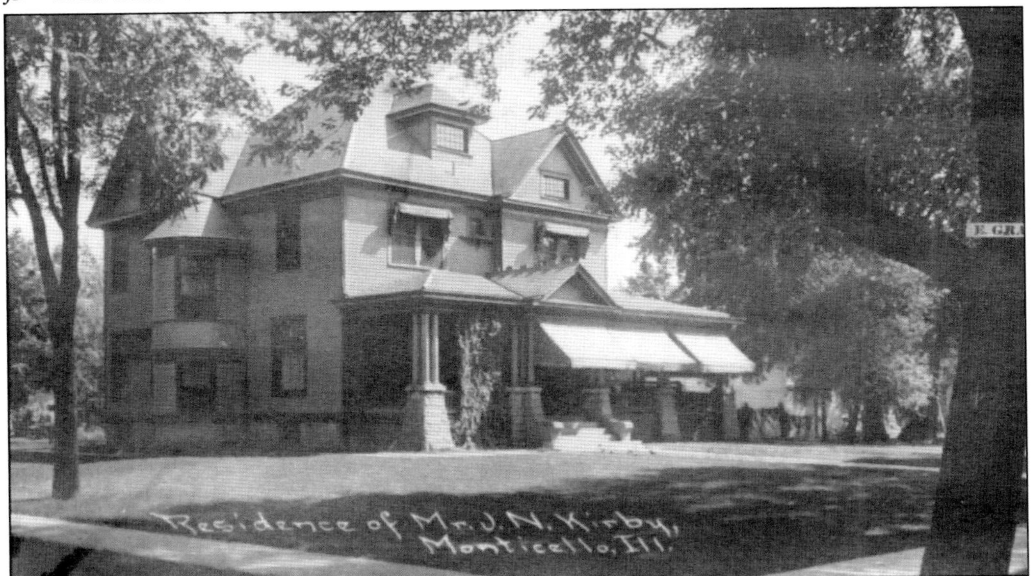

This Queen Anne house with a stair turret was built at 619 North State Street in 1903 for John N. Kirby. The original hip roof has since been replaced with nested half-timber gables. The master bedroom had a mouthpiece to call the kitchen. Born in Limerick, Ireland, in 1842, Kirby married Mary Marquiss, the granddaughter of Monticello founder Abraham Marquiss. The Kirbys established a trust that funded Kirby Hospital. (APL.)

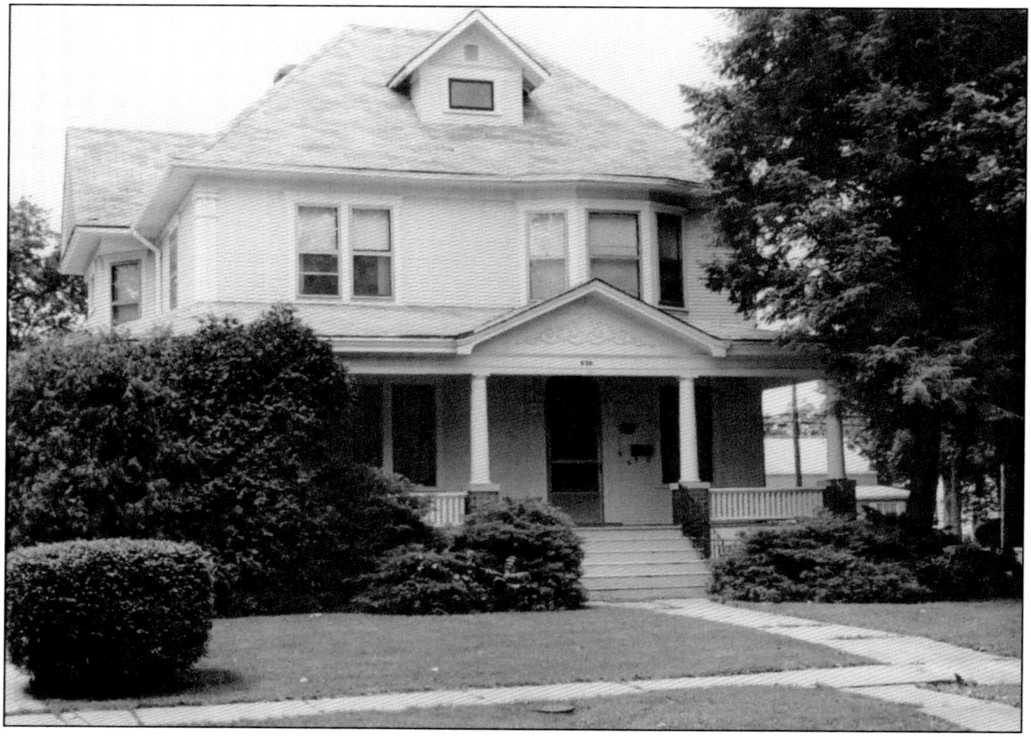

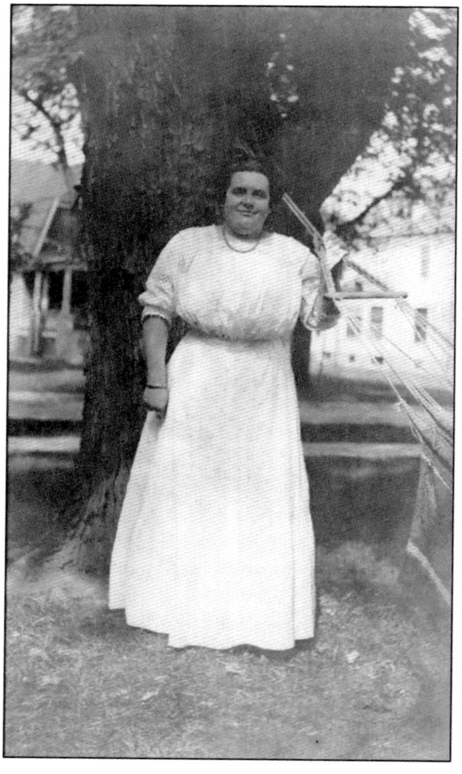

After amassing wealth through land speculating and other ventures, Albert T. England and his wife, Harriet (daughter of Sheriff W.H. Plunk), built a Queen Anne home in 1906 at 620 North State Street, directly across from John and Mary Kirby. Two years earlier, their son William Herbert had married the Kirbys' daughter Nell. (APL.)

Born in 1879, Nell Kirby married William Herbert England in 1904. After her parents' bequest funding Kirby Hospital, Nell served from 1941 to 1950 on Kirby Hospital's board of directors. Nell died a childless widow in 1950. As a result, her entire estate was donated to the John and Mary Kirby Hospital. (APL.)

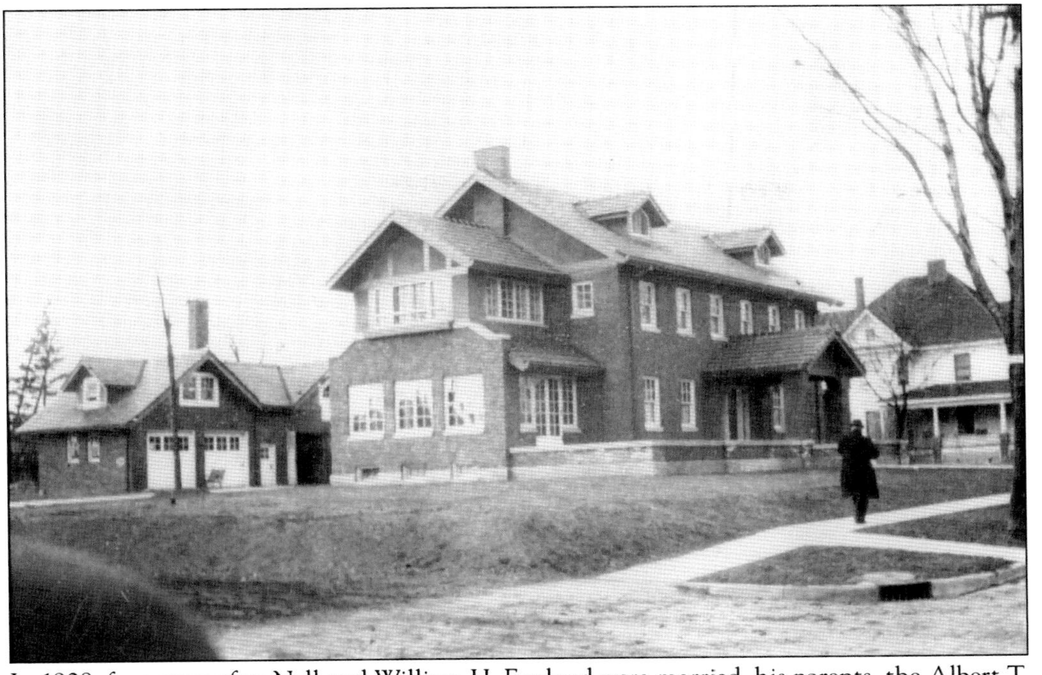

In 1908, four years after Nell and William H. England were married, his parents, the Albert T. Englands, built this 4,600-square-foot Tudor-style house at 612 North State Street as a late wedding present for the couple. It included a ballroom in the basement and a tunnel to the carriage house, which had its own 850-square-foot apartment. (SR.)

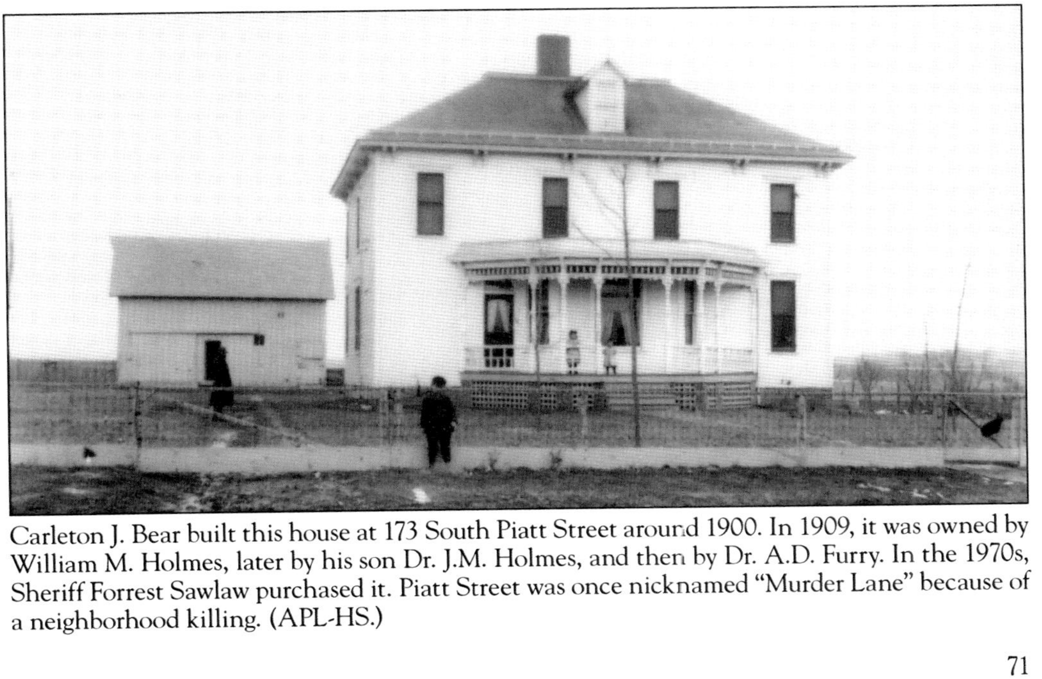

Carleton J. Bear built this house at 173 South Piatt Street around 1900. In 1909, it was owned by William M. Holmes, later by his son Dr. J.M. Holmes, and then by Dr. A.D. Furry. In the 1970s, Sheriff Forrest Sawlaw purchased it. Piatt Street was once nicknamed "Murder Lane" because of a neighborhood killing. (APL-HS.)

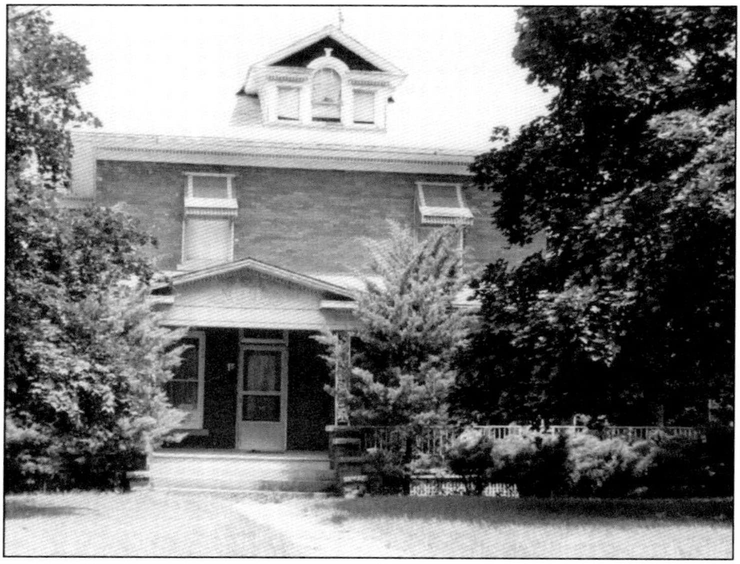

Seymour Marquiss built this large brick house at 125 South Piatt Street in 1903. The downstairs woodwork matches that from the Voorhies Castle, several miles south of Bement, Illinois. Three upstairs bathrooms contained marble sinks. Later owners included Marquiss's son-in-law Dr. Frederick Keele and Charles McIntosh, school superintendent and author of a history of Piatt County. (APL.)

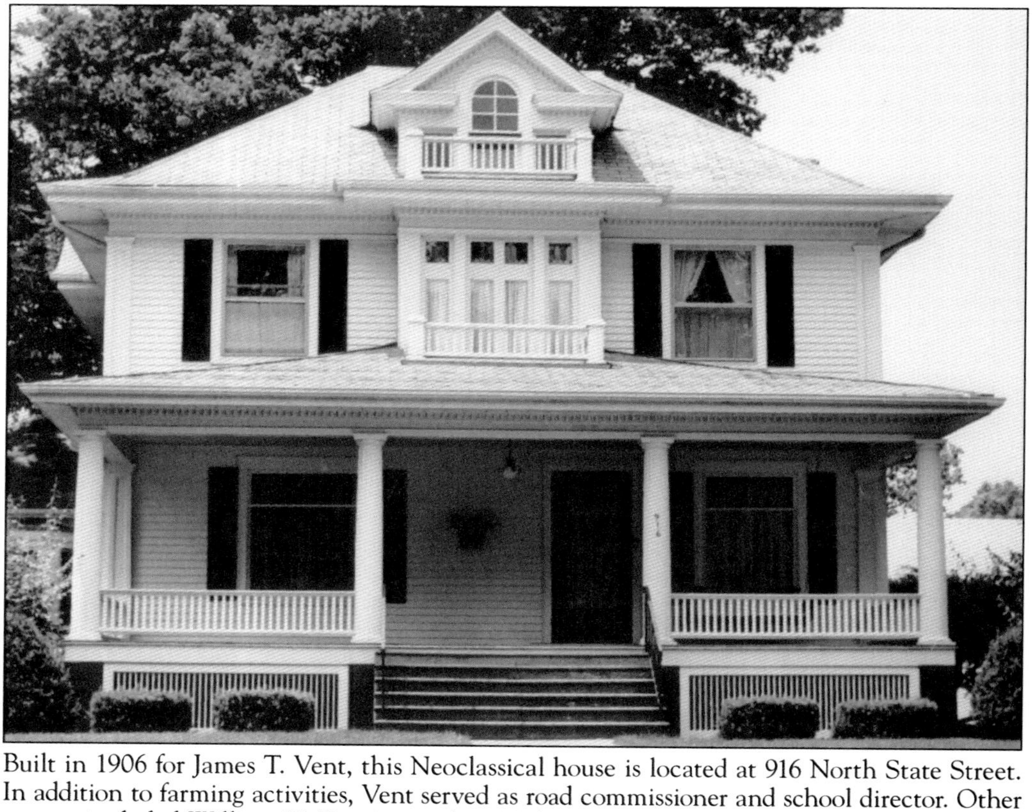

Built in 1906 for James T. Vent, this Neoclassical house is located at 916 North State Street. In addition to farming activities, Vent served as road commissioner and school director. Other owners included William H. Piatt's grandson Kirby Smith and, for decades until 2009, Donn Piatt, a descendant of one of the city's founders, James Piatt. (APL.)

Henry Timmons built this Queen Anne house at 506 North Charter Street in 1905. John Dighton's family lived there from 1916 until 1971. Timmons and Dighton came from two of Monticello's wealthiest families. It was Timmons's hope that Dighton's only son, John, might marry any of Timmons's three daughters. Mary Timmons married the son in 1907, but she died in 1909. The next year, her sister Olive married him. (APL.)

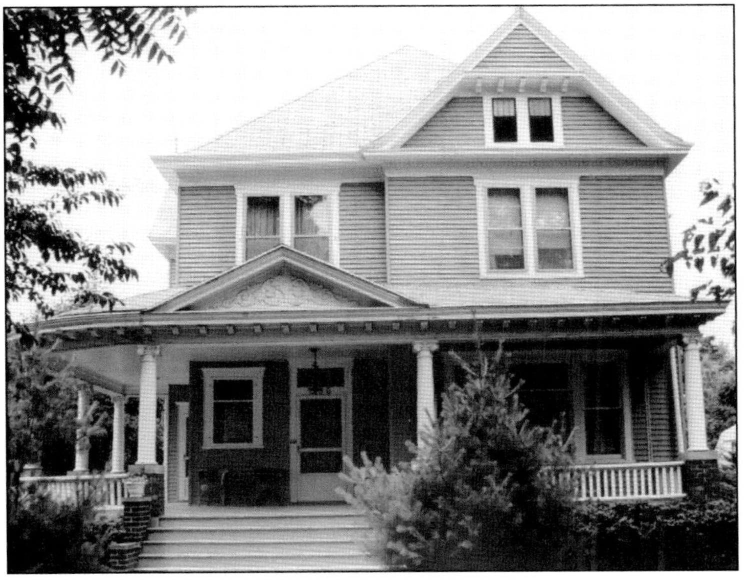

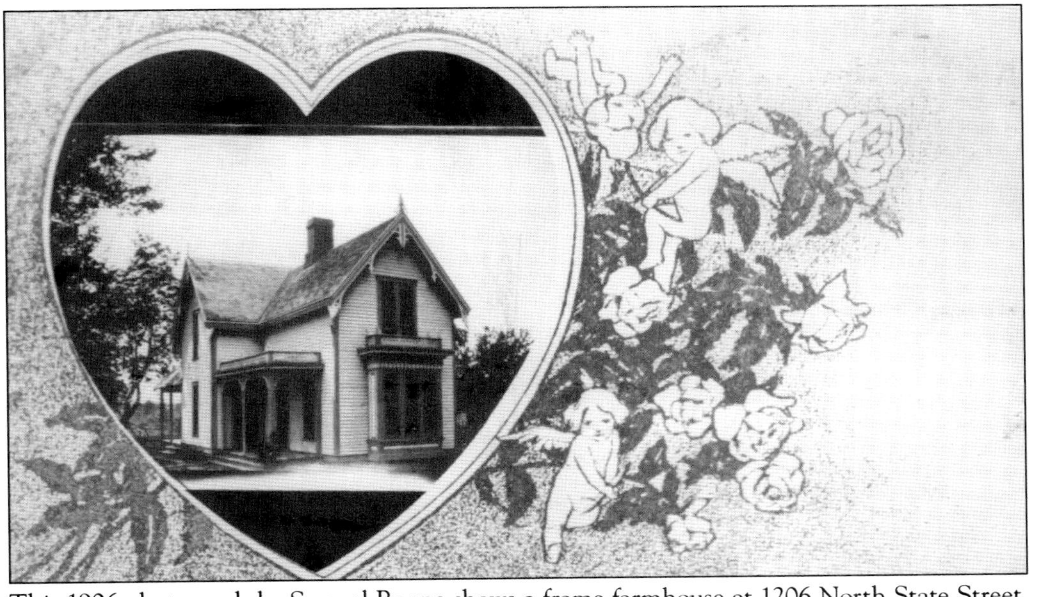

This 1906 photograph by Samuel Roane shows a frame farmhouse at 1206 North State Street. The property was deeded to James Piatt in 1843 and later owned by William Piatt. Roane and his family lived there from 1902 until 1908. As a rural mail carrier, Roane supplied many photographs of life in and around Monticello from the early 1900s through the 1970s, with a particular relish for the Piatt County Fair. (SR.)

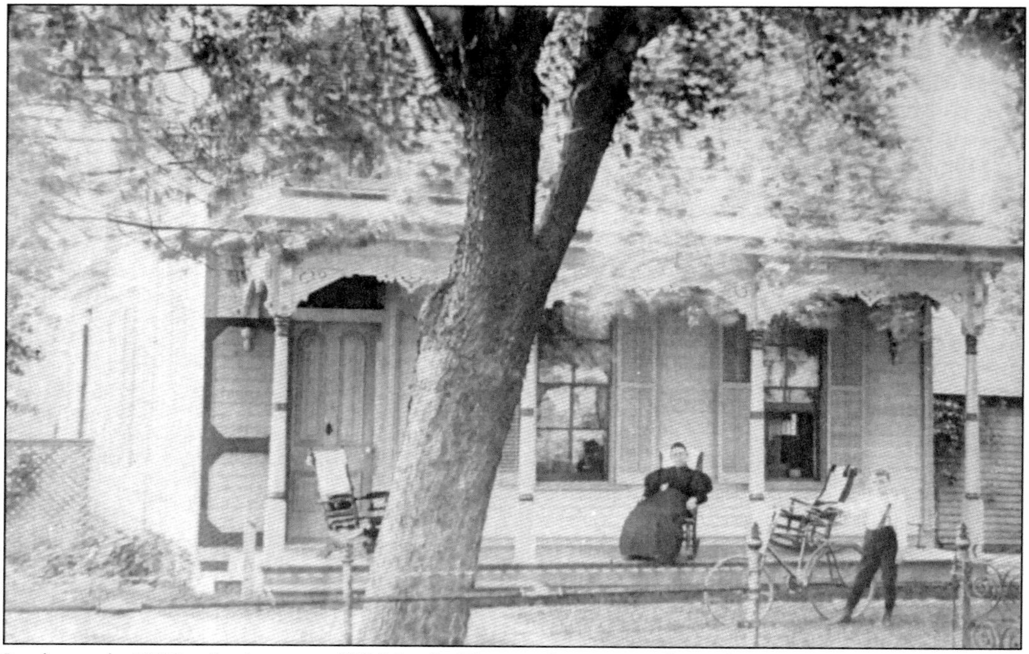

In the early 1900s, the home at 520 North Charter Street was that of Dr. William Burr Caldwell, creator of the laxative known as Pepsin Syrup. Lena Bragg, Allerton Library head librarian from 1913 until 1955, also once lived there. For a period of time, the house was segmented into apartments. Passersby may notice how the Victorian porch makes the house seem almost like a steamboat. (APL.)

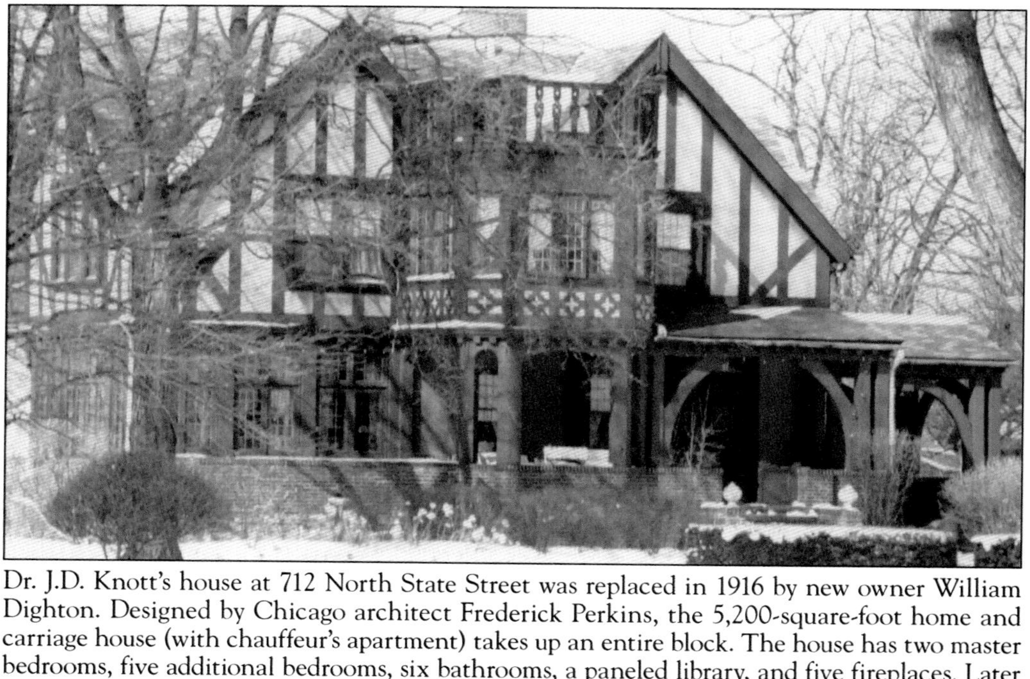

Dr. J.D. Knott's house at 712 North State Street was replaced in 1916 by new owner William Dighton. Designed by Chicago architect Frederick Perkins, the 5,200-square-foot home and carriage house (with chauffeur's apartment) takes up an entire block. The house has two master bedrooms, five additional bedrooms, six bathrooms, a paneled library, and five fireplaces. Later owner Henry Dighton kept a small donkey for children to enjoy. (APL.)

Allen Moore bought controlling interest in the Pepsin Syrup Company in 1899, selling out to Sterling Products in 1925. He served as a Monticello alderman and mayor and, from 1920 to 1924, as Congressman from the 19th Congressional District. In the 1920s, he and his wife donated $150,000 for a new Monticello High School gymnasium. He eventually became involved in Texas oil development. He died in San Antonio in 1945. (APL.)

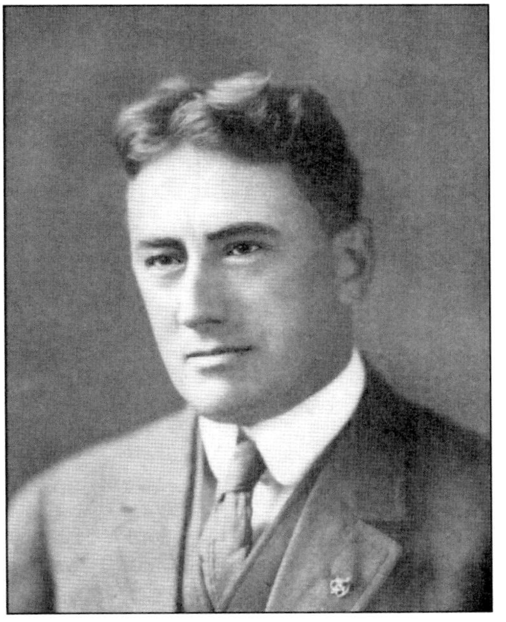

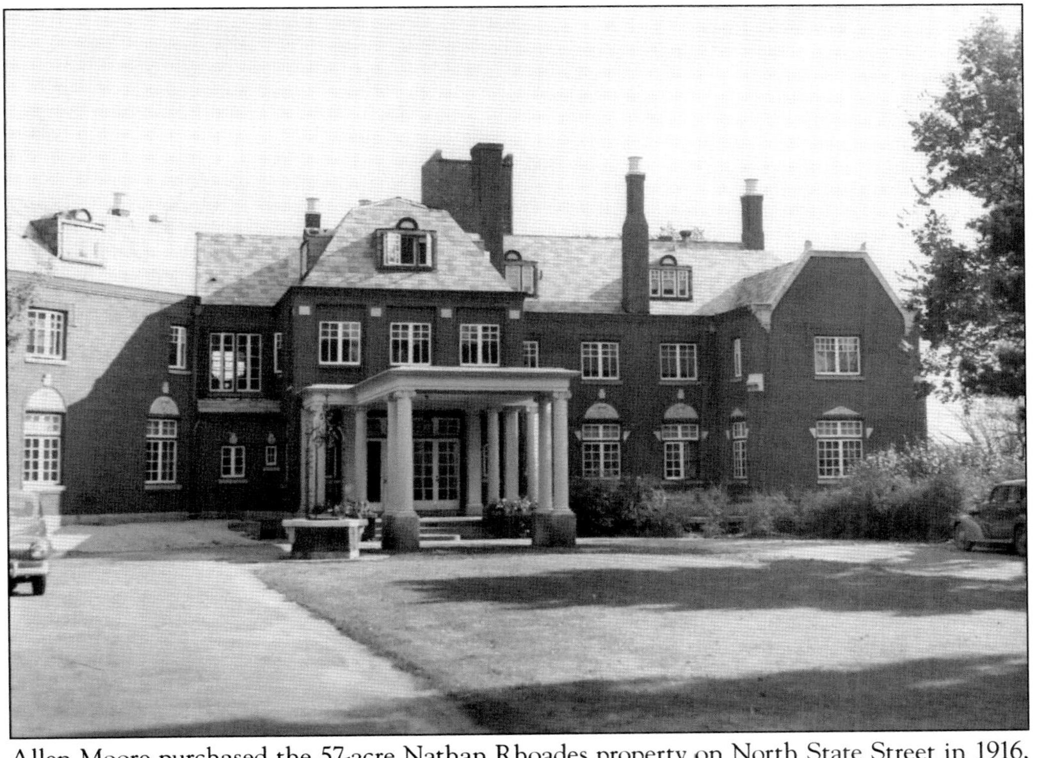

Allen Moore purchased the 57-acre Nathan Rhoades property on North State Street in 1916, demolished the 50-year-old house, and replaced it with a 20,000-square-foot mansion. After Moore declared bankruptcy during the Depression, the Kirby Hospital trust fund purchased the property. In 1939, it became Kirby Hospital. It was razed in 1974 for a new facility. In 2011, the hospital moved near Lodge Park. (PCHGS.)

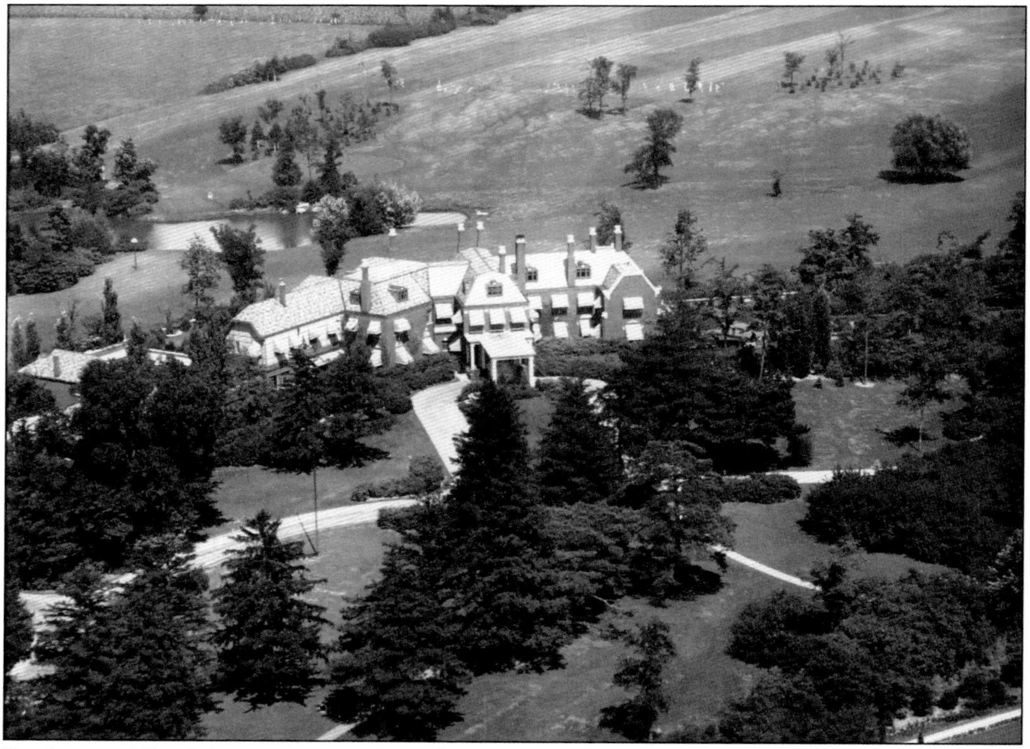

Bradmore, Allen Moore's estate on North State Street, is seen in this aerial view. Moore filled the property with formal English gardens, paved terraces, a pond, tennis courts, rock gardens, and his own nine-hole golf course. For privacy, he erected a low brick wall along the State Street side of the property. (APL.)

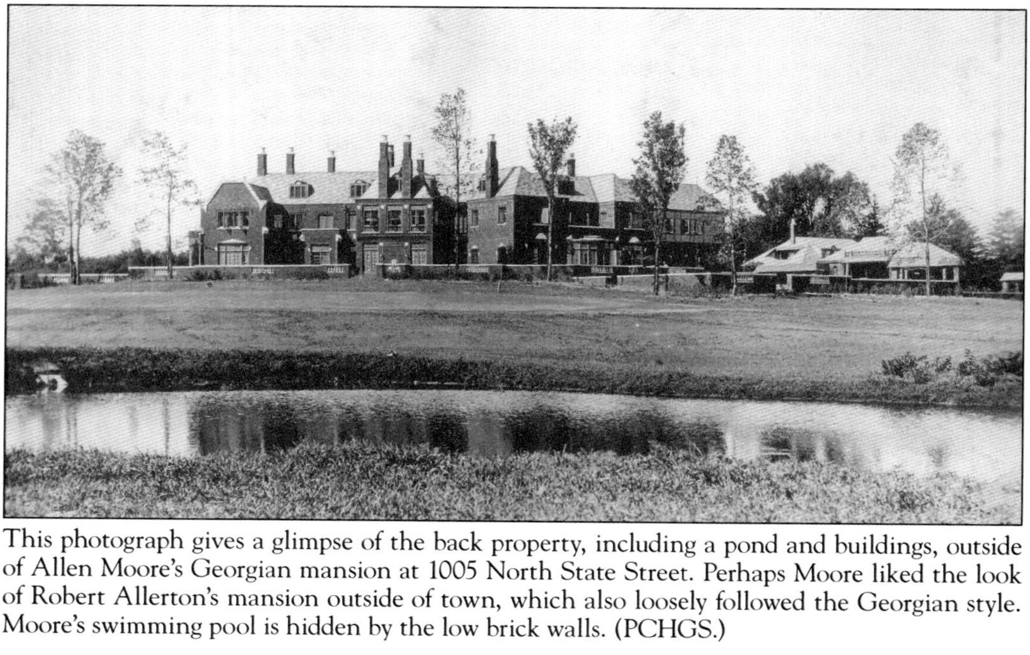

This photograph gives a glimpse of the back property, including a pond and buildings, outside of Allen Moore's Georgian mansion at 1005 North State Street. Perhaps Moore liked the look of Robert Allerton's mansion outside of town, which also loosely followed the Georgian style. Moore's swimming pool is hidden by the low brick walls. (PCHGS.)

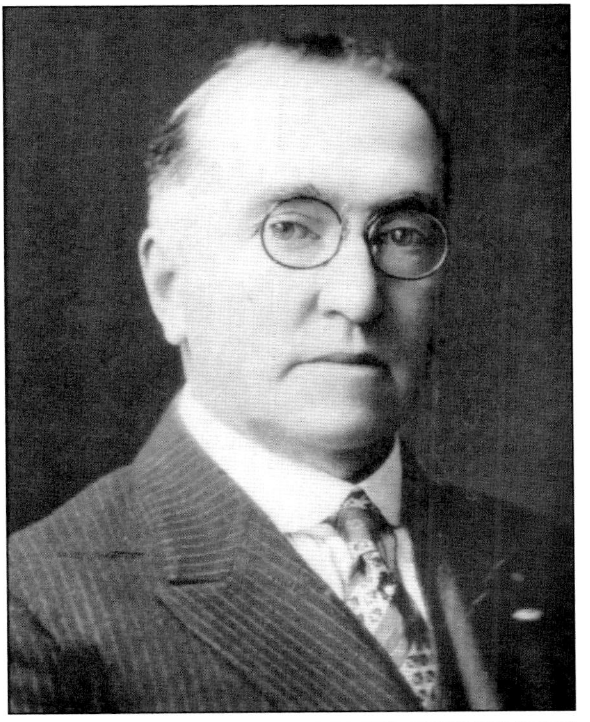

Pharmacist John Hott purchased the Chenoweth Drug Store in the early 1900s. He sold the business when an opportunity arose to become partner and sales manager of Pepsin Syrup Company. He served as the company's general manager until ill health forced him to retire in 1934. He then bought Pinus Medicine Company from William Dighton. Hott was also vice president and director of the National Bank of Monticello. (PCHGS.)

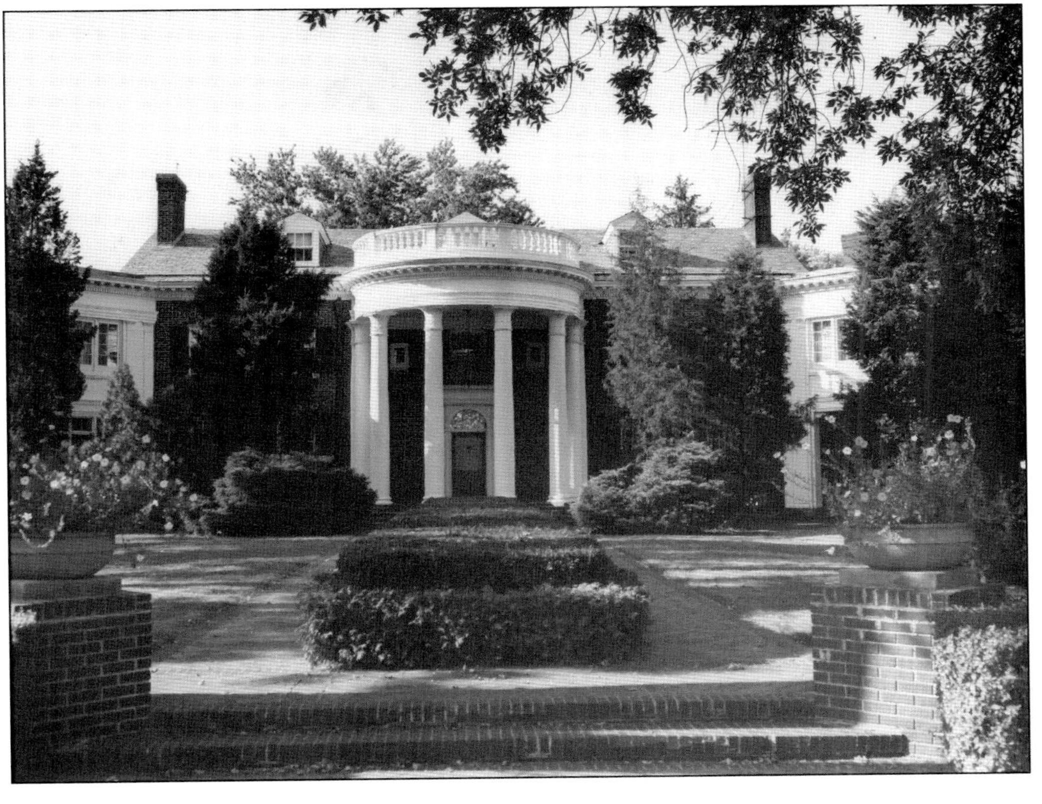

In 1925, John Hott purchased a house at 810 North State Street once owned by Sheriff Plunk, demolished it, and, at the cost of $40,000, built a 23-room mansion with a two-story, semicircular portico. Hott's son Maxwell donated the property to the University of Illinois Foundation in 1960. Again a private residence, it is still referred to as the "Hott House." (APL.)

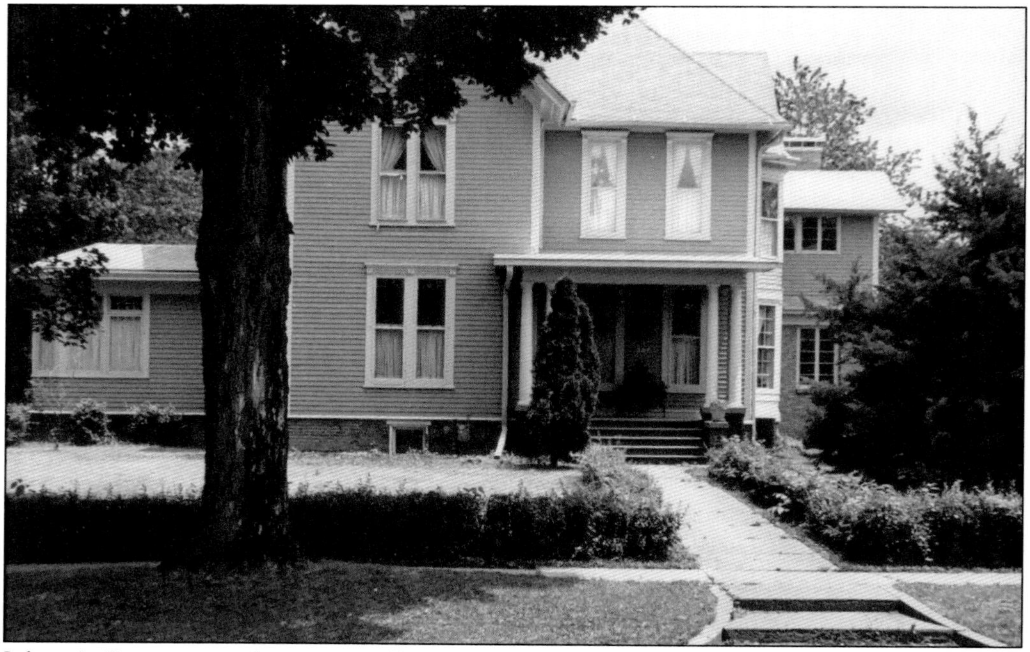

Julius A. Brown arrived in Monticello in the 1870s and, after starting a hardware business on the square, built a steep-gabled farmhouse at 807 North State Street. The columns and wings were added at a later date. A descendant of John Britton, one of Monticello's early settlers, later owned this house, as did Maxwell Hott, who lived there from the mid-1930s through the early 1940s. (APL.)

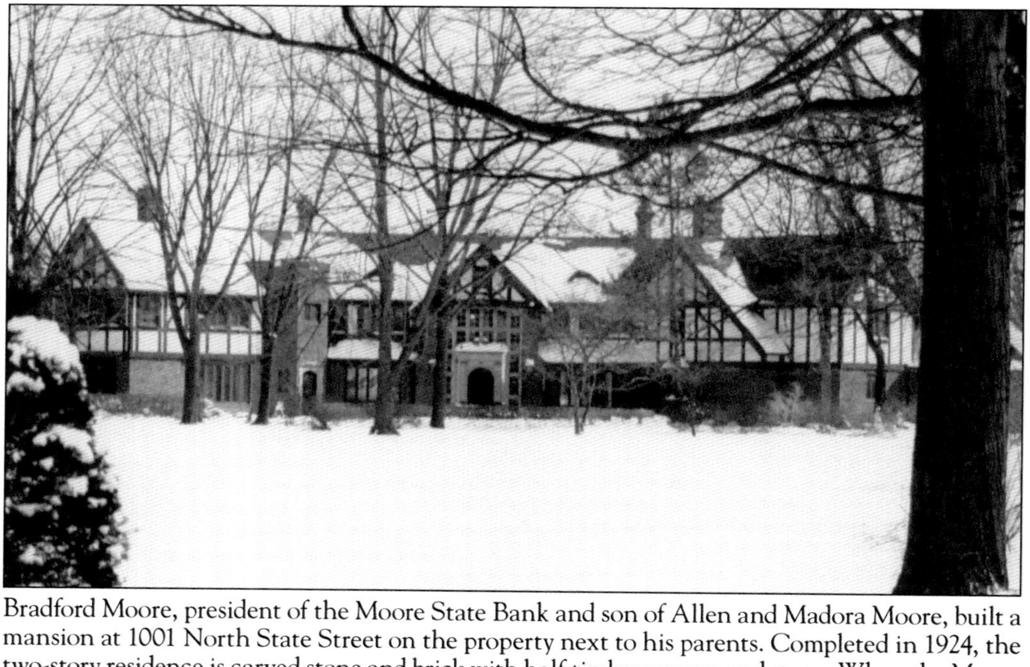

Bradford Moore, president of the Moore State Bank and son of Allen and Madora Moore, built a mansion at 1001 North State Street on the property next to his parents. Completed in 1924, the two-story residence is carved stone and brick with half-timber cypress and stone. When the Moore State Bank failed in 1933, Moore sold his estate for less than 25 percent of its cost. (APL.)

William Edmund Lodge was a farmer and self-educated lawyer who arrived in Monticello in 1859 from Edgar County, Illinois. Lodge bought a newspaper that had originally been named the *Monticello Times* before being changed to the *Sucker State*. Lodge named it the *Conservative* and operated it from 1862 until 1864 before selling to Nathan Rhoades. Lodge was the first Piatt County farmer to use tile for draining land. (PCHGS.)

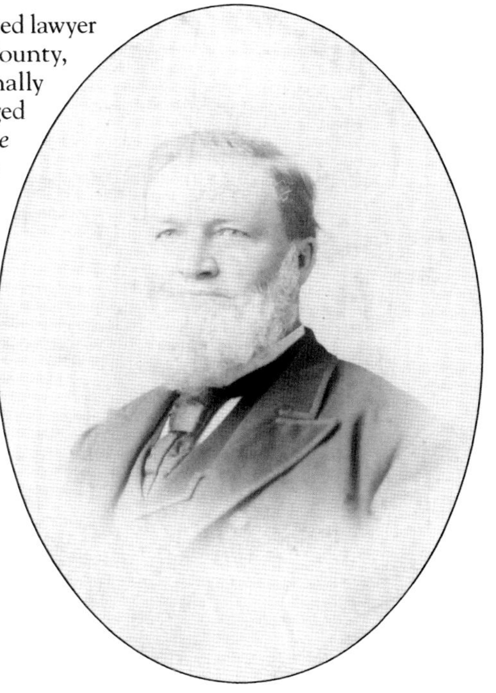

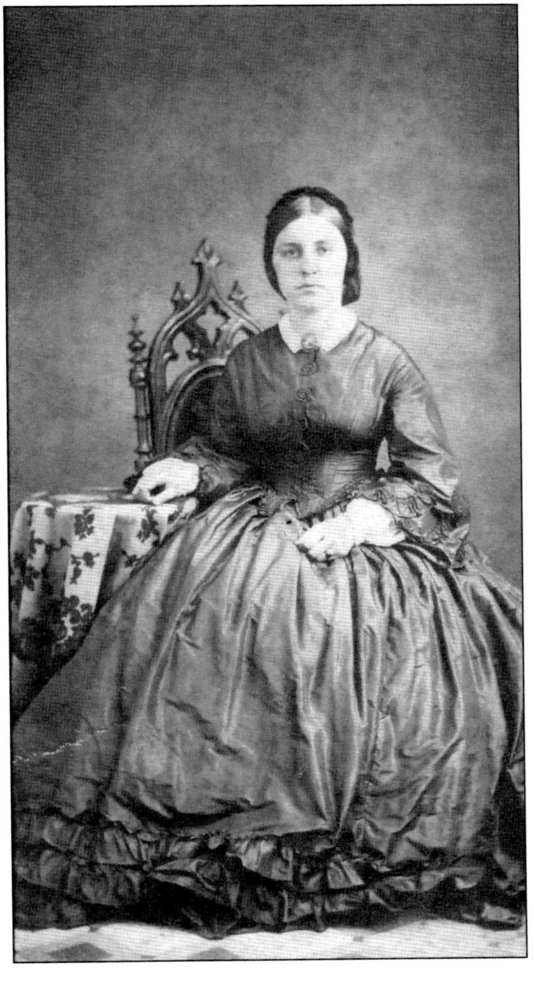

Frances "Frankie" A. Piatt, was born in 1843 to Clarinda and William Hart Piatt. She married William Edmund Lodge in 1866 and, in 1868, gave birth to son William Franklin Lodge. William and Frances, and later their son, owned a great deal of property directly north and west of Monticello city limits. She died in 1895. (APL.)

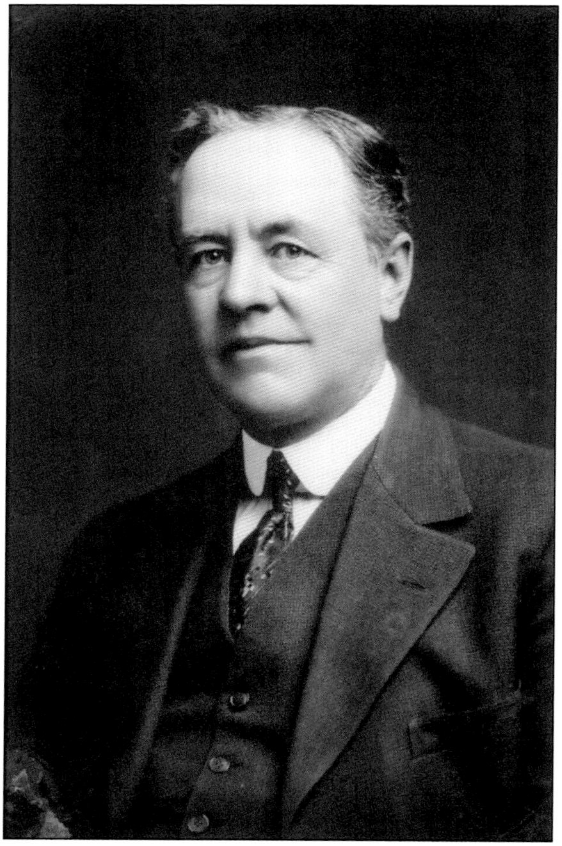

William Franklin Lodge was a general contractor who operated tile and brick mills, orchards, and greenhouses. He founded the Monticello Mutual Telephone Company in the 1890s and helped organize the Boys Scouts, the Rotary, the cemetery association, and the Piatt County Historical Society. After his 1935 death, his estate north of town—now called Lodge Park—was sold to the forest preserve. (APL.)

An eastward view in 1904 shows Bridge Street running under the Wabash trestle, alongside the Illinois Central Railroad. The Lodge residence and greenhouses at 416 Elm Boulevard lay west of Market Street between High Street and the Illinois Central Railroad. The Lodge house was demolished in August 1962 to make way for a store at Center and Market Streets. Until the 1940s, Center Street ended at Market Street. (RS.)

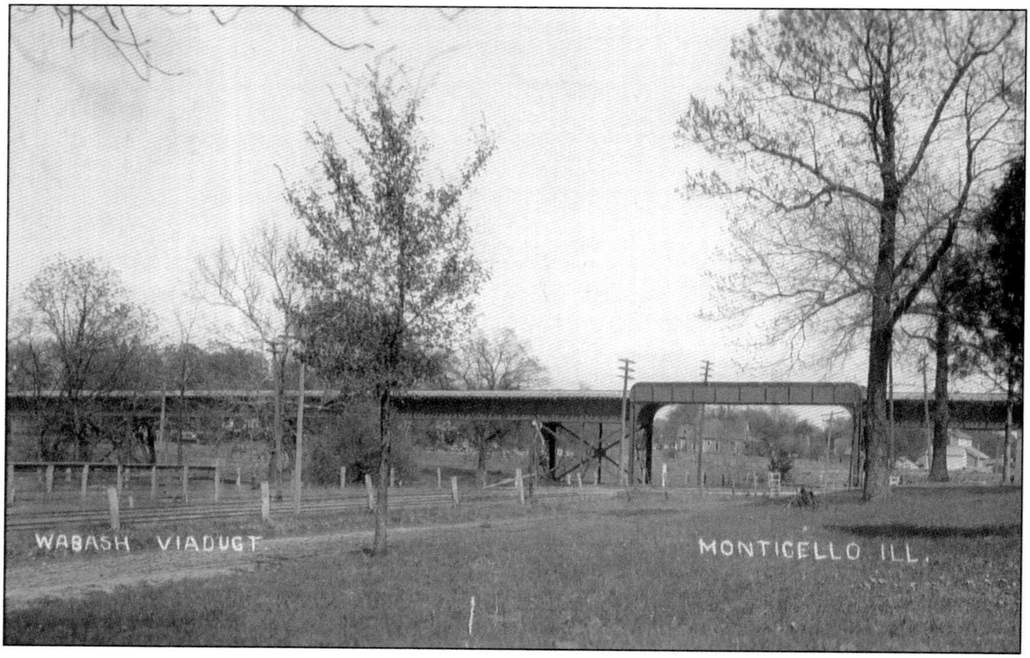

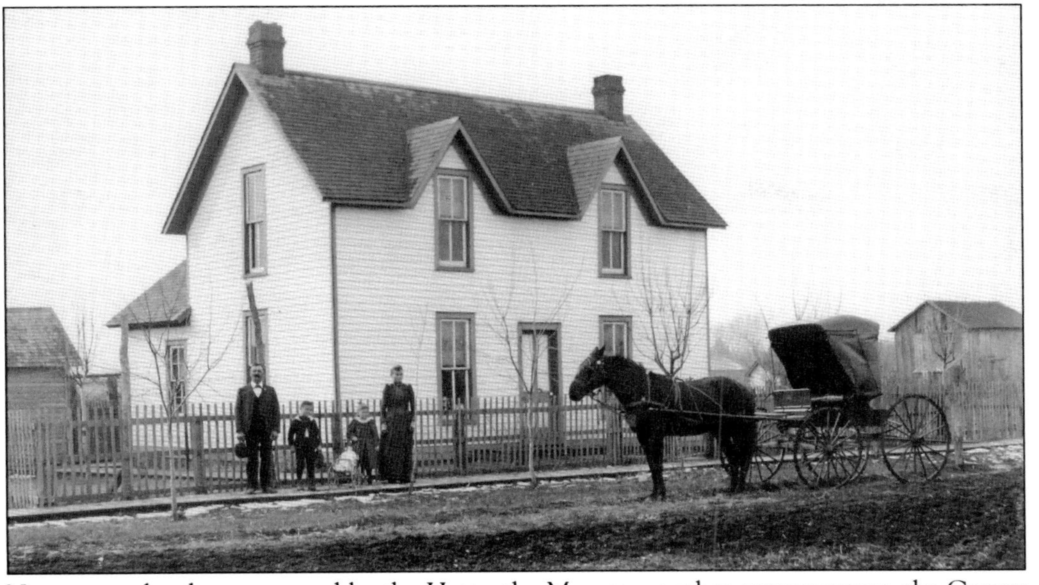

Not as grand as houses owned by the Hotts, the Moores, or other entrepreneurs, the George Mench house at 913 East Center Street was photographed in the early 1900s. George and Rosa Mench stand with their children, John and Mary, on a wooden sidewalk in front of the house. The house, with a modified entryway, is still there. (PCHGS.)

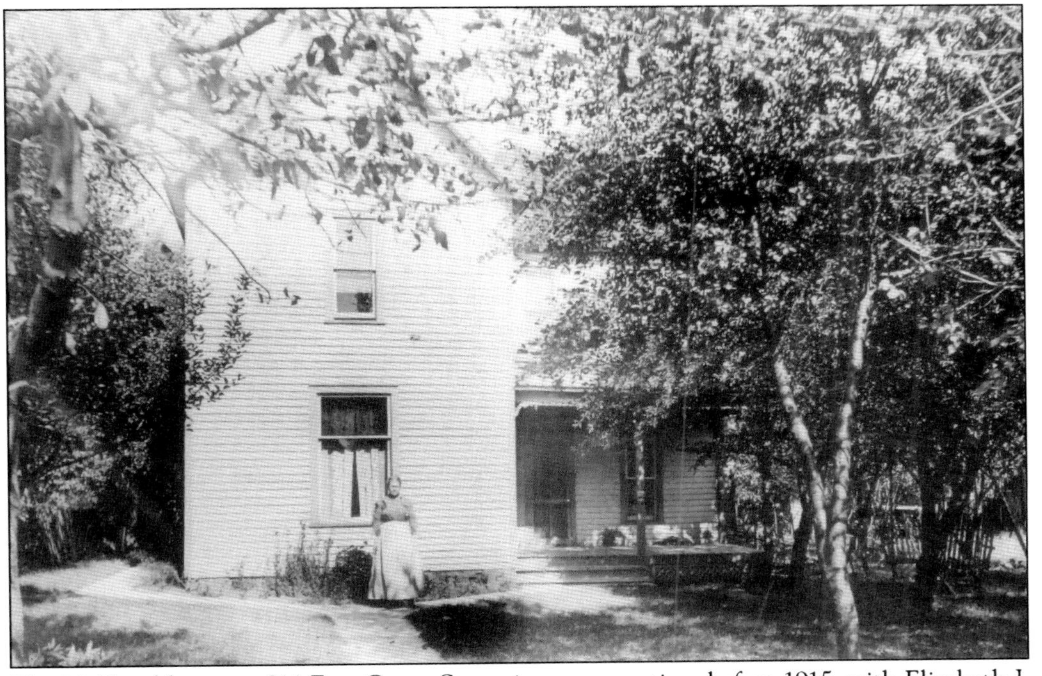

The Hubbard home at 214 East Grant Street is seen sometime before 1915, with Elizabeth J. Walker Hubbard posing in front. Her husband, Albert Hubbard, operated a dray line—a hauling and delivery business—from 1896 until 1912. Later, their son Robert lived there and also ran a delivery service. The casual observer of the still existing house would now see an added front porch. (APL.)

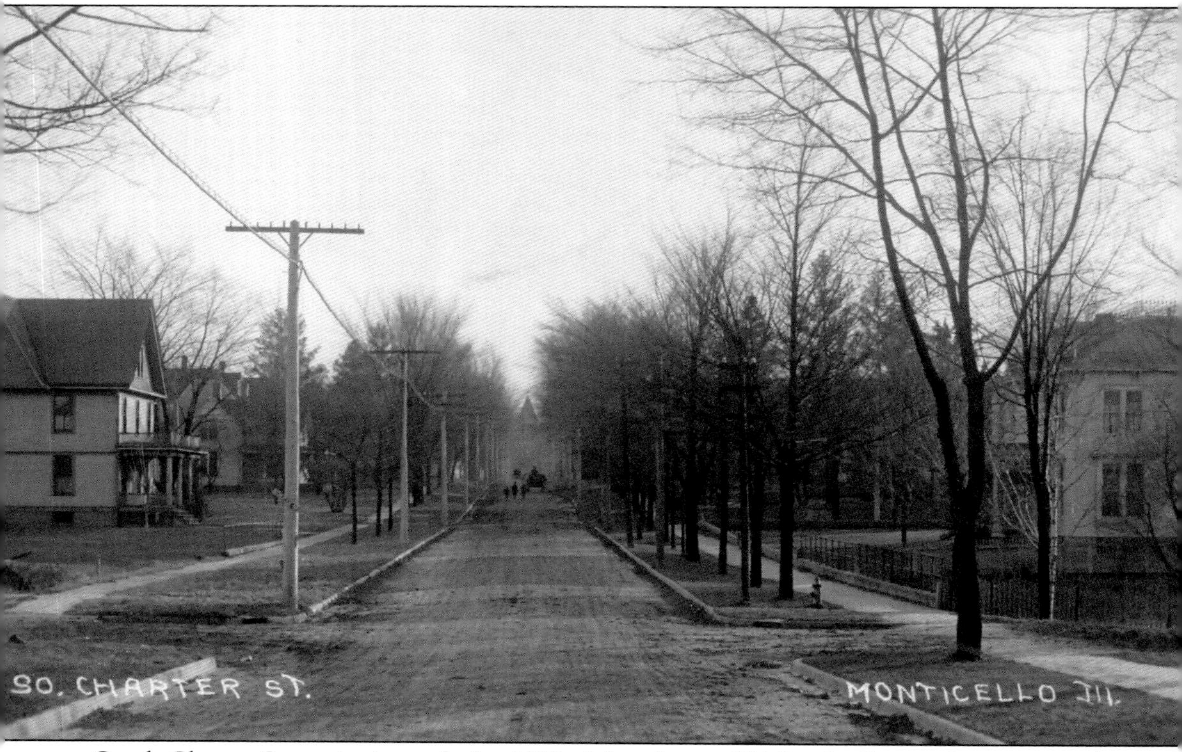

South Charter Street is pictured after 1909. A law firm at 316 South Charter Street currently occupies the house in right foreground. Built for Wilbur Fisk and Alice Stevenson, it was Dr. William B. Caldwell's home from 1914 until 1921 and then a funeral home for 30 years. The Fisks' daughter Mary wed Piatt County attorney (and later judge) Elim Hawbaker. The Hawbakers lived at 816 South Charter Street. (SR.)

Four

Old Settlers and New Changes 1900–1920s

Early settlers, many of whom were lionized at every August fair, were dying away by the early 1900s. Bricks paved the square between 1903 and 1905, covering more alleys and streets, including Market and Bridge Streets. In 1905, as downtown wooden sidewalks were deteriorating, concrete sidewalks replaced them. Ornamental lights appeared along Main and State Streets and, by 1909, the city required lights anywhere the railroad intersected with streets or alleys. Street addresses changed to today's numbering scheme. The Interurban Transit System established a station in Monticello in 1907, connecting to the bigger towns east and west. At the end of 1909, more than 1,200 citizens had telephones. Monticello drilled three more city wells in 1915.

The new city hall, built at the corner of State and Main Streets, housed the post office and firefighting equipment on the first floor, with city council and mayoral chambers on the second. More structures were added near the square, including the two-story brick Pembroke Building constructed as an automobile dealership and garage. The Pembroke displayed the only electric sign in town and advertised Kelly Springfield Tires.

Entertainment included several movie theaters, fairs, local bands, and parades. New and larger churches replaced older ones, and an attempt was made to persuade evangelist Billy Sunday or his colleague to preach in Monticello as they traveled nearby.

Armed men roamed the Allerton estate in 1917 for a lion—undoubtedly a hoax—that "attacked" the butler. That same year, as the country plunged into war, more than 1,200 Piatt County men registered for the draft. In 1918, Roy Hamm became the first Monticello resident killed in action. To help support the war effort, Robert Allerton donated $200,000 in cash and the proceeds from his crop sales from 10,000 acres of farmland. Generosity continued after the war when Allen Moore donated $150,000 (approximately $2 million in 2012) for a high school gymnasium in memory of the soldiers.

In 1919, the courthouse lawn displayed Monticello's first municipal Christmas tree, wired with electric lights. As Monticello entered the 1920s, many older landmarks were remodeled or demolished and more houses extended the city limits.

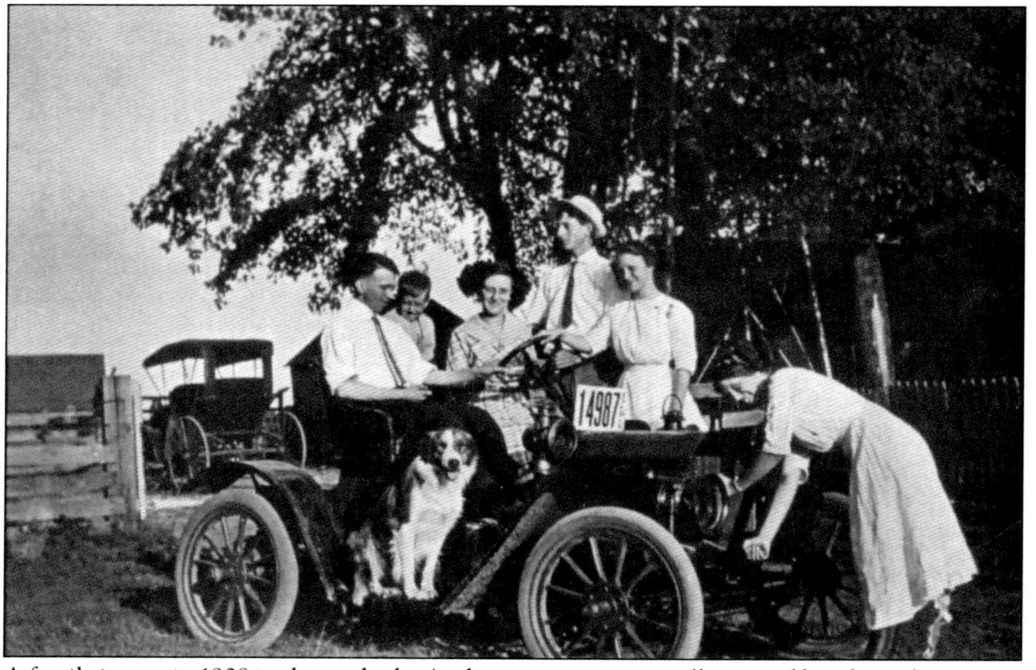

A family is seen in 1908 in their vehicle. At the time, many cars still required hand-cranking. Most automobiles sold after 1919 were started electrically by a small, round foot-operated button switch on the floor. The average cost of a car in 1919 was $850. By 1925, because of mass production, the average cost decreased to $290. (PCHGS.)

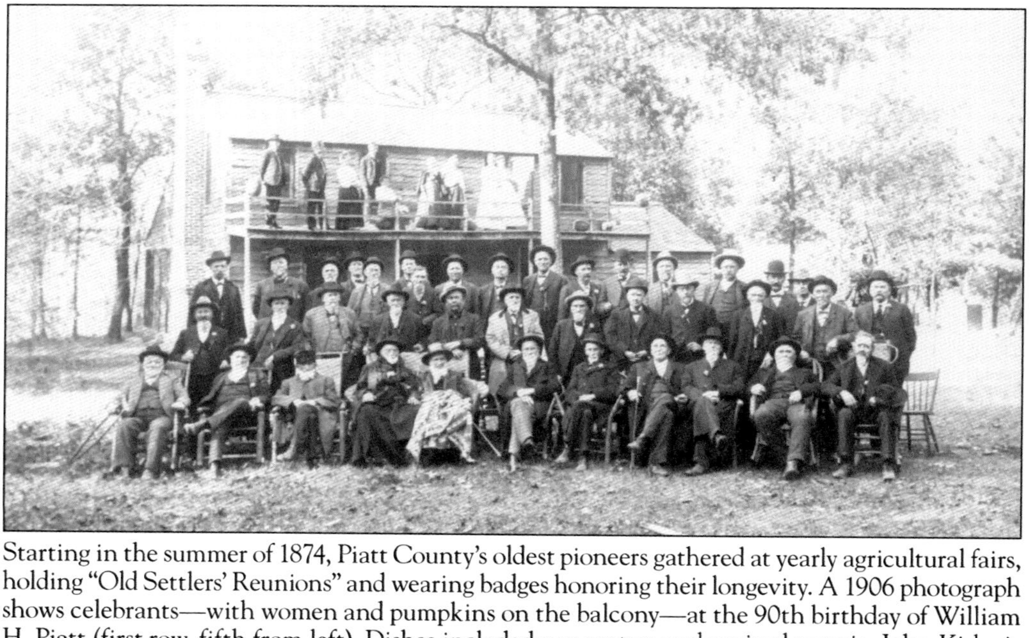

Starting in the summer of 1874, Piatt County's oldest pioneers gathered at yearly agricultural fairs, holding "Old Settlers' Reunions" and wearing badges honoring their longevity. A 1906 photograph shows celebrants—with women and pumpkins on the balcony—at the 90th birthday of William H. Piatt (first row, fifth from left). Dishes included raw oysters and squirrel pot pie. John Kirby is third from left in the second row. (APL.)

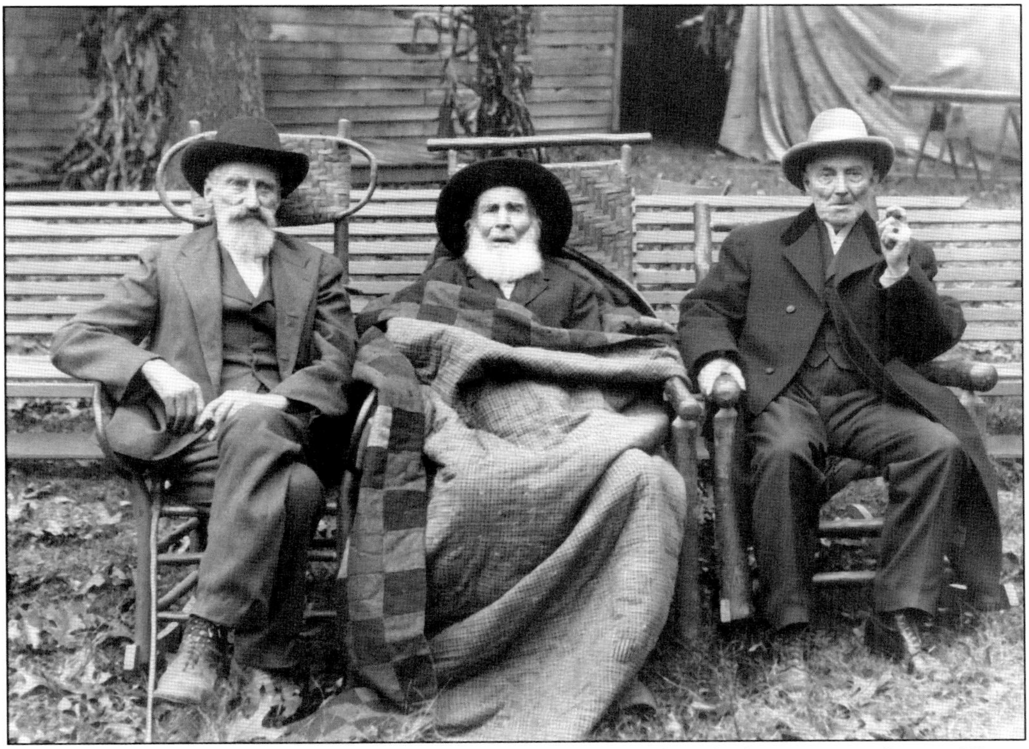

Allen Sadorus (left), William H. Piatt (center), and an unidentified man sit in front of Briar Crest cabin in 1906 at Piatt's 90th birthday party. Briar Crest was located within what is now Lodge Park. The Hayworth cabin adjoined Briar Crest when the cabin was moved to Lodge's estate. (PCHGS.)

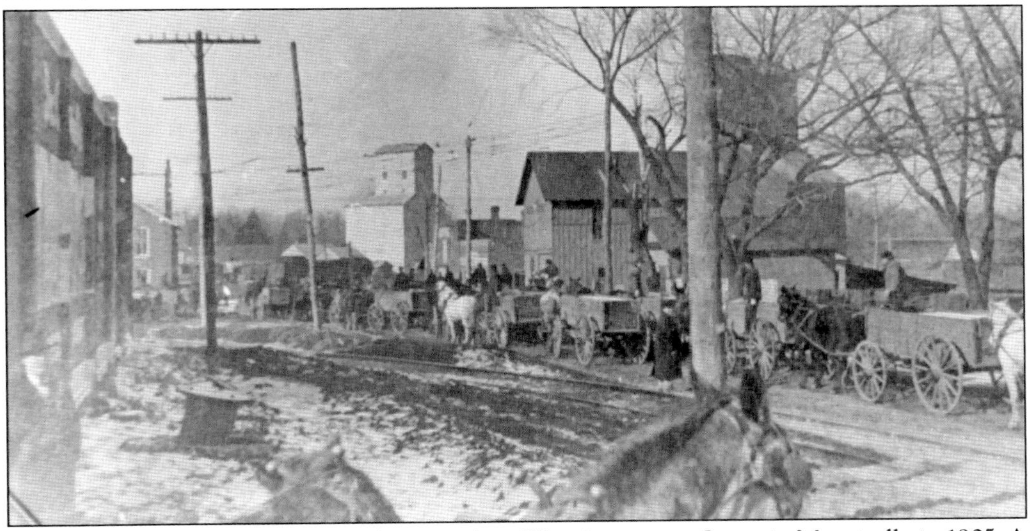

Farmers and their wagons head to elevators along West Livingston Street in Monticello in 1905. A number of grain merchants operated elevators for corn, wheat, or oats. One firm—Piatt, Hubbell and Company—opened a grain elevator as early as 1873 or 1874. Another such business was the E.G. Knight and Company Elevator, which eventually became Finson Grain Company. (PCHGS.)

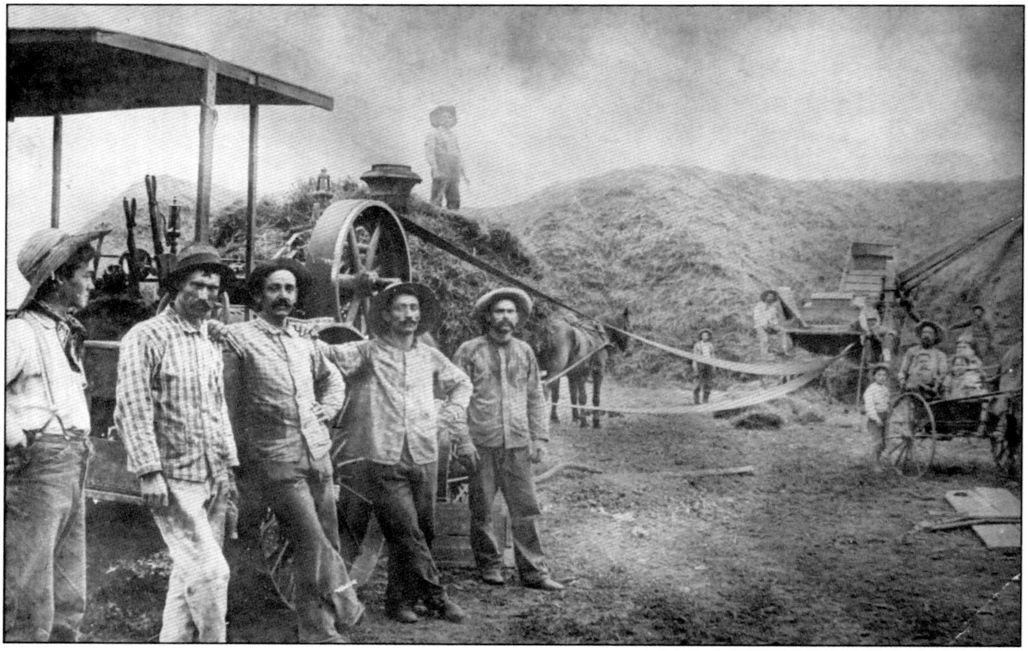

A group of hired men stop its work and poses on the Conard farm east of Monticello around 1900. The men in front of the wagon are, from left to right, J. Miller, T. Miller, D. Hubbard, H. Anderson, and B. Griffith. John Ray stands on top of the wagon, and the P. Conard family sits inside the buggy. (PCHGS.)

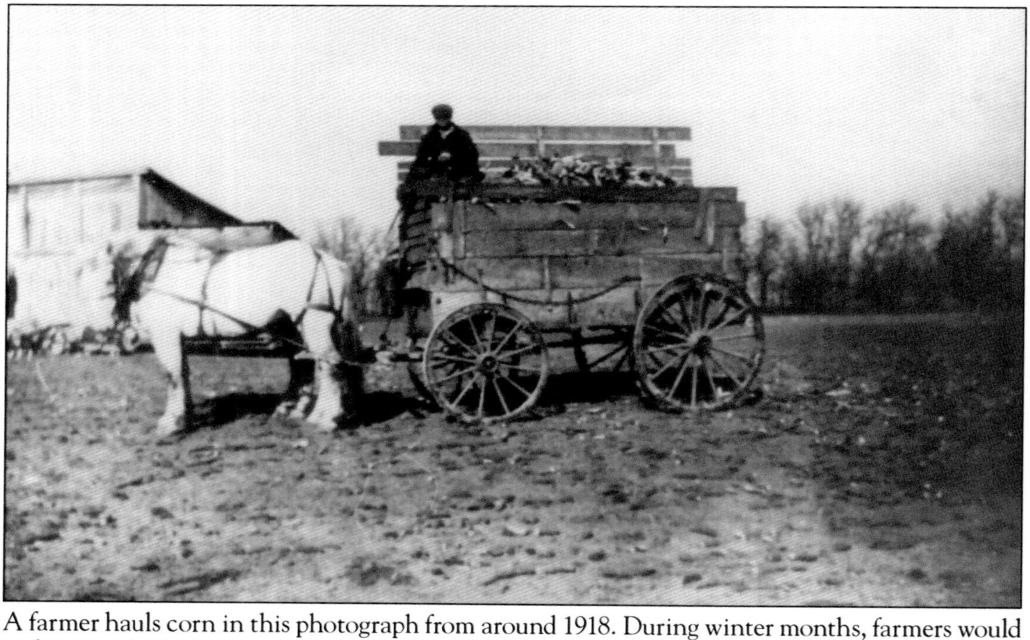

A farmer hauls corn in this photograph from around 1918. During winter months, farmers would gather together in cooperative efforts to shell the harvested and stored corn. Changes had already affected some farms by the early 1900s, as threshing machines powered by steam engines and tractors replaced many of the horse teams. (PCHGS.)

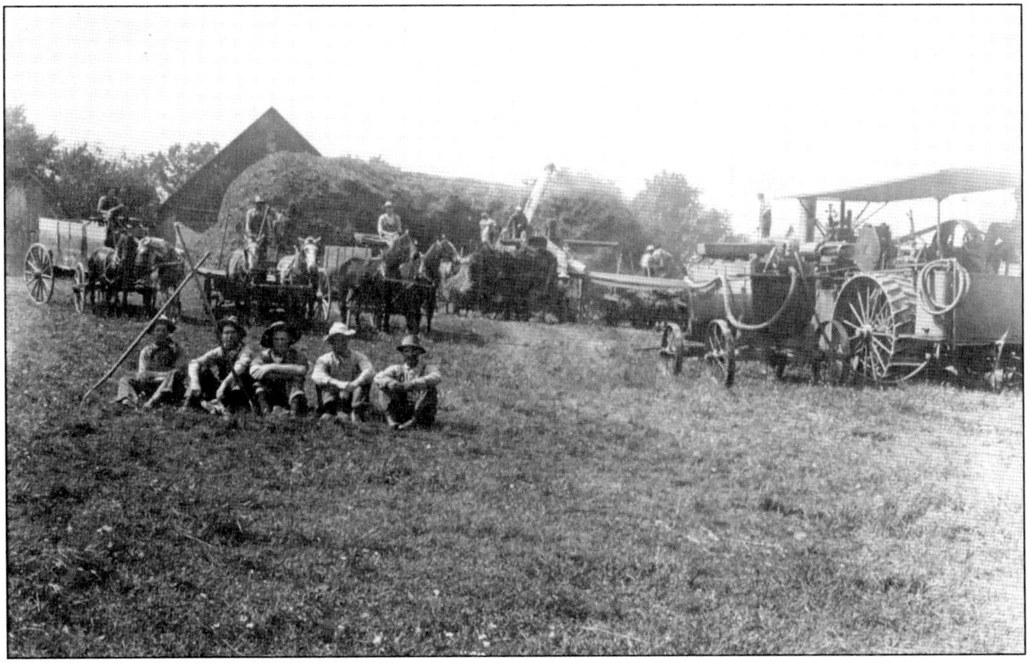

A group of farmers and laborers takes a rest while being photographed in the early 1900s. From 1860 to 1900, the percentage of people in the United States who were involved in agriculture dropped from 58 to 38 percent. The number of farms in Illinois peaked in 1900 at 260,000, averaging 125 acres. (APL.)

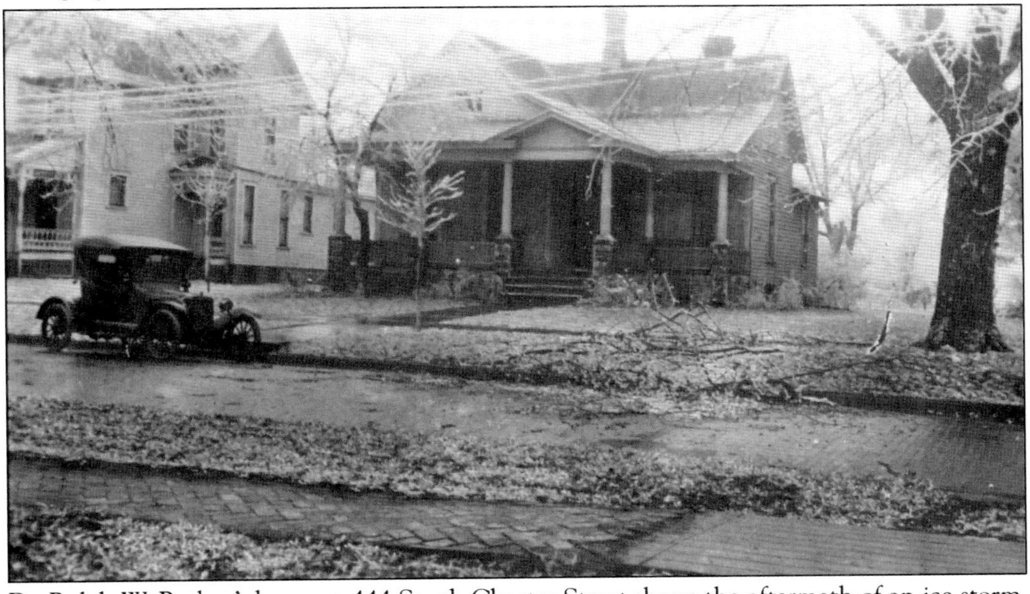

Dr. Ralph W. Bushee's house at 444 South Charter Street shows the aftermath of an ice storm, with downed limbs blocking sidewalk and street. The white house to the left was built around 1880 and owned at one time by Illinois state legislator William Hubbart. Hubbart's first wife was another Clarinda Marquiss, granddaughter one of the town founders, Abraham Marquiss, and niece to Clarinda Marquiss Piatt. (PCHGS.)

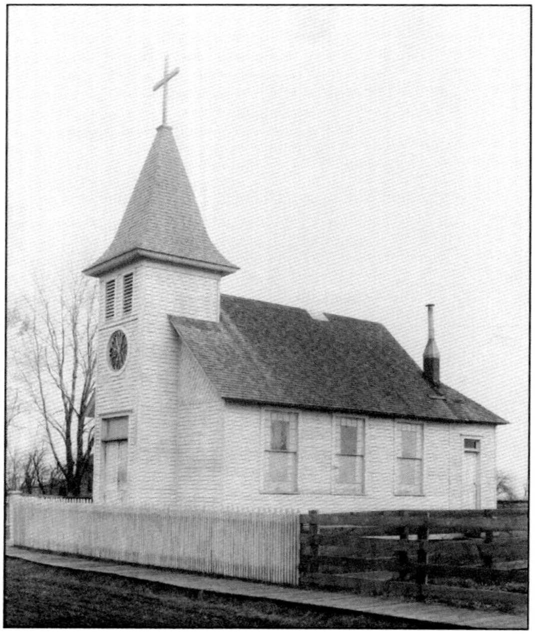

Before 1872, Monticello Catholics met in private homes and were visited by traveling priests about six times a year. Eventually, county officials allowed them to use the courthouse. After the first St. Philomena Catholic Church was built in 1889 at North and Buchanan Streets, services were held twice a month. The frame building was torn down in 1906 when a new brick church was built near the courthouse square. (PCHGS.)

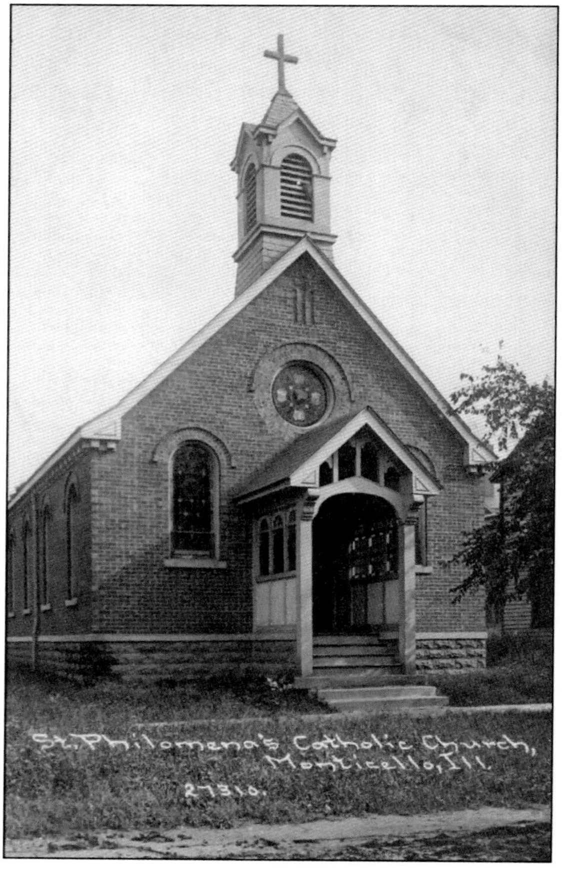

The second St. Philomena Catholic Church was built at the corner of State and Lafayette Streets in 1906. A basement was added later. Robert Allerton, a friend of the priest, Father Selva, donated funds to decorate the new brick church. After World War II, the congregation grew larger than the original 10-family membership. A new and larger church was built along Route 105 in 1964. (APL-SR.)

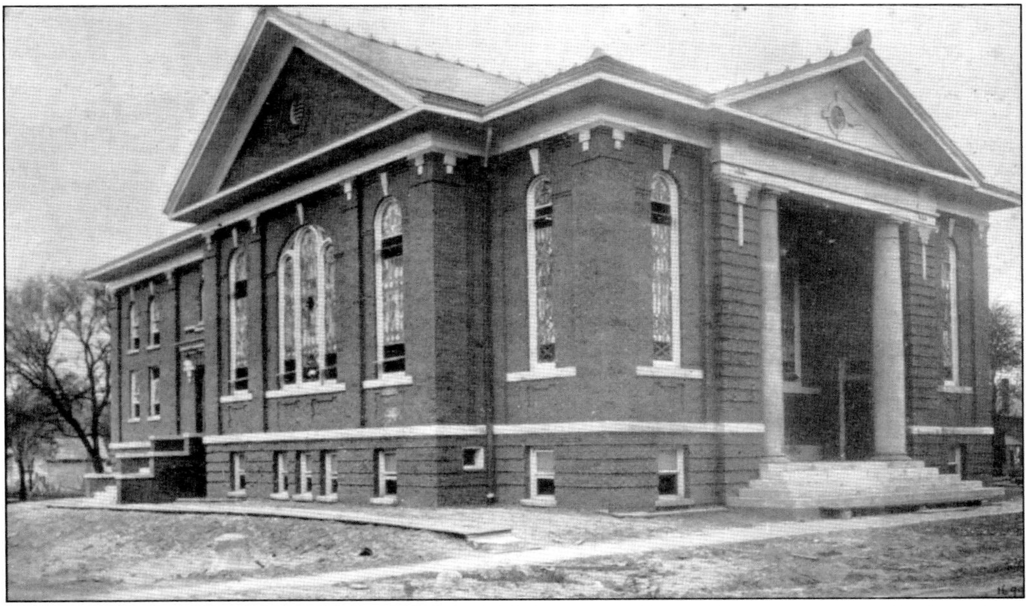

Methodist services began in Monticello in 1842. Five years later, the congregation built its first church at the northwest corner of Marion and Market Streets. Men entered through the right front door and women used the left. The sanctuary was also split into separate seating sections for men and women. The photograph shows the current brick structure that was built in 1911. (APL.)

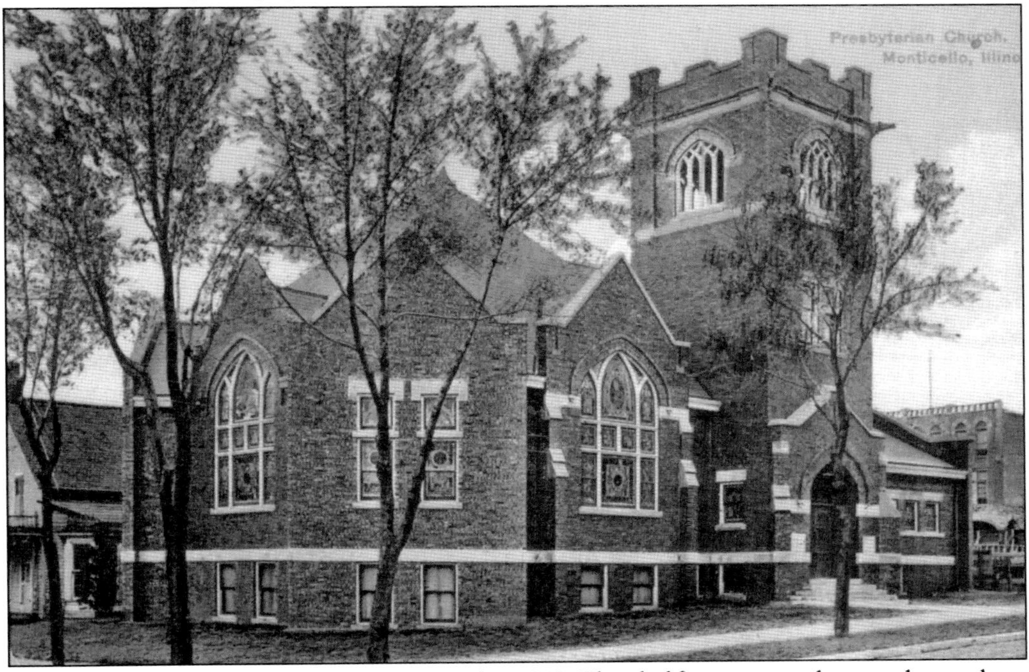

Like the Methodists, Presbyterians organized in 1842. They held services in the courthouse, later using the Methodist church after its construction. Services faltered until the late 1850s. The Presbyterian congregation finally had its own church in 1869, replacing it in 1907 at what is now 215 South Charter Street. It was redecorated in 1939 and remodeled in 1955. (APL.)

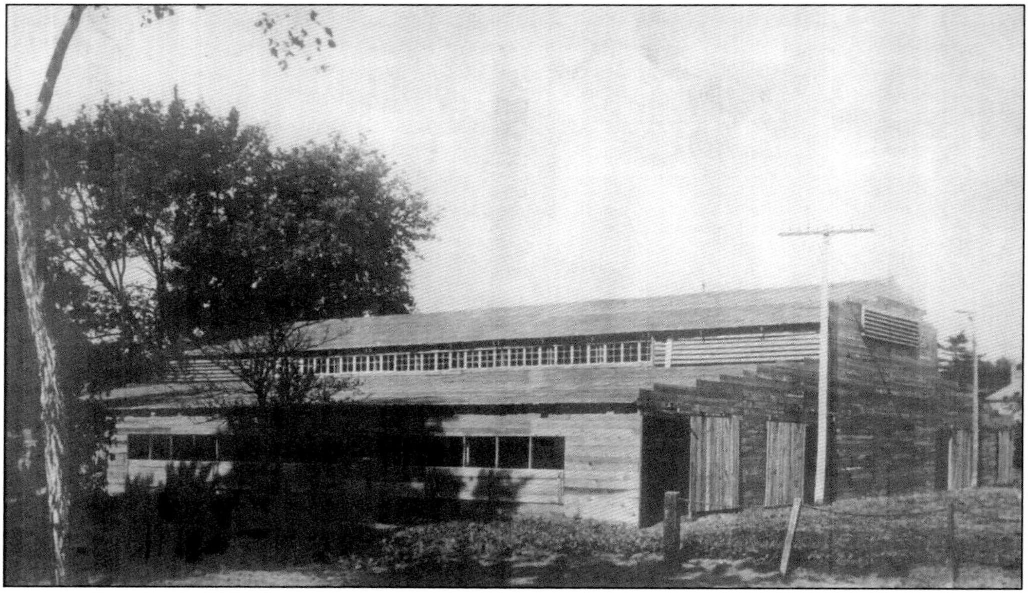

In 1908, citizens wanted traveling evangelist Billy Sunday or a colleague to preach in Monticello. Unsuccessful in their attempts, residents still erected a 2,000-seat tabernacle south of the Methodist church, where local pastors delivered sermons from July 5 to August 16, 1908, earning Piatt County the name "Pious County." James Rankin later purchased the building for $415 to use as a barn. (RS.)

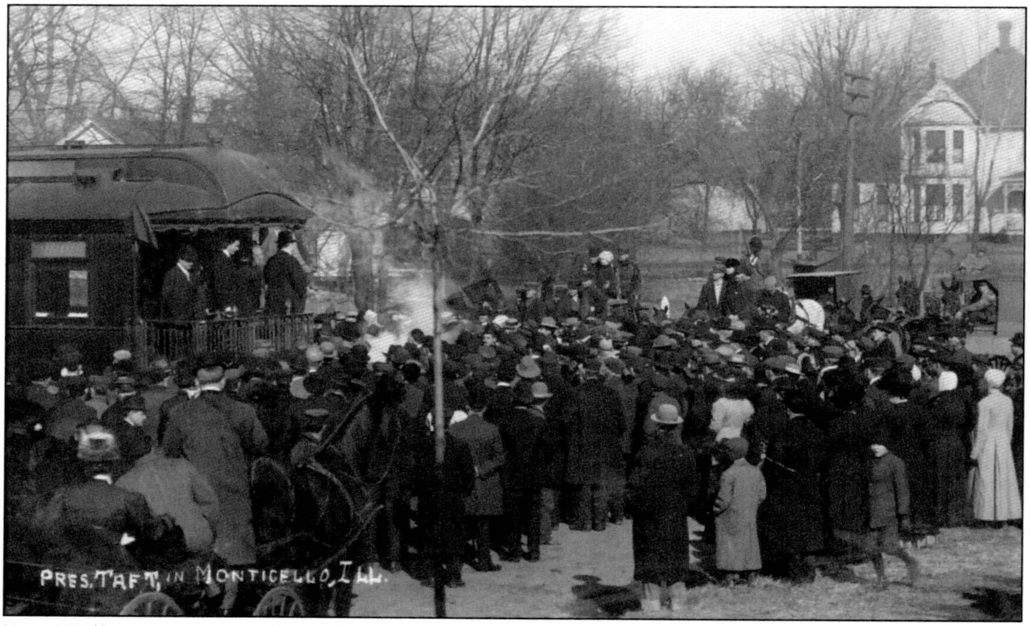

Pres. William Howard Taft speaks from the back of an Illinois Central train at North State Street near Allerton Library in 1909. Dempsey Cline is in the wagon. Others included Philip Johnson, John Dighton, Thomas Ball, A.T. Vent, and L. Hammerschmidt. Taft served as president from March 4, 1909, until 1913. (APL-SR.)

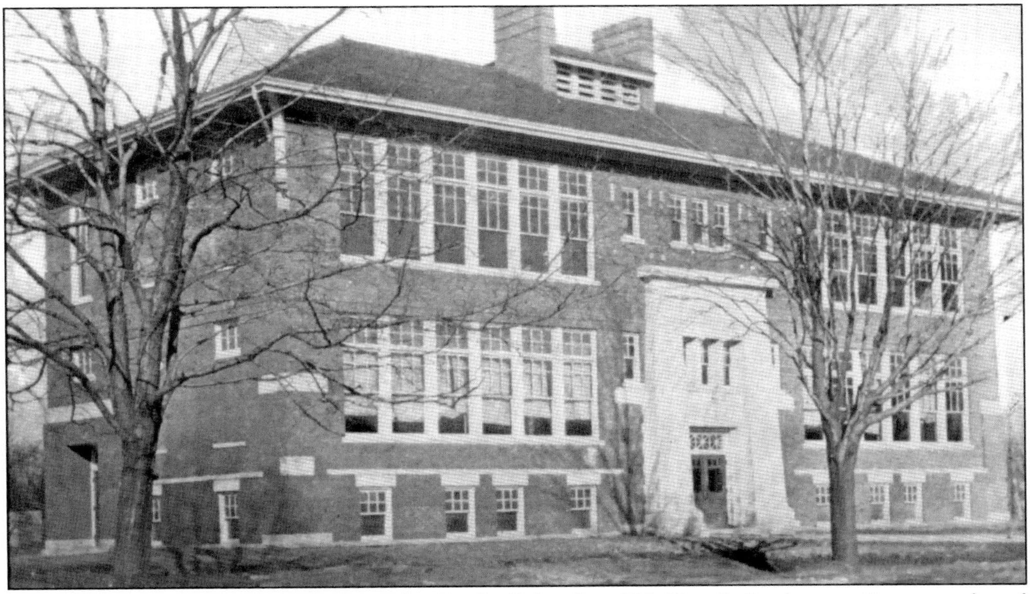

Constructed in 1911, the new Lincoln Grade School at 700 North Buchanan Street replaced the North School, which had been built in 1877. George Lux oversaw the work and replaced workmen who refused to correct their bricklaying errors. Although this delay required immediate rebuilding, the 14,490-square-foot school was dedicated the following year. The total cost was $18,000. (APL-SR.)

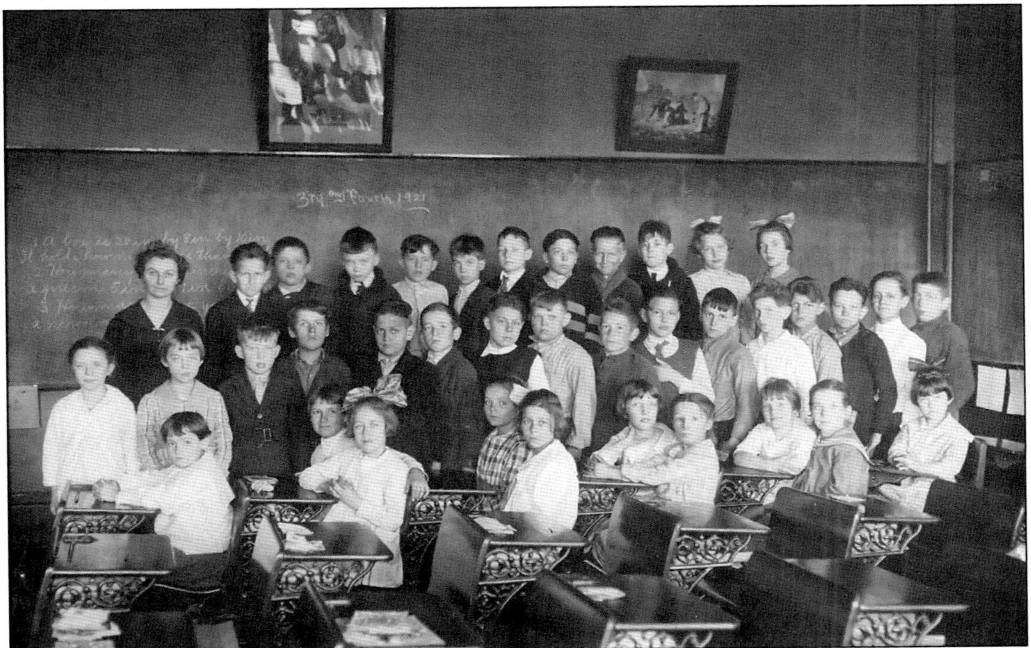

Kathryn L. Valentine appears with her third-and-fourth-grade class in 1921. Born in 1896, she began teaching in 1914, retiring in 1968 after 50 years at Washington School. She died in 1977 and donated 18 acres near the north cemetery to establish Valentine Park with the forest preserve district. The land was purchased from William E. Lodge in the late 1800s. (APL.)

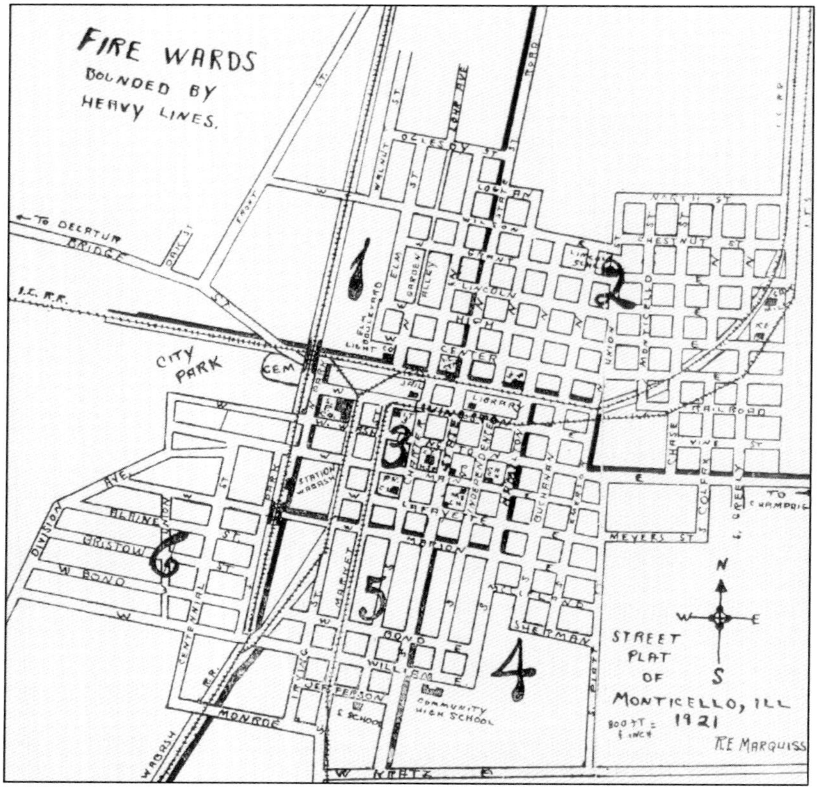

As seen in this 1921 map, Monticello was comprised of six fire wards. Center Street ended at Elm Boulevard where the Lodge family lived (near the "1" by the north-south railroad tracks). The old cemetery sat east of the city park, near where the swimming pool is now located. The city limits stopped just north of Oglesby Street and south of Kratz Road. (APL.)

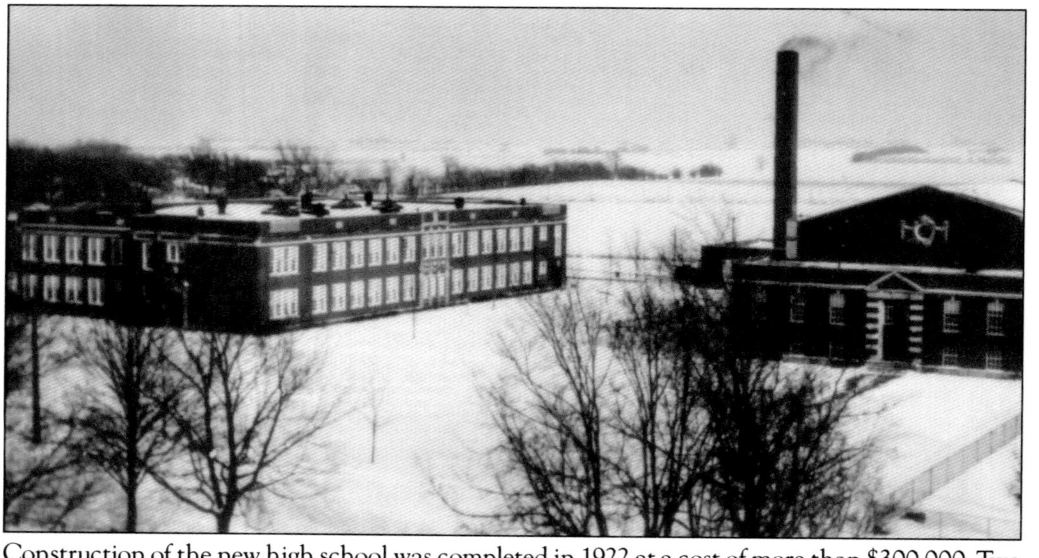

Construction of the new high school was completed in 1922 at a cost of more than $300,000. Two years later, Allen and Madora Moore donated $150,000 for a new gymnasium in memory of the valor and patriotism shown by the community's soldiers during World War I. The gymnasium's construction commenced in June 1925, with dedication of the completed building in August 1926. All merchants closed their businesses during the dedication. (APL.)

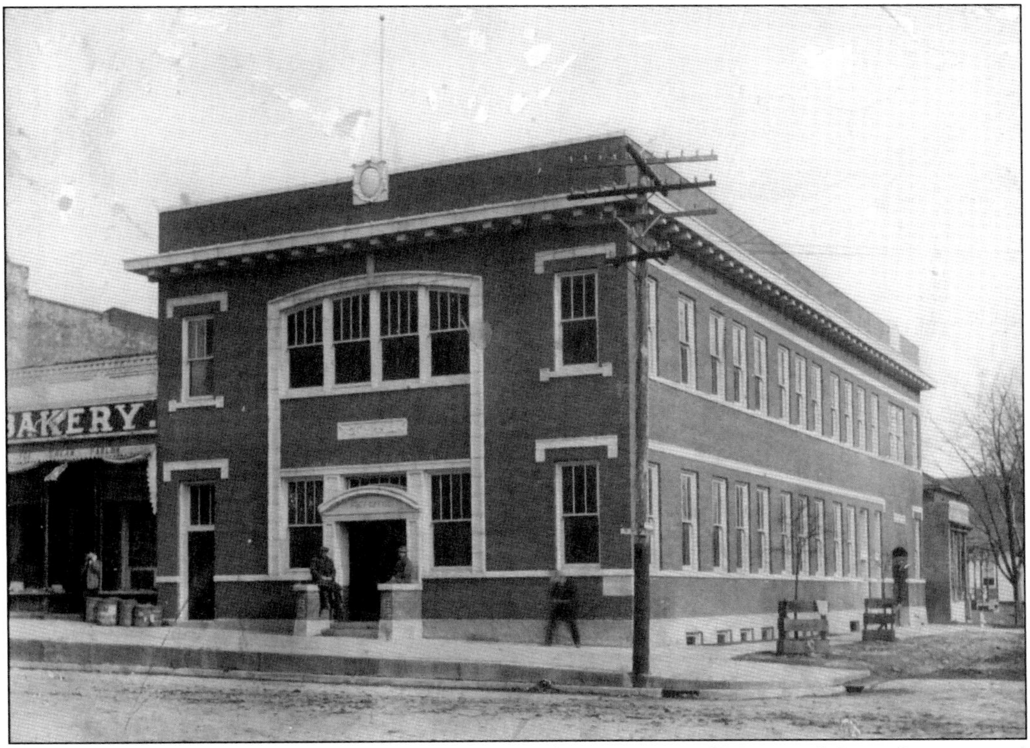

Rains hampered completion of city hall at the northeast corner of Main and State Streets until January 1913. Previously, the post office had been inside houses or stores, such as 108 West Washington Street; here, both it and the firehouse were located on the first floor. The second floor housed the council room, reception room, vault, and mayor's office. The back of the building housed a police courtroom. (PCHGS.)

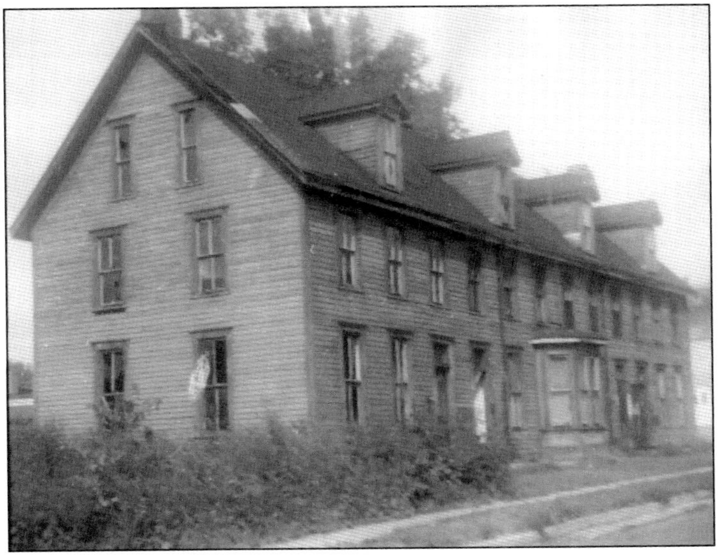

The Lewis Flats Building provided Monticello's first public housing. Constructed in 1861, the building was located on the grounds of what is now 310 West Washington Street, immediately west of where the old Honselman cabin originally sat. Close to the ditch, it would sometimes flood. After deteriorating, Lewis Flats was razed in 1962 and replaced by a Laundromat. Now, Kelly's Accounting occupies the site. (PCHGS.)

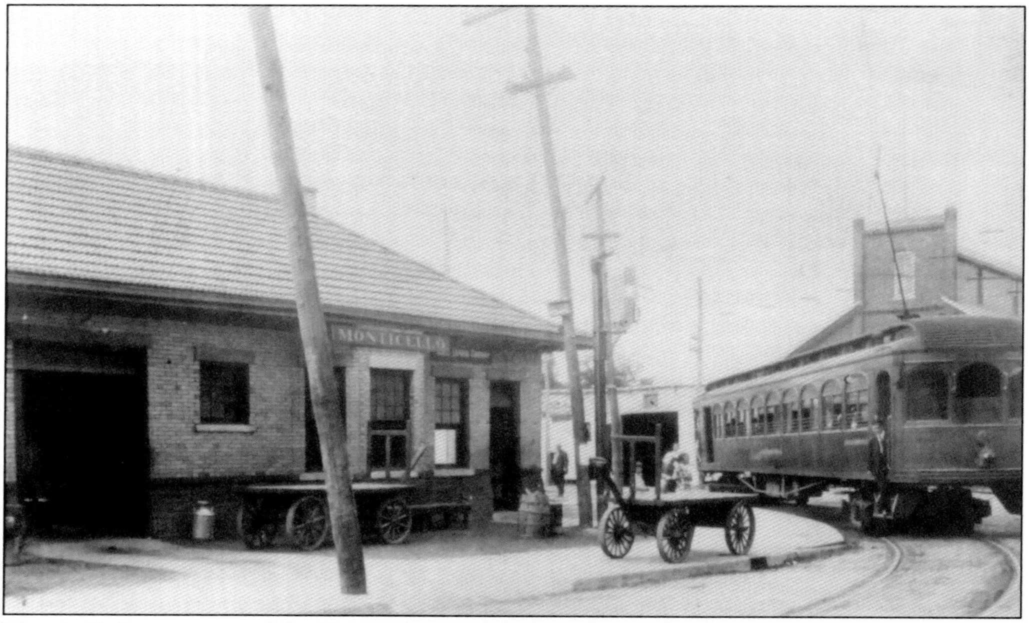

Monticello became part of the Illinois Terminal Railway System (ITS) in 1907. Daily trains operated every two hours and connected Danville, Champaign, Monticello, Decatur, and Peoria. People could get on or off anywhere along the line. Entering the town from Bement, the Interurban followed Market Street north and turned right onto Livingston Street. (PCHGS.)

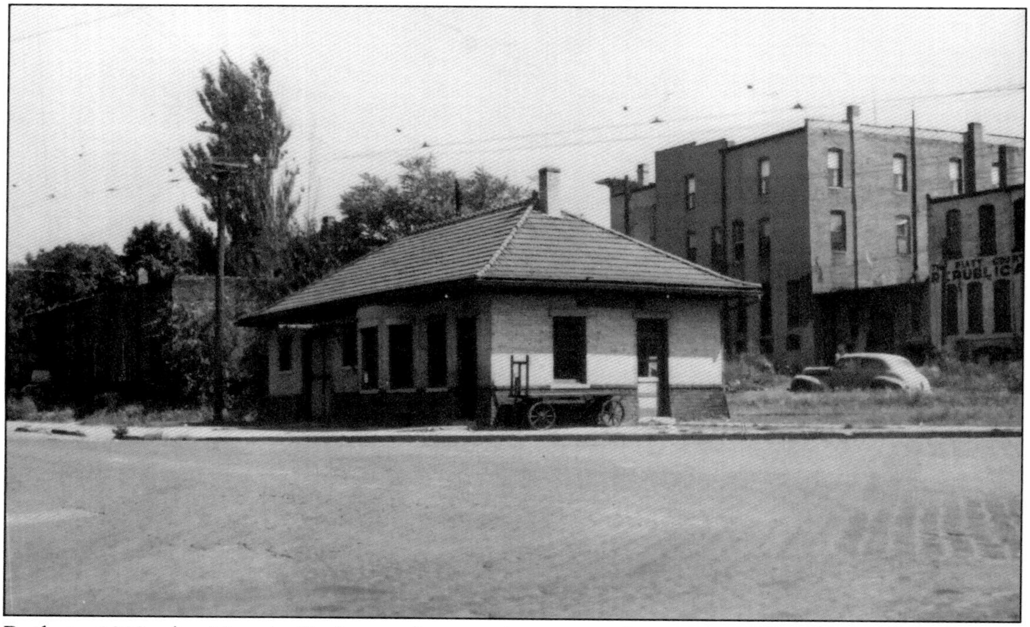

Built in 1912, the Monticello Interurban station sat at the corner of Market and Livingston Streets until it was demolished in 1962, seven years after the last train ran. Some said the "ITS" for Illinois Traction (or Terminal) System meant "I Travel Slow" as they traveled to Champaign, Danville, Decatur, or Peoria. Local businesses, such as the Camp Creek Duck Farm, shipped their live ducks using the Interurban. (RS.)

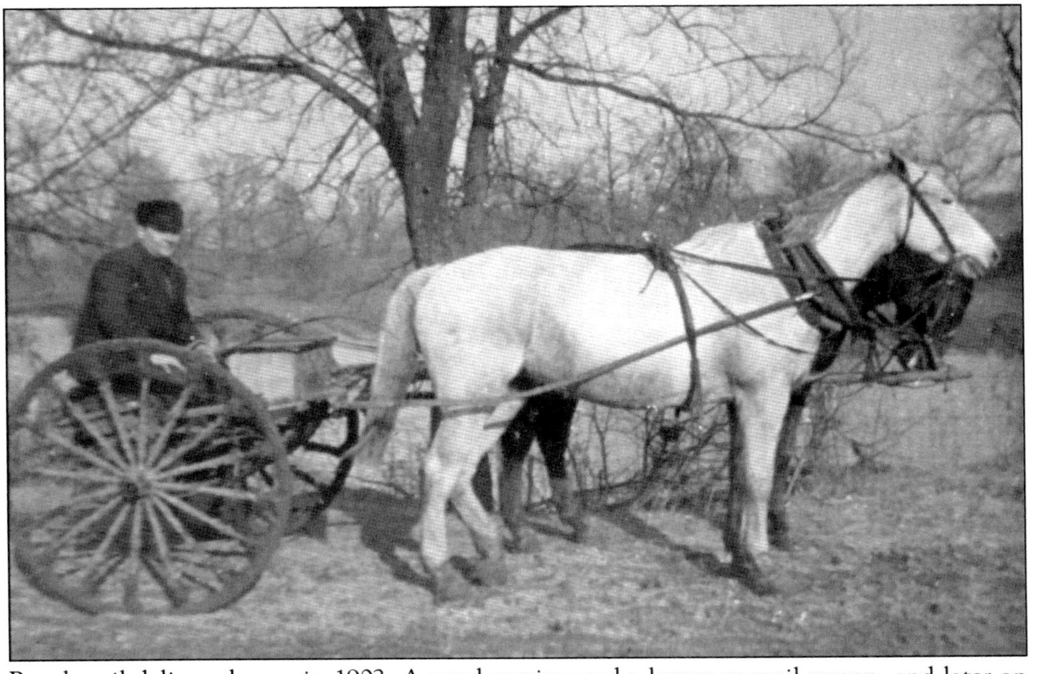

Rural mail delivery began in 1902. A rural carrier used a buggy or mail wagon, and later an automobile, to travel the assigned route. People who did not live on the route were allowed to erect a mailbox along the route or have their mail delivered to a neighbor. (PCHGS.)

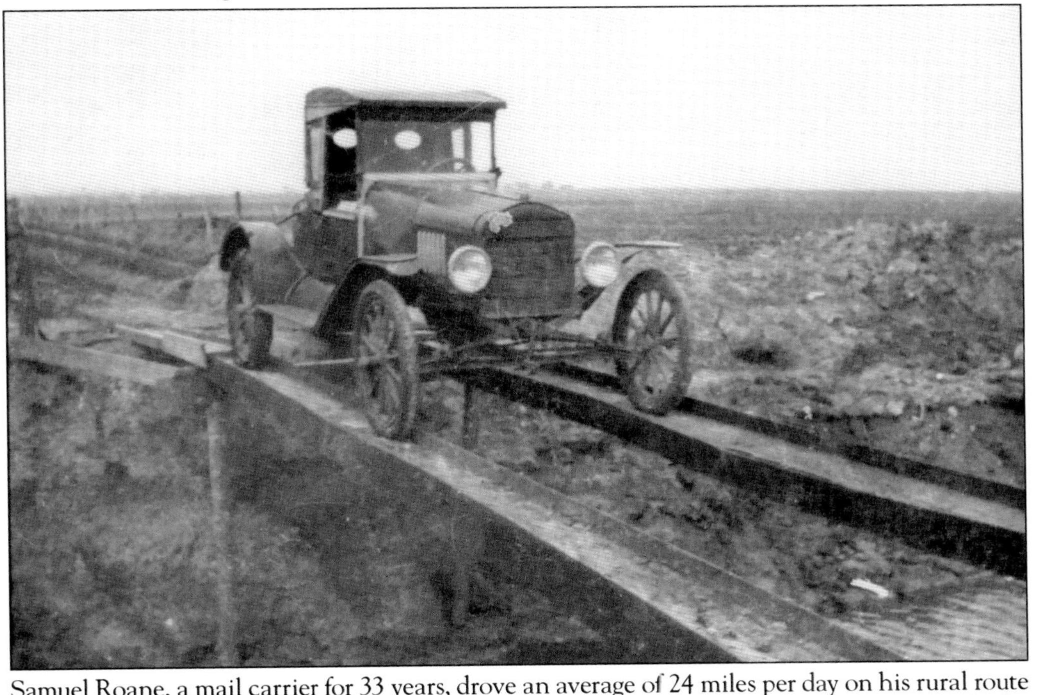

Samuel Roane, a mail carrier for 33 years, drove an average of 24 miles per day on his rural route delivering mail. He used I beams in 1921 to cross a stream when the bridge went out. Because vehicles had different widths, not every car could use the unconventional I-beam bridge. (APL-SR.)

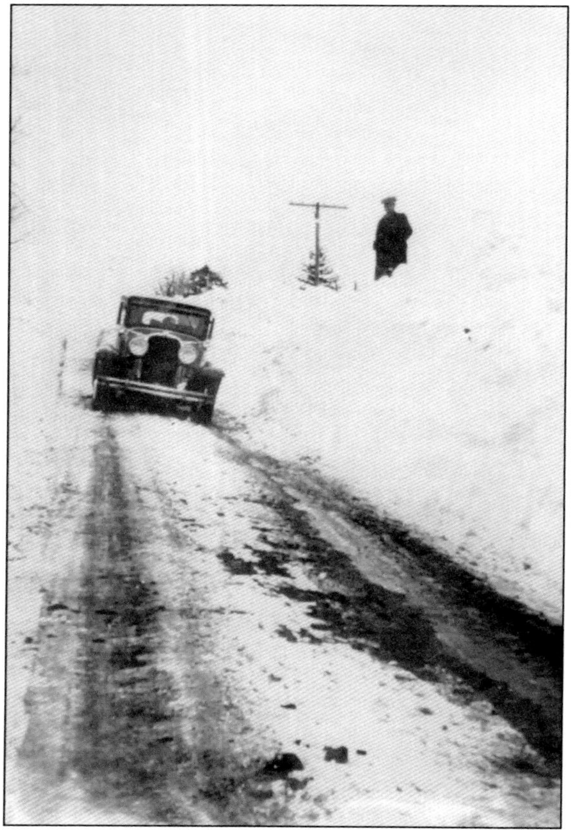

On February 22, 1914, after a blizzard, the snow was so deep and heavy that two trains were snowed under in a 16-foot drift about two miles south of Monticello at what was called Sulu Switch. Sleds brought the passengers to farmhouses or into town, bypassing other drifts up to eight feet high. Trains did not move for three days. (APL-SR.)

In this view from along the Illinois Central Railroad, one can look east over the growing town of Monticello around 1912. The first train scheduled between Monticello and Urbana ran in January 1872. Allerton Library appears in the background near Lizard Run behind the elevator (with "Monticello Grain" at the top). The tall chimney in the photograph's center is assumed to be part of the Monticello Water Works. (PCHGS.)

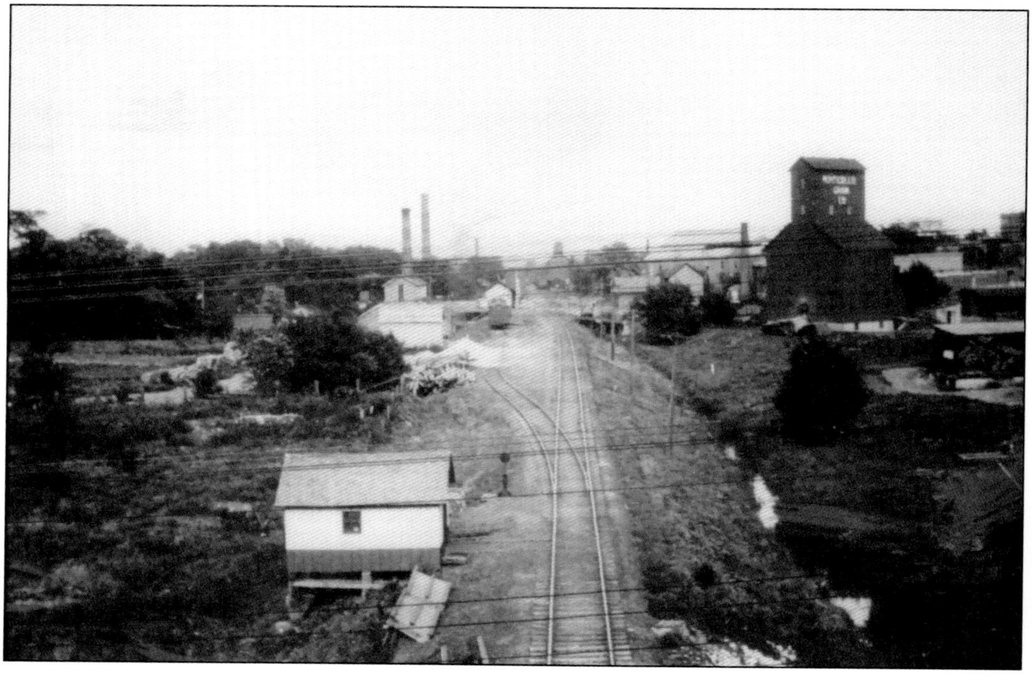

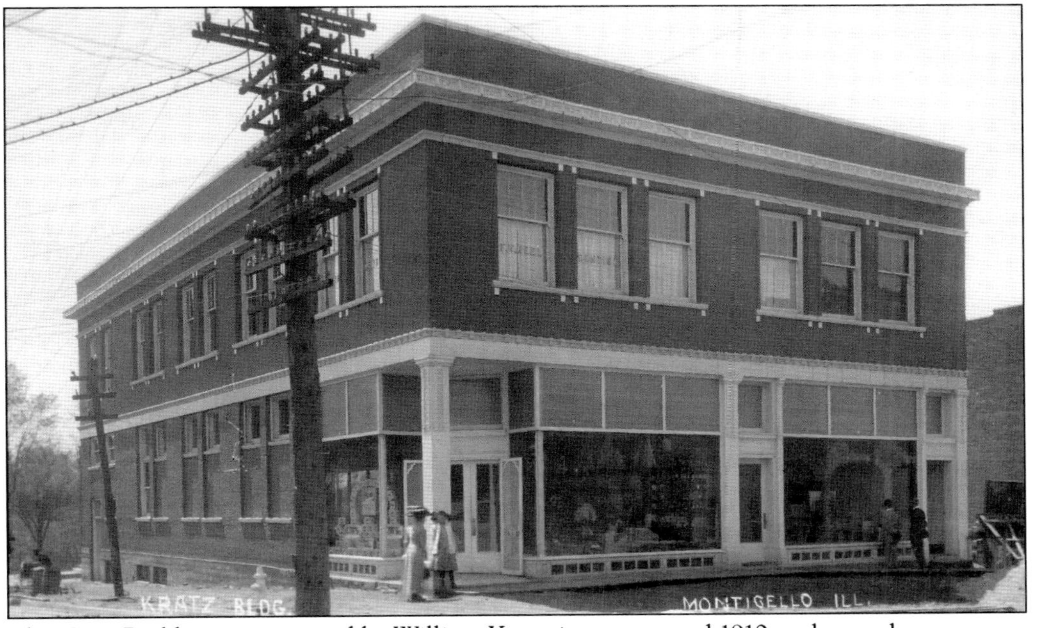

The Kratz Building, constructed by William Kratz, is seen around 1910 at the southwest corner of Main and Charter Streets. A small frame building erected in the late 1800s once sat on the lot, which was originally owned by James Piatt. In 1908, the building was moved and the lot became an open-air theater called the Airdome, with benches at the north end and a screen at the south. (APL.)

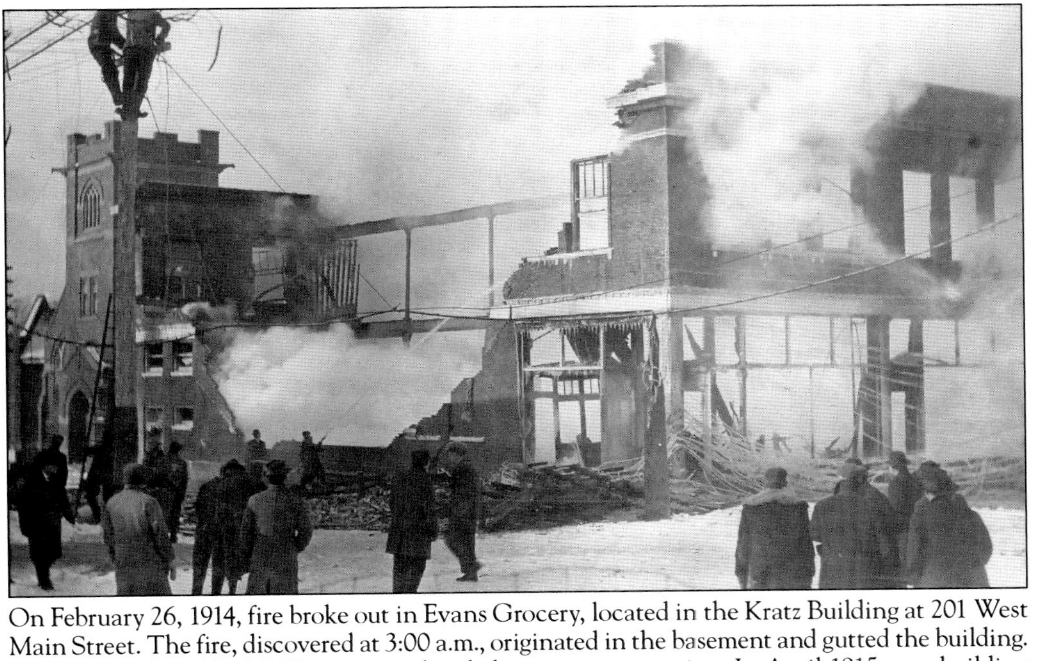

On February 26, 1914, fire broke out in Evans Grocery, located in the Kratz Building at 201 West Main Street. The fire, discovered at 3:00 a.m., originated in the basement and gutted the building. George Lux, hired by J.P. Kratz, immediately began reconstruction. In April 1915, as rebuilding of the lower floor continued, the Kratz family celebrated the upper floor's reopening with the performance of a ballet. (APL.)

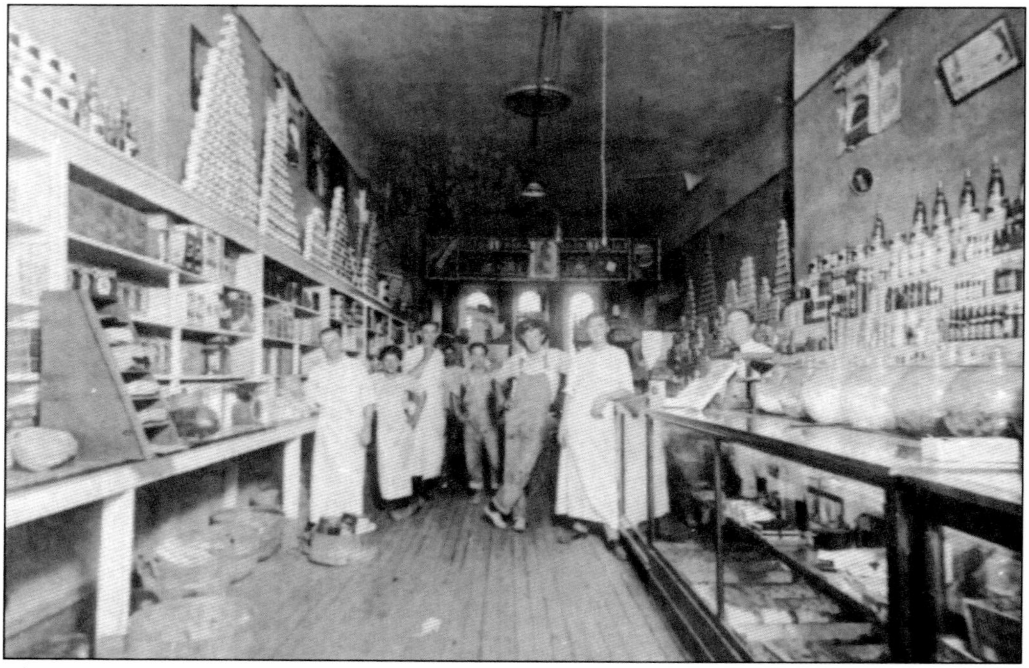

The interior of the Fred Edie Grocery Store at 105 South State Street is shown in 1915 with Fred Edie standing behind the counter. He had operated the dry goods portion of Michael Hazzard's store after 1904 when Hazzard retired. Open many hours, non-self-service stores were particularly busy on Saturday nights when people paid their bills. Grocery stores sometimes gave a free bag of candy to the bill payers. (PCHGS.)

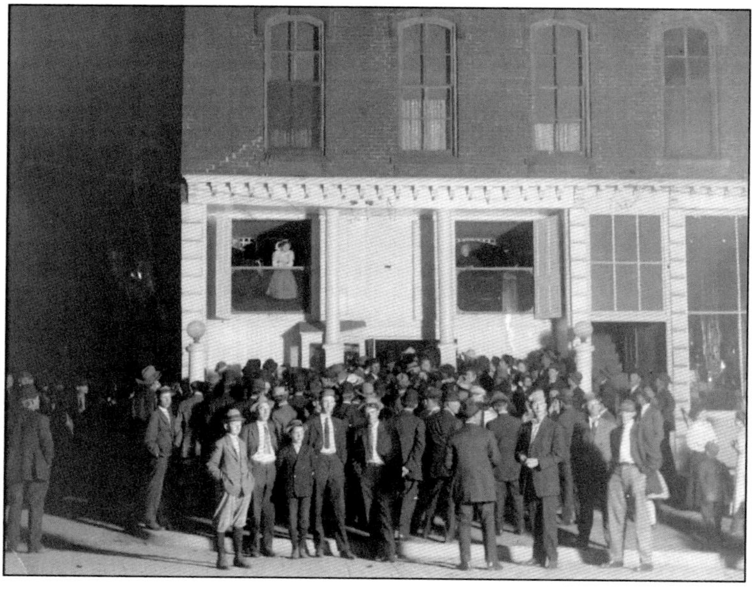

The Nickelodeon, an early movie theater in Monticello, was photographed around 1907 by Creech Photographers. The approximate address is 113 East Washington Street. The man in a light-colored cap facing the camera is Claude Freeman, an employee with the Interurban train. Freeman died in 1911 from injuries suffered after being shocked on the tracks by 600 volts. (PCHGS.)

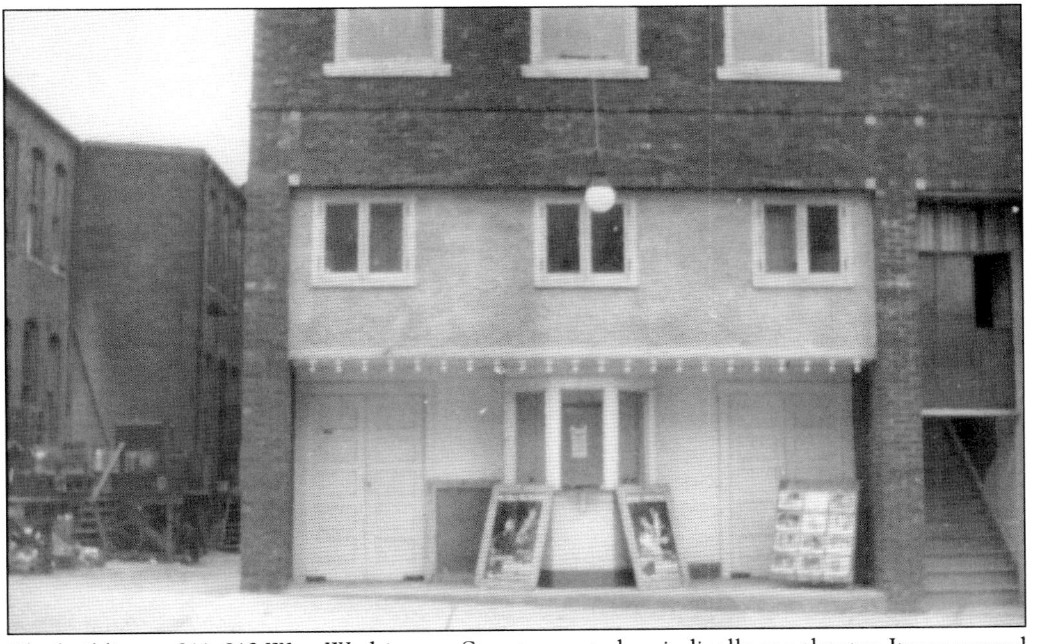

The building at 211–213 West Washington Street operated periodically as a theater. It was named the Star in 1917 and later was the Globe, managed by Frank Norris. He renovated it by lowering the floor to street level and erecting a new stage with suitable scenery for vaudeville acts. In earlier years, the building housed Steele and Searfoss Jewelry and, from 2007 to 2013, Pearls and More Jewelry. (PCHGS.)

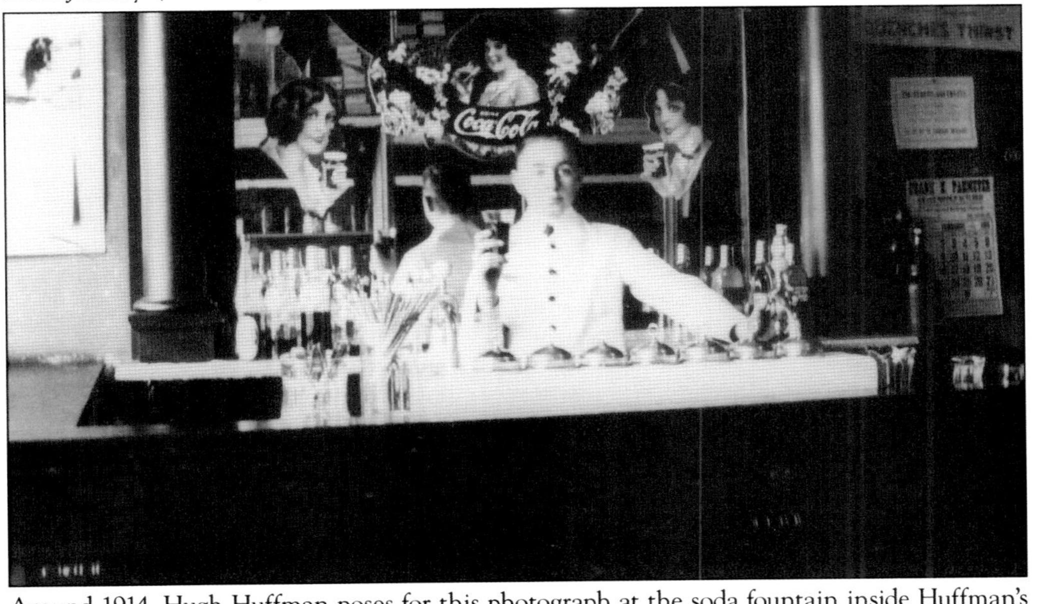

Around 1914, Hugh Huffman poses for this photograph at the soda fountain inside Huffman's Bakery at 101 South State Street. Fred Dresback owned the bakery from 1916 until 1938. A two-story building used for the Masonic hall and nicknamed "Old Romeo" was built on the property in 1850 but was repeatedly relocated over many years. The current structure was built in 1875. (APL-SR.)

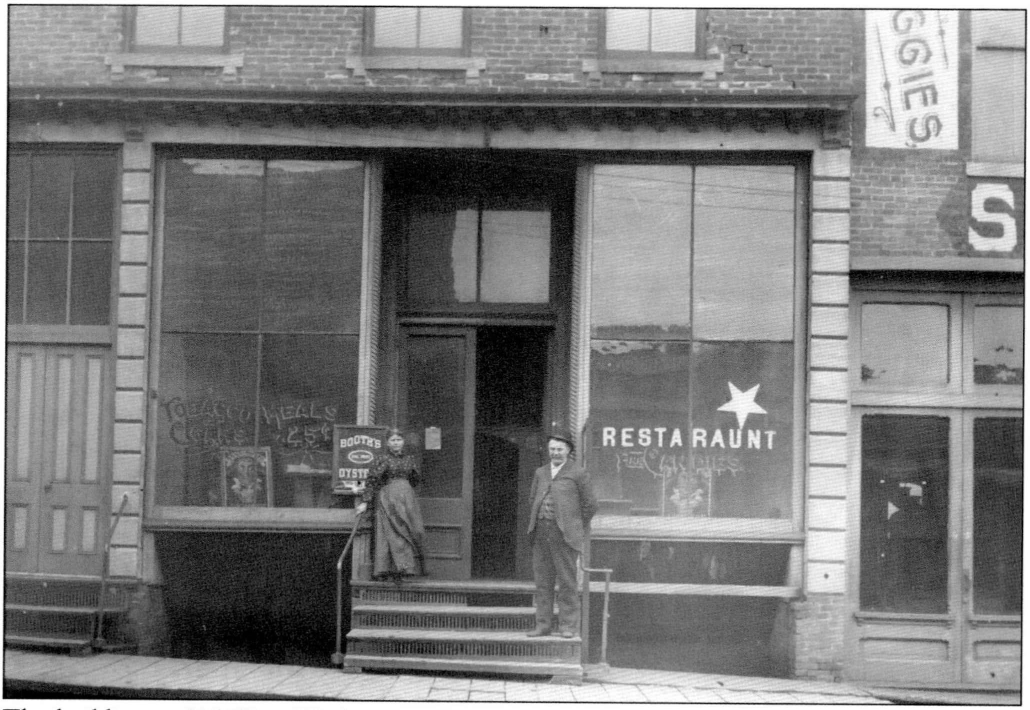

The building at 215 West Washington Street was constructed around 1910 and may be Lew Durbin's Lunch Counter. According to the window advertisements, it sold meals for 25¢, candies, tobacco, cigars, and Booth's Oysters. Oysters were shipped in two-gallon wooden buckets. The oysters were then sold in half-pint to quarter-sized pasteboard containers. Buyers could also bring their own pint or quart jars. (PCHGS.)

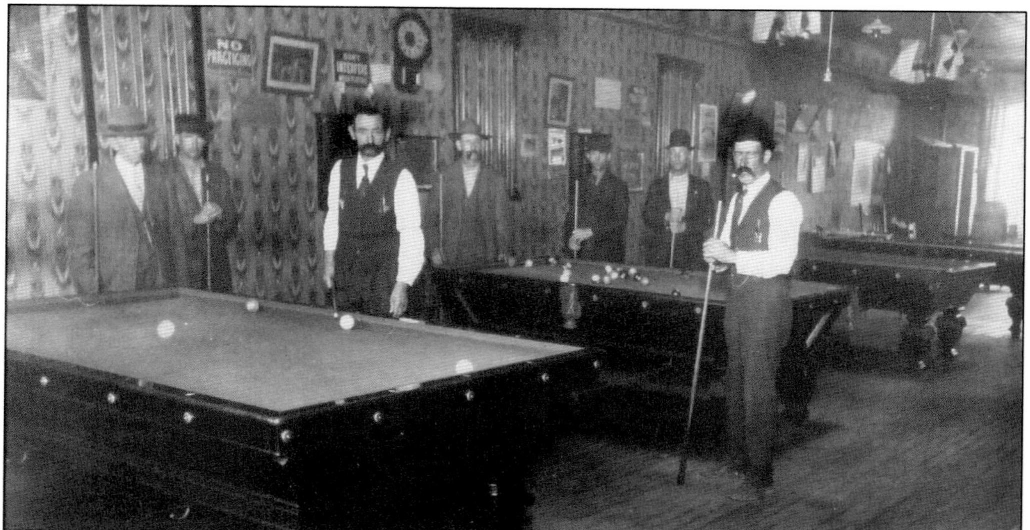

No Practicing and Do Not Interfere signs warn visitors at Robert Griffith's billiard parlor to behave themselves. The parlor was located on the second floor of 215 West Washington Street above Lew Durbin's Lunch Counter. Griffith and his wife lived at 603 East Center Street, the home that had previously been owned by Dr. William Noecker and then moved from the square. (APL.)

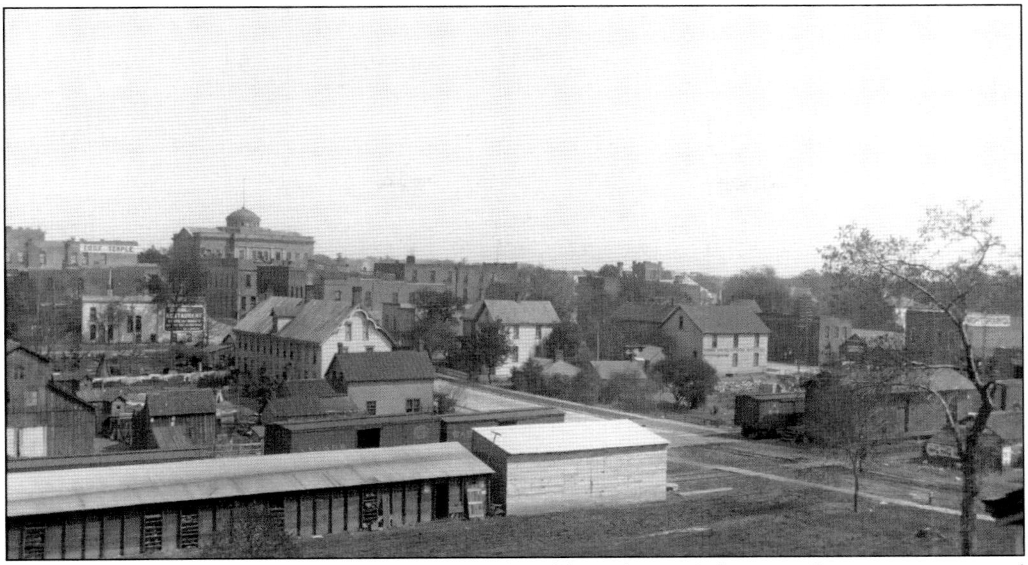

The west side of Monticello near the Wabash railroad line along Washington Street is seen around 1909. The large two-story, light-colored building with laundry billowing in the backyard is Lewis Flats, public housing. Across Washington Street stands a two-story brick building now called the Red House Gallery. The courthouse cupola can be seen in the distance. (APL-SR.)

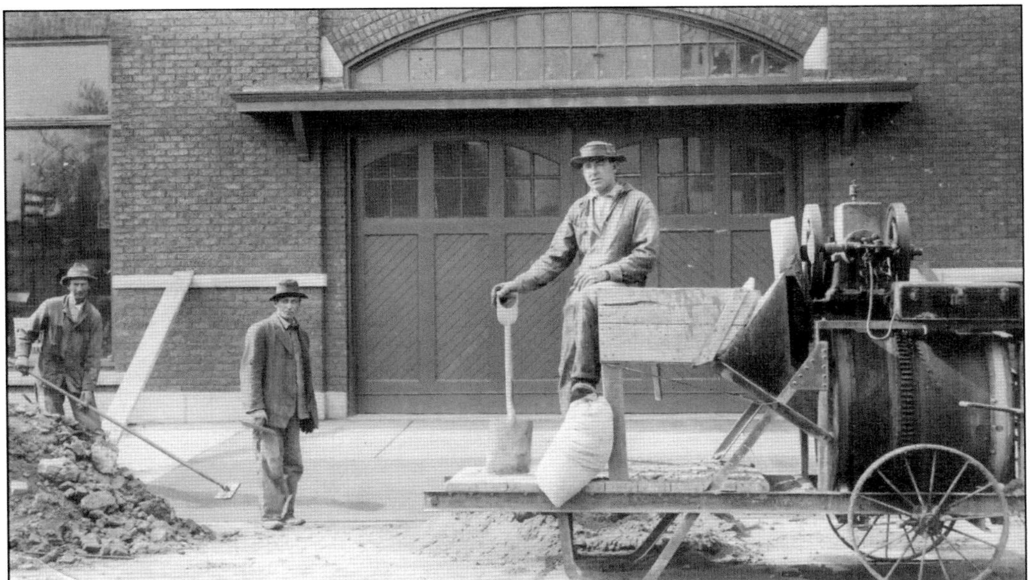

Keith Knott, Bill Longworth, and ? Fisler lay a sidewalk in 1914 in front of the Fireproof Garage at 119 East Washington Street. The garage was built by John Pembroke after a fire demolished the frame building there, which was at one time the Woolington Hotel and Empire Laundry, later the Hop Sing Laundry. The elevator installed for hauling cars to the upper level for repair work was removed in 1995. (APL-SR.)

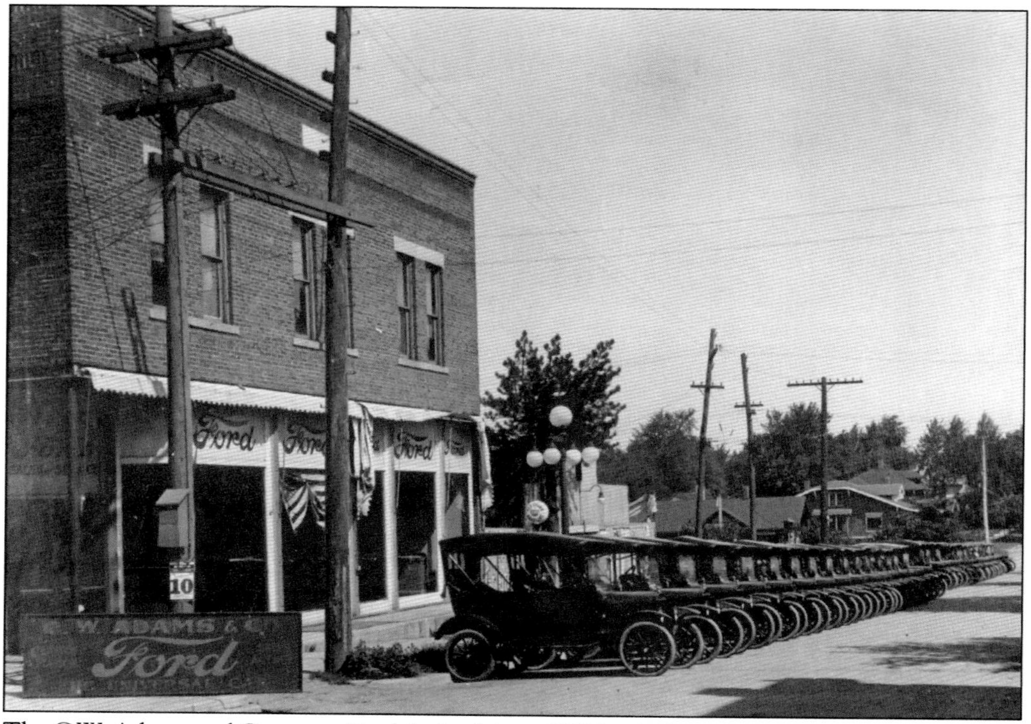

The C.W. Adams and Company Ford dealership at 112 North State Street is seen in 1916 behind the Moore State Bank. The Illinois Central Depot appears where the two telephones lean toward each other. Beyond that is a bungalow that is still standing. In 1979, the National Bank tore down old buildings on East Livingston Street across from the post office for a parking lot. (PCHGS.)

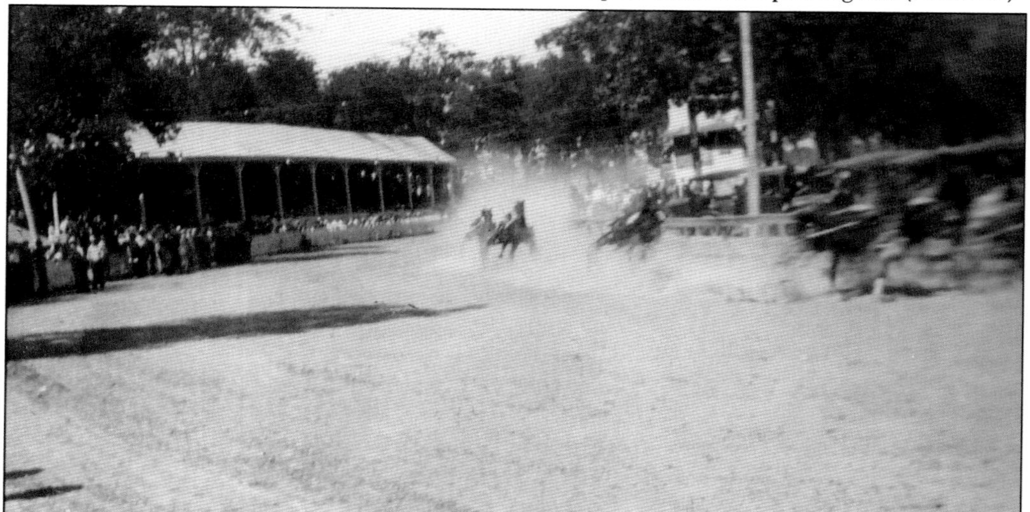

In 1861, the Piatt County Agricultural Society bought 15 acres of land north of town, now the State Street Forest Preserve. The society reorganized in 1869 and decided to hold county fairs instead. The weeklong summer event was especially popular for horse-racing, as seen in this photograph from 1913. The half-mile track was constructed around 1877. Later, the track was widened and a 3,000-seat amphitheater was constructed. (APL-SR.)

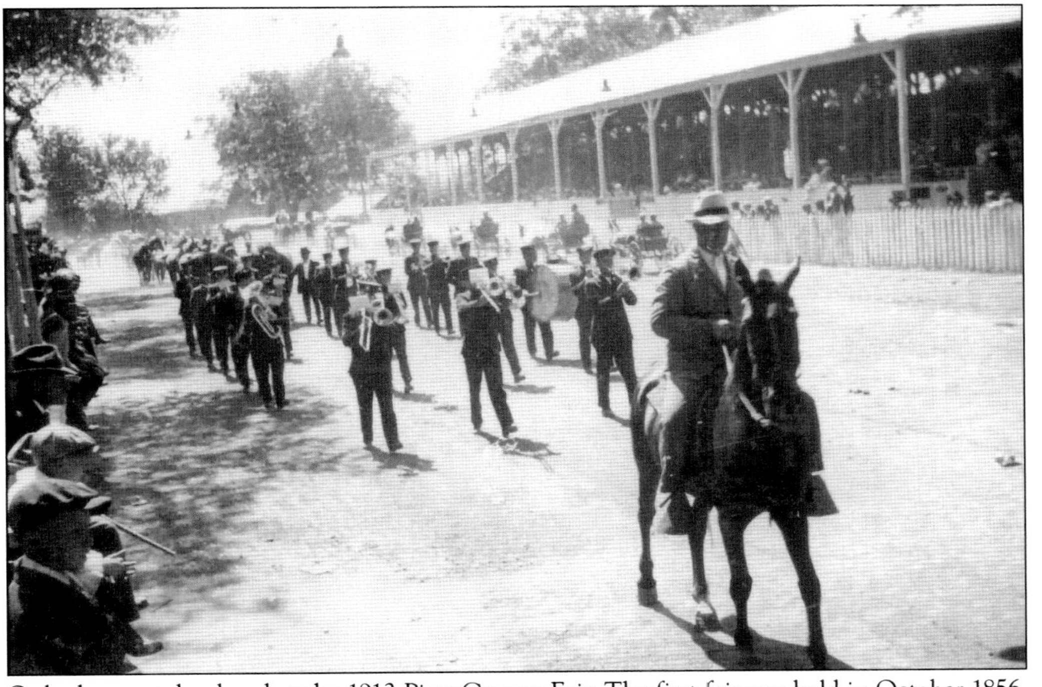

Onlookers watch a band at the 1913 Piatt County Fair. The first fair was held in October 1856, with later fairs held every August. In 1888, W.E. Lodge donated the Hayworth cabin for exhibition at the fair. By then, the fair was Illinois's largest. The biggest attractions in 1900 were a 45-foot Ferris wheel and Jesse James's brother officiating as the starter of the race. (APL-SR.)

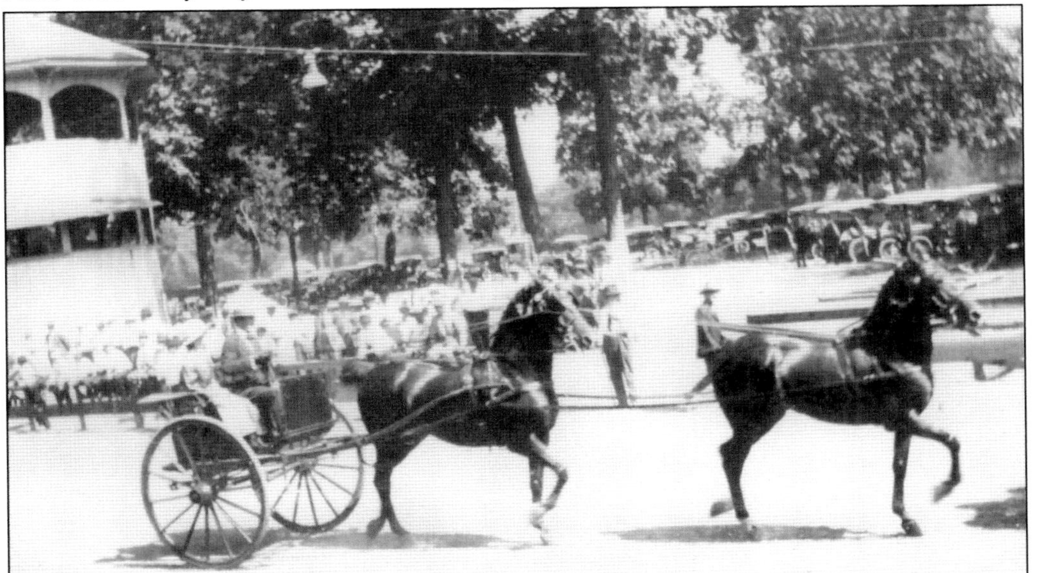

In addition to watching parades and races, visitors to the county fair could get a tattoo for a $1 or watch sharpshooters wowing the crowd with their prowess. Little did onlookers realize that the marksmen were shooting blanks at cigarettes spring-loaded to blast apart. A Ford touring car could be ogled at the C.W. Adams Ford dealership before the final day's raffle in 1914. (APL-SR.)

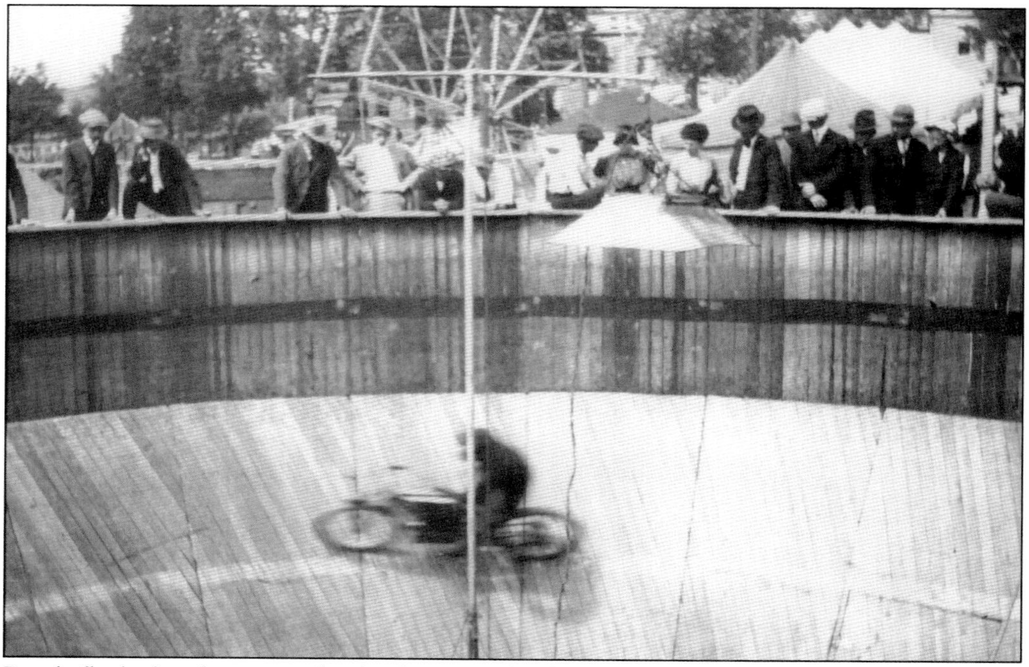

People flocked to the county fair for the entire day, bringing their dinner as well as feed for their horses. By afternoon, the town was deserted. Each year, something new attracted townsfolk: a Wild West show, clowns, dollar rides for children in an air balloon pulled by a steam engine, hoochie-coochie dancers, or as shown here in 1913, the Motordome attraction. (APL-SR.)

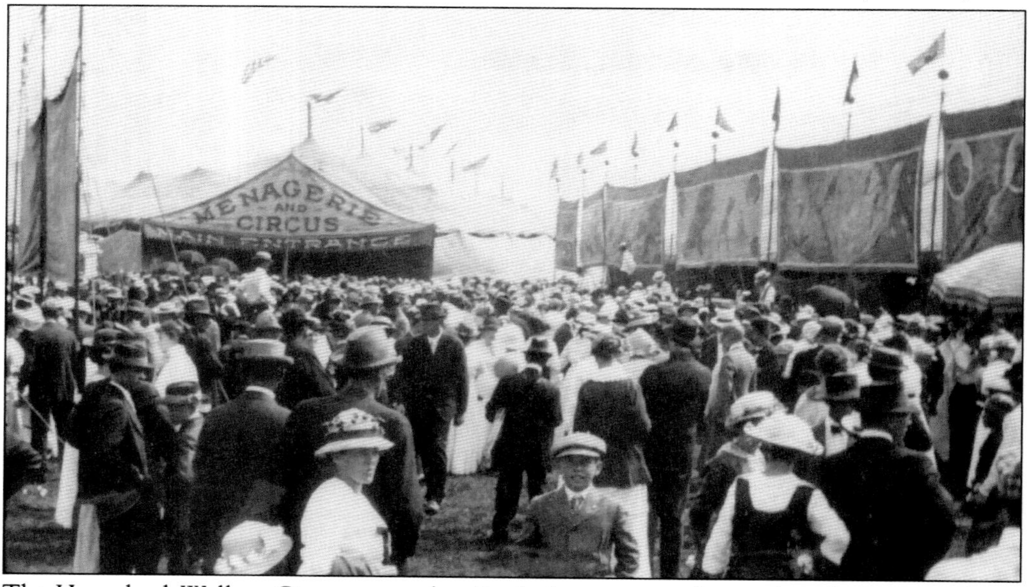

The Hagenbeck-Wallace Circus camped at Bryden's pasture at the south end of Monticello in 1915. Charles Bryden gave permission to use the land as long as all children whom he named (of lower income) received free admission. At its peak, the Hagenbeck-Wallace Circus was the second-largest circus in America, after the Ringling Bros. and Barnum & Bailey Circus, which performed in Rhoades's pasture on East Washington Street in 1895. (APL-SR.)

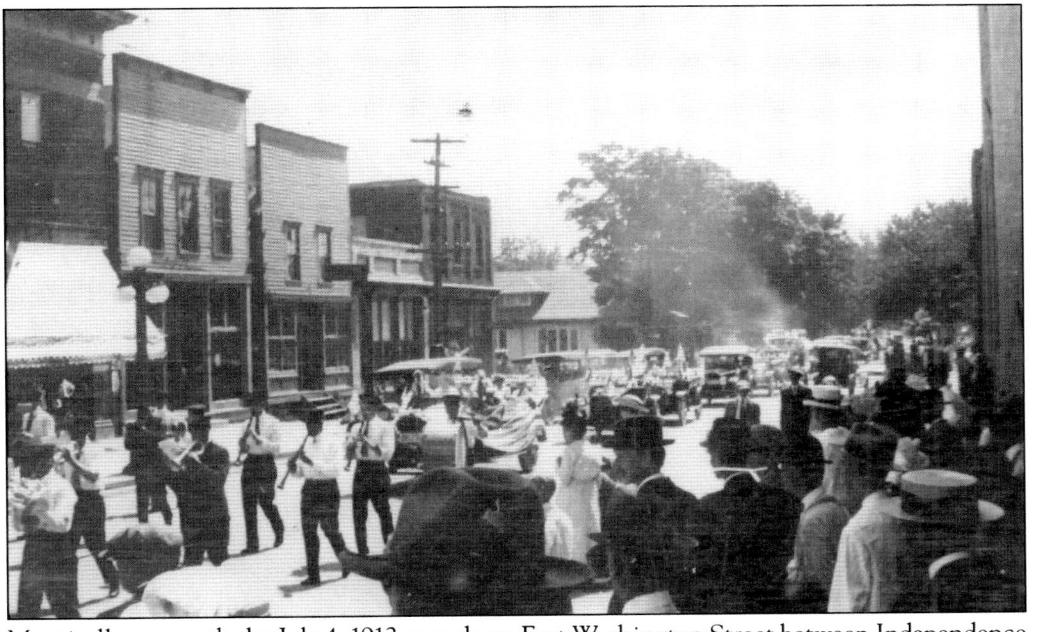

Monticelloans watch the July 4, 1912, parade on East Washington Street between Independence and State Streets. Note the now gone frame buildings along the street's north side. The brick building at 112 East Washington Street was constructed around 1883 by a Mr. Farra. Early in William F. Lodge's career, he operated a bowling alley at 114 East Washington Street. Later, it housed Charles Anderson's barbershop and bathhouse. (APL-SR.)

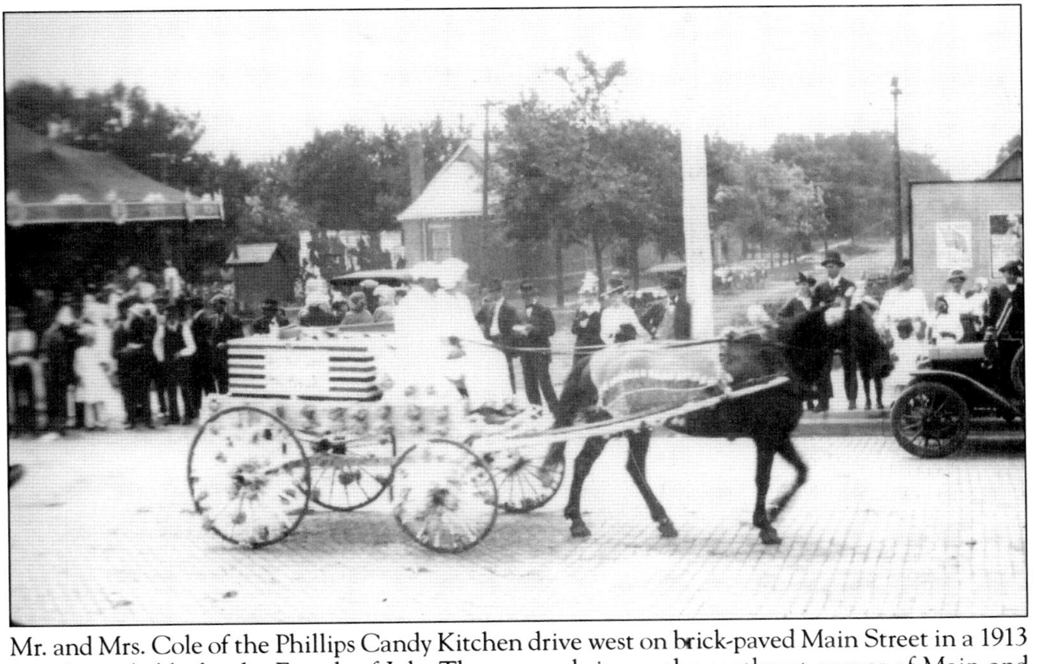

Mr. and Mrs. Cole of the Phillips Candy Kitchen drive west on brick-paved Main Street in a 1913 parade, probably for the Fourth of July. The carousel sits on the southeast corner of Main and State Streets where a small park is now located. At the far right is an empty lot where the Dairy Queen is currently located. (APL-SR.)

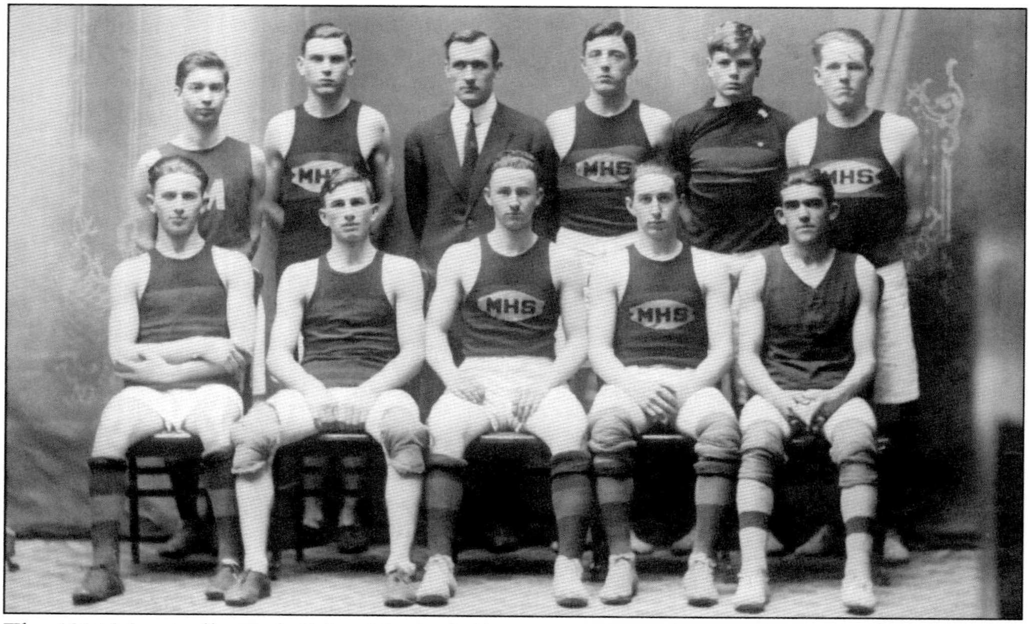

The 1914 Monticello High School basketball team sits for a photograph. Pictured, from left to right, are (first row) Dwight Duvall, John Kelly, H. Thompson, Murray Collyer, and R. Marquiss; (second row) Burl Edie, unidentified, coach Lynn Robison, Jesse Adkins, Eugene Marquiss, and Homer A. Marquiss. (APL-SR.)

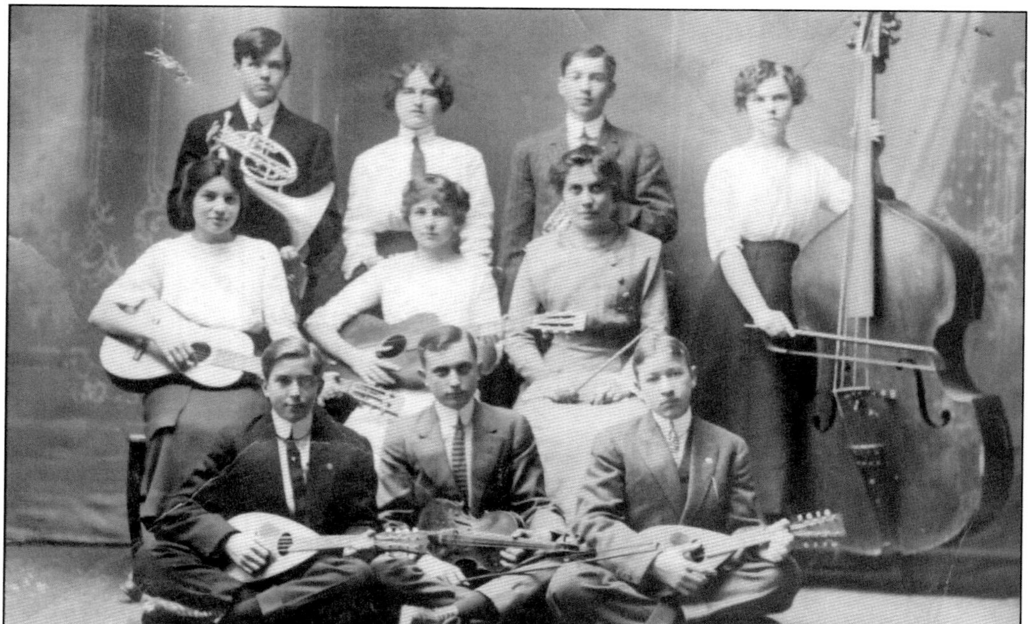

A high school student band appears in this photograph from 1913. Pictured, from left to right, are (first row) Maxwell Hott (son of John Hott), Joseph Raycraft, and Harold Pinkard; (second row) Doris White, Marion Smith, and Lois Evans; (third row) Harry Nichols, Gladys Reecer, Burl Edie, and an unidentified student with the double bass. (APL-SR.)

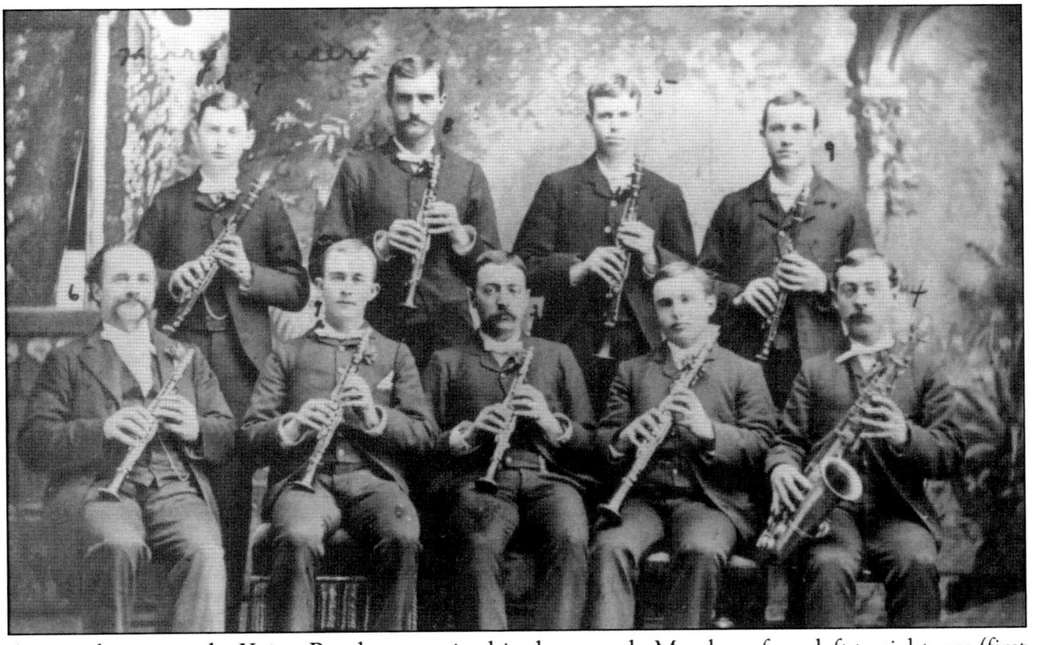

A group known as the Kaiser Band appears in this photograph. Members, from left to right, are (first row) unidentified, possibly Cory Rhoades, William Smith, unidentified, and James Smith; (second row) Harry Kaiser (of Kaiser Abstract), unidentified, Charles Bryden, unidentified. (PCHGS.)

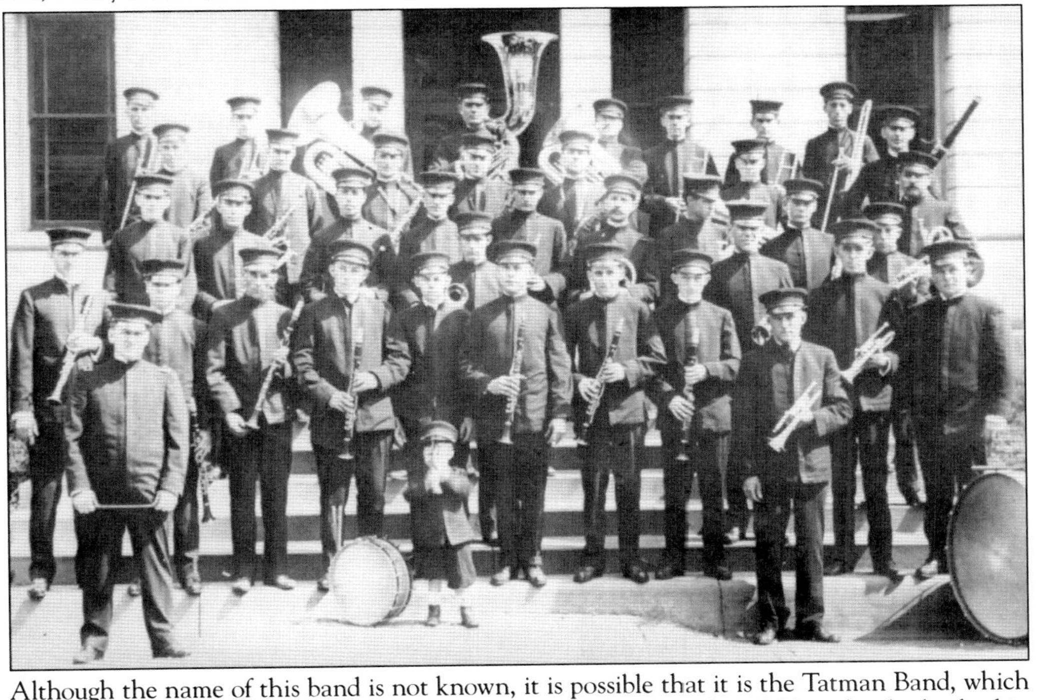

Although the name of this band is not known, it is possible that it is the Tatman Band, which was organized in 1892 by Thomas Tatman. The band reorganized in 1900 under the leadership of John Andrew and became known as the Pepsin Band. It gave weekly public concerts in the summer. (PCHGS.)

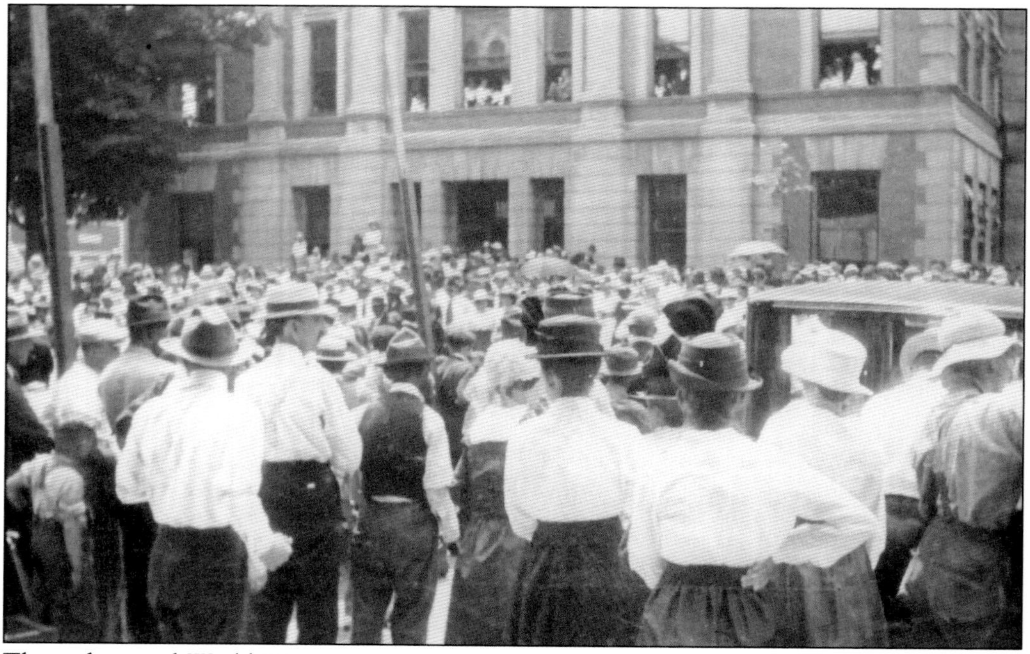

Three thousand World War I patriots filled the square and courthouse windows in a farewell celebration for draftees. The 1918 draftee contingent was made up of 100 men, the largest at that time from Piatt County. The Methodist Guild served dinner to the men and their friends and families before they left for Camp Wheeler in Macon, Georgia. (APL-SR.)

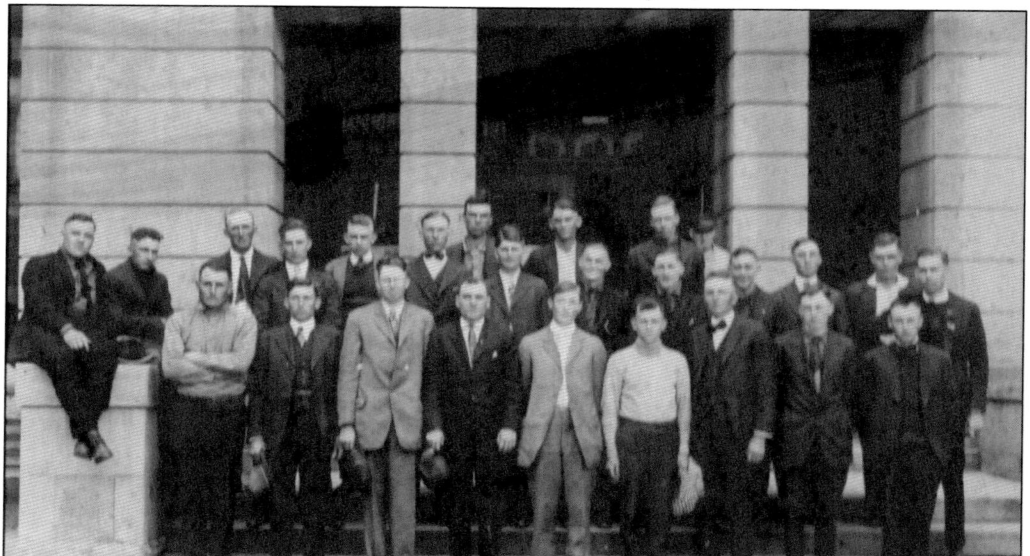

Draftees pose in front of the courthouse in 1918, prior to being sent—most probably—to Jefferson Barracks, Missouri. On June 5 that same year, 1,261 young men registered for military service following the United States declaration of war against Germany. The Piatt County Exemption Board included Allen F. Moore and several doctors as medical examiners. (PCHGS.)

Abraham Lincoln encountered Stephen A. Douglas on July 29, 1858 on the road from Monticello to Bement and later agreed to meet in joint debates. Had they not met and not debated, Lincoln may have not become president. A pyramid-shaped monument was erected in 1918 on the east side of the road to commemorate the occasion. It was replaced by a stone marker around 1957 when the road was widened. (APL-SR.)

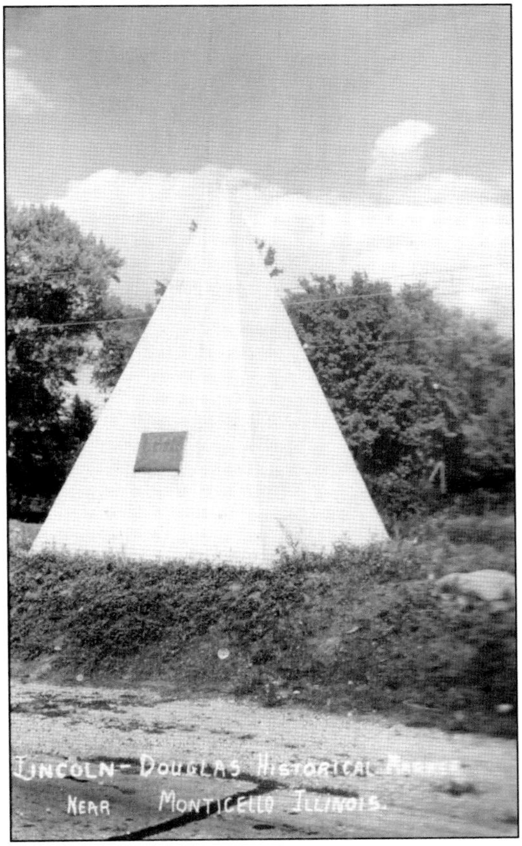

Some of the people in this July 4, 1920, parade include Dr. Bushee, Albert Priebe, Obert Kilton, Ora Stiverson (the tuba player nearer the onlooking man in the hat), and J. Gregory. The merry-go-round sits at the southeast corner of State and Main Streets. The small building immediately to the right of the carousel is an outdoor privy. The building next to that is St. Philomena Catholic Church. (APL-SR.)

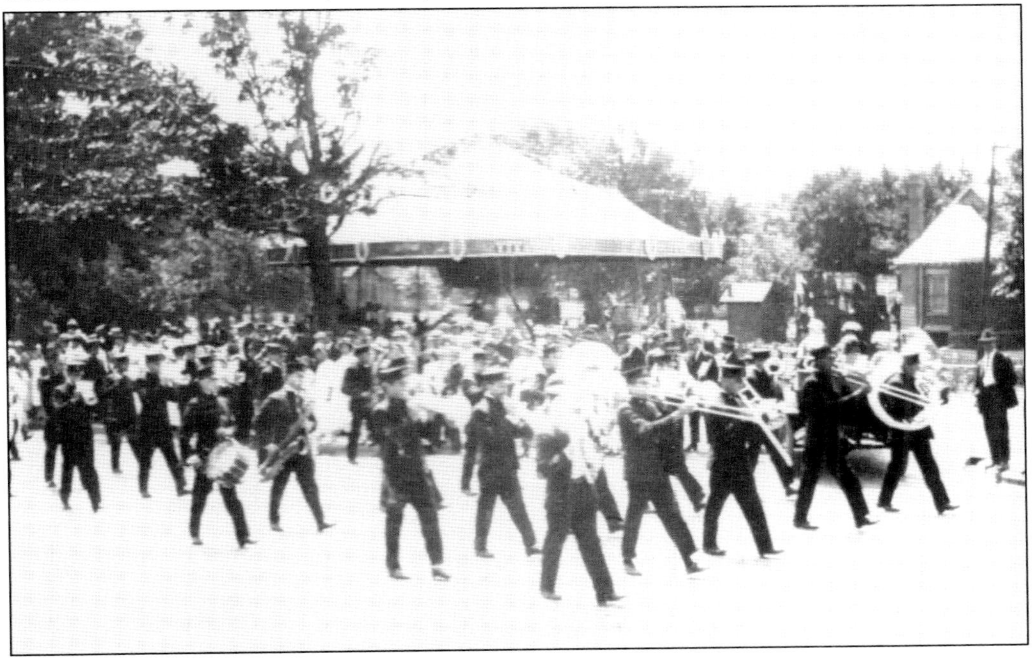

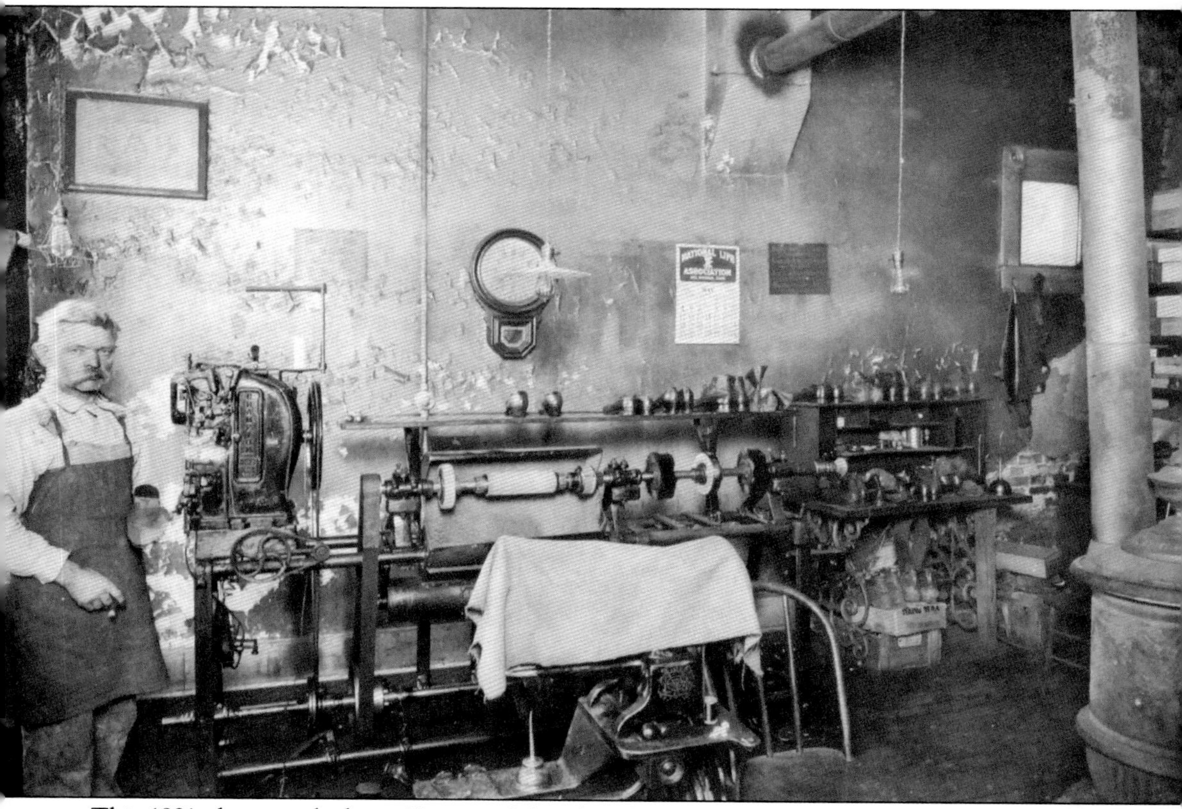

This 1921 photograph shows Herman Schmidt in his shoe repair business, located at 208 West Main Street from 1914 to 1921. He apparently did not mind the paint peeling off the walls. Born in Germany in 1862, Schmidt had made his way to America and served in the 1898 Spanish-American War. He died in 1951. (PCHGS.)

Five

Keeping Pace 1920s–1980s

As the 1920s ended, Monticello's major employers included banks, Pepsin Syrup, and the Tylac Company. In 1933, as the Depression deepened, every Monticello bank closed its doors. By the end of November, the newly organized National Bank replaced the Moore State Bank. Eventually, the closed institutions returned between 80 to 100 percent of the depositors' money.

Monticello rebounded in the late 1930s with more banks and gas stations in and around the courthouse square. The Honselman cabin, which sat at Washington and Market Streets since 1843, was moved to the countryside, its spot later supplanted by one of those many gas stations. In the 1940s, the square boasted seven grocery stores, four barbershops, two newspapers, and at least six dry goods businesses.

During World War II, Piatt County reached its bond sales quota before any other Illinois county. The *Piatt County Journal* published names and addresses of residents in the armed forces so friends could stay in contact. On August 15, 1945, the town closed all businesses and schools to join in celebrating Victory in Japan Day. By the end of the war, a total of 1,767 Piatt County men had served their country.

Monticello was able to start a hospital in 1939 through the munificence of the Moore and Kirby families. Other generous citizens included Robert Allerton, who, in 1946, donated a portion of his estate to the University of Illinois, and Maxwell Hott and his wife, who gave their home at 810 North State Street to the university for conference and seminar use.

As cars became more plentiful, the Interurban Train lost popularity, closing entirely in 1955. In 1962, Market Street was resurfaced, covering up the tracks. The Interurban train station was demolished to make way for a parking lot.

Parking lots and modern houses replaced many old businesses and homes. Faster roads to Champaign and Decatur meant more commuting possibilities for Monticello citizens. Mom-and-pop stores decreased, replaced by bigger and more modern stores.

Dial telephone service was installed in 1952. Until the early 1990s, residents could call other Monticelloans using only the last four digits of the phone number.

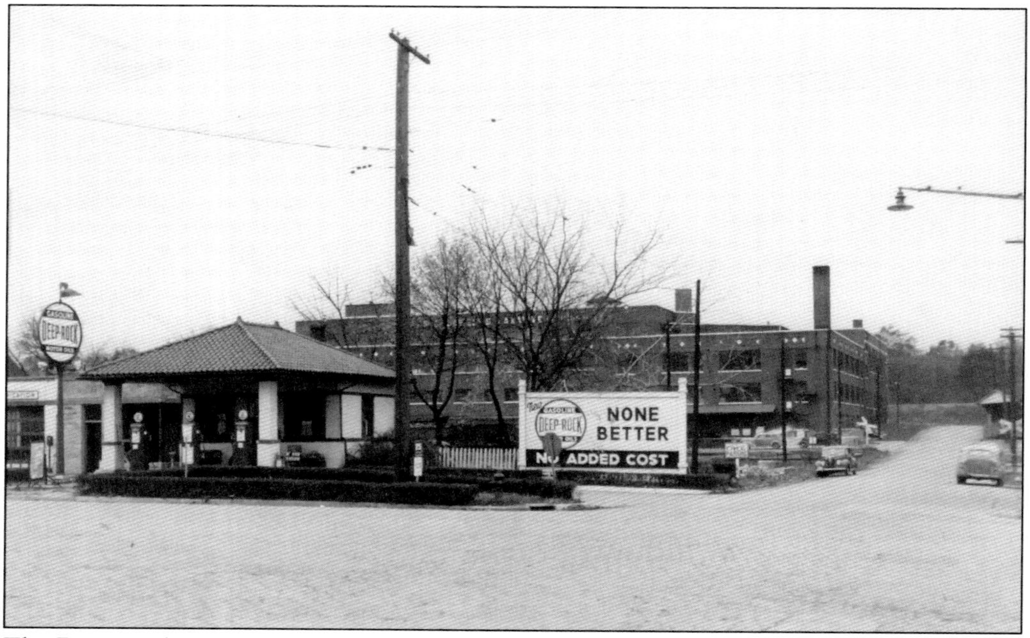

The Deep Rock gas station opened in 1922 at the southwest corner of Livingston and Market Streets and offered a men's "retiring room" and a ladies' parlor. Since then, the spot has been continuously used for a gas station. The E.D.S. Station was established in 1977 and offered full service until 2012. (PCHGS.)

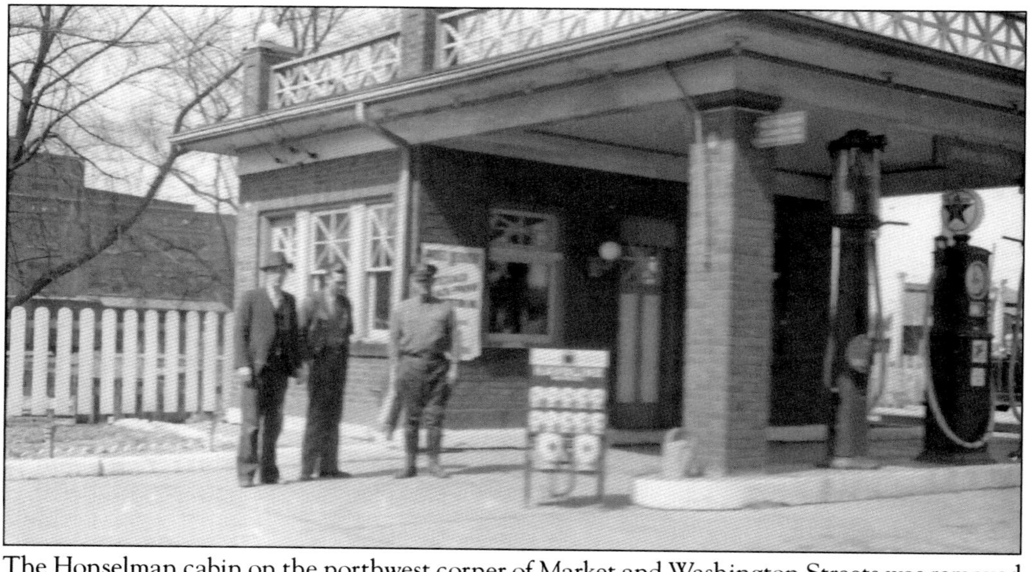

The Honselman cabin on the northwest corner of Market and Washington Streets was removed in 1920. By 1932, a Texaco gas station was constructed in its spot. In this photograph, brothers Ernie (left) and Harry (center) Parker stand next to a uniformed John Doss in front of the station. Pepsin Syrup Company appears in the background. A bank claimed the location in 1982 and, in the 1990s, a drugstore took over. (PCHGS.)

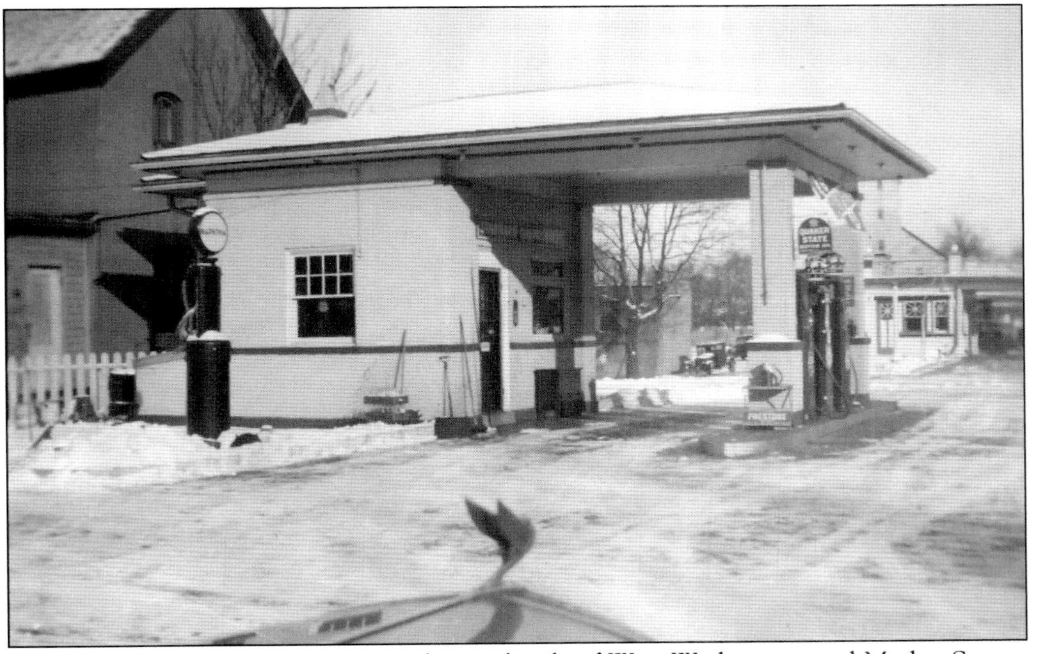

Standard Oil purchased two lots on the south side of West Washington and Market Streets in 1926. By 1928, its new gas station served the public. Over the decades, several gas stations operated there. To the station's west, at 315 West Washington Street, looms what was once the home of the lots' prior owner, Christian Wengenroth. In this photograph, the Texaco station is seen across the street. (PCHGS.)

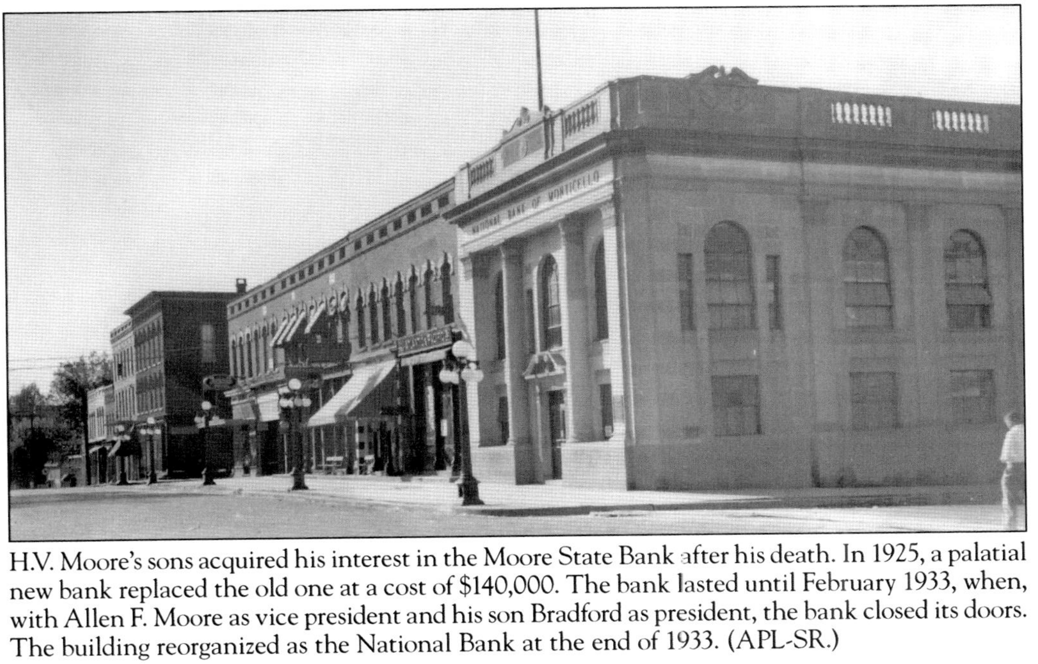

H.V. Moore's sons acquired his interest in the Moore State Bank after his death. In 1925, a palatial new bank replaced the old one at a cost of $140,000. The bank lasted until February 1933, when, with Allen F. Moore as vice president and his son Bradford as president, the bank closed its doors. The building reorganized as the National Bank at the end of 1933. (APL-SR.)

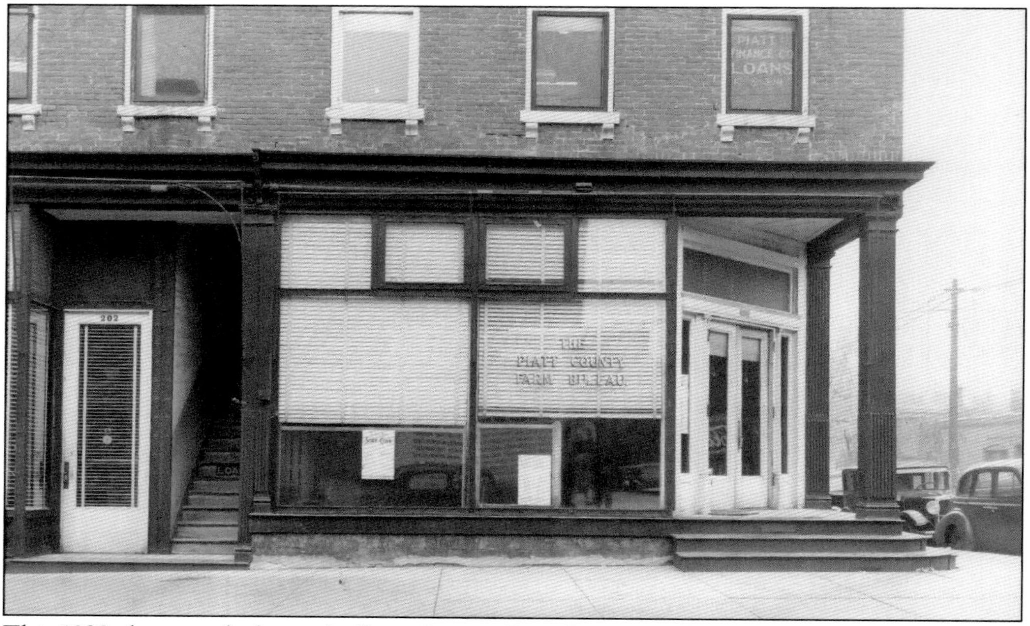

This 1938 photograph shows the Piatt County Farm Bureau at the northwest corner of Charter and Washington Streets (200 West Washington Street) after it took over a defunct bank. The original structure had to be rebuilt when it collapsed in 1868 halfway through its construction. Dr. Noecker's drugstore occupied the east half of the first floor in 1869. (PCHGS.)

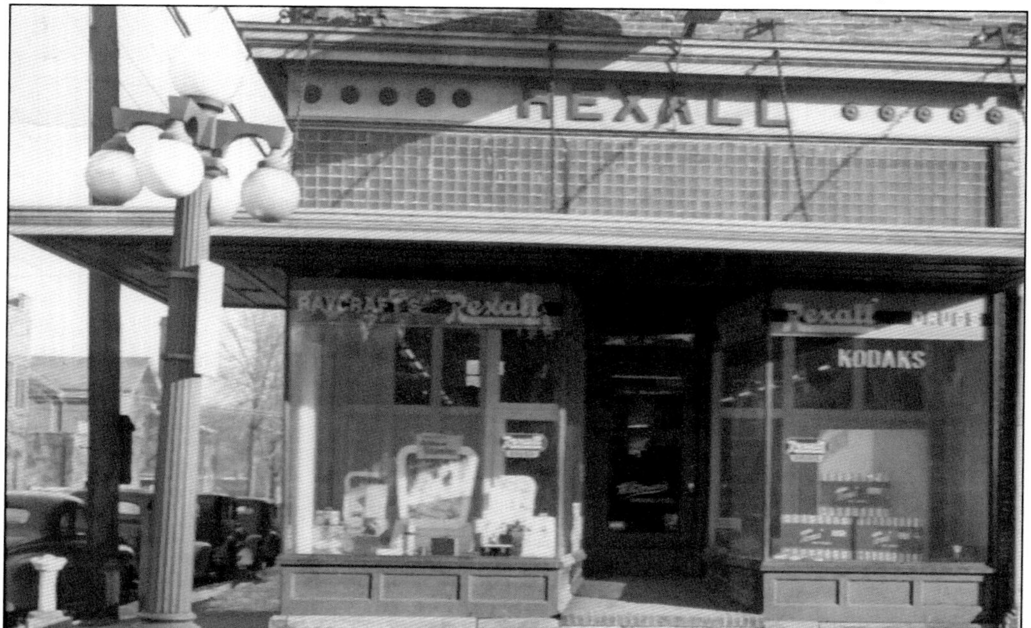

Raycraft's Rexall Drugs sat on the northeast corner of Charter and Washington Streets. Joseph Raycraft and Maxwell Hott purchased the business in 1916 from Charles H. Ridgely, who had operated the drugstore for years. The store stayed open until 1994, when it was sold to Carle Rx Express and left the building's ground floor empty for the first time in a century. (PCHGS.)

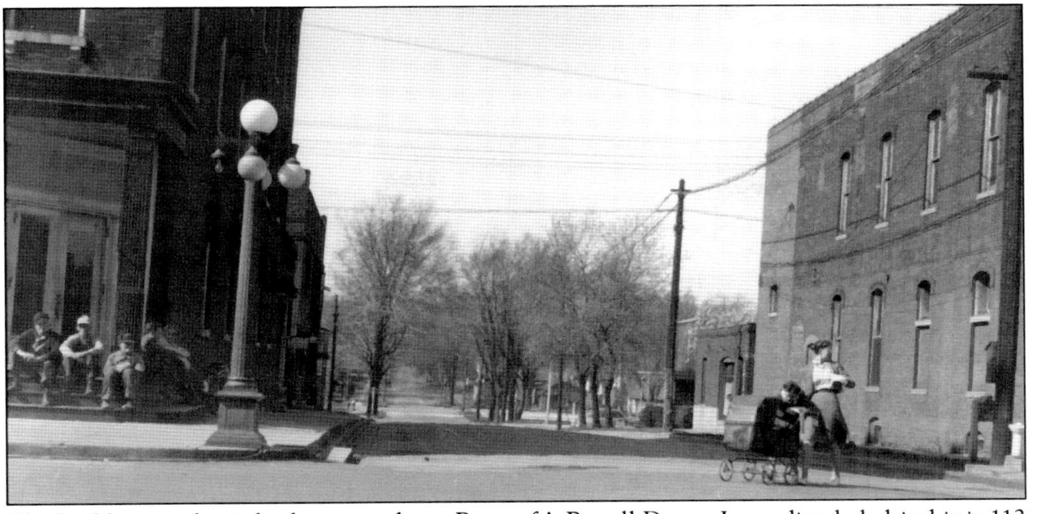

The building in the right foreground was Raycraft's Rexall Drugs. Immediately behind it is 113 North Charter Street, the current home of Carlton Cleaners and previous business address of Dr. Nelson Coffin. Starting in 1865, Abstract Title Service was established across the street at number 110. By 1889, it was Harry Kaiser Abstract. Kaiser Abstract is still there. (PCHGS.)

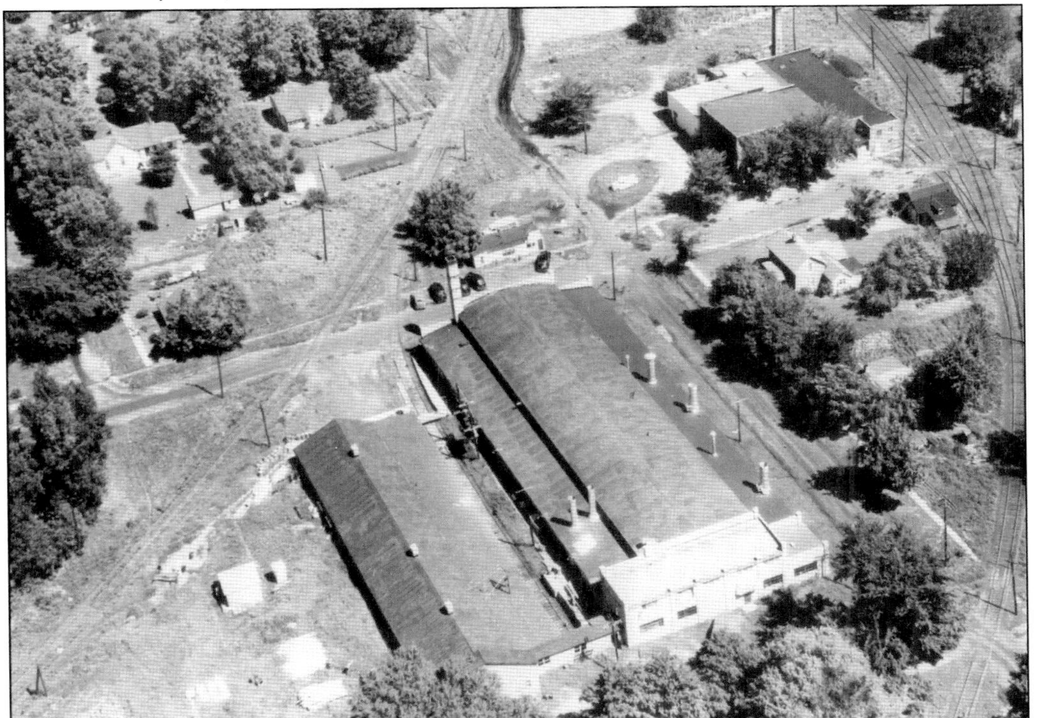

Allen Moore brought the Tylac Company to Monticello in the late 1920s. The factory, completed in 1929, sat at Greeley and High Streets. Tylac produced a low-cost substitute for ceramic tile, later adding refrigerator door molding, wooden ammunition boxes during World War II, and green chalkboards. The next owner, Loxit Systems, sold part of the business and auctioned off the property in 1963. The building burned down in 1974. (PCHGS.)

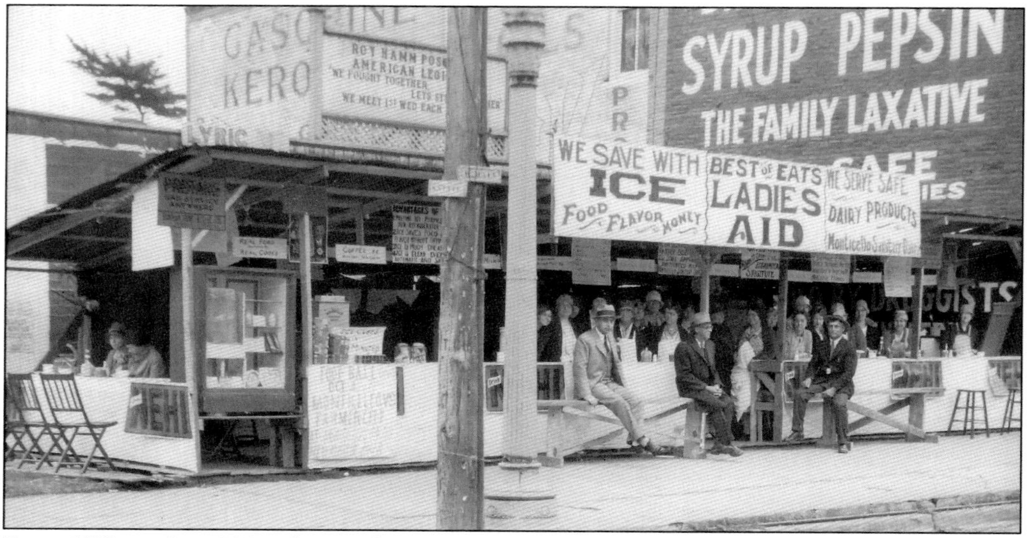

From 1893 to the 1930s, the southwest corner of Main and State Streets was an empty lot. During a 1935 festival, the Ladies' Aid Society sponsored and helped out at a food stand. This was the location of the Tenbrook Hotel, where Lincoln usually stayed when in town. Harold Hammerschmidt's popcorn stand opened there around 1938, and in 1951, the Hammerschmidts erected the Dairy Queen. (RS.)

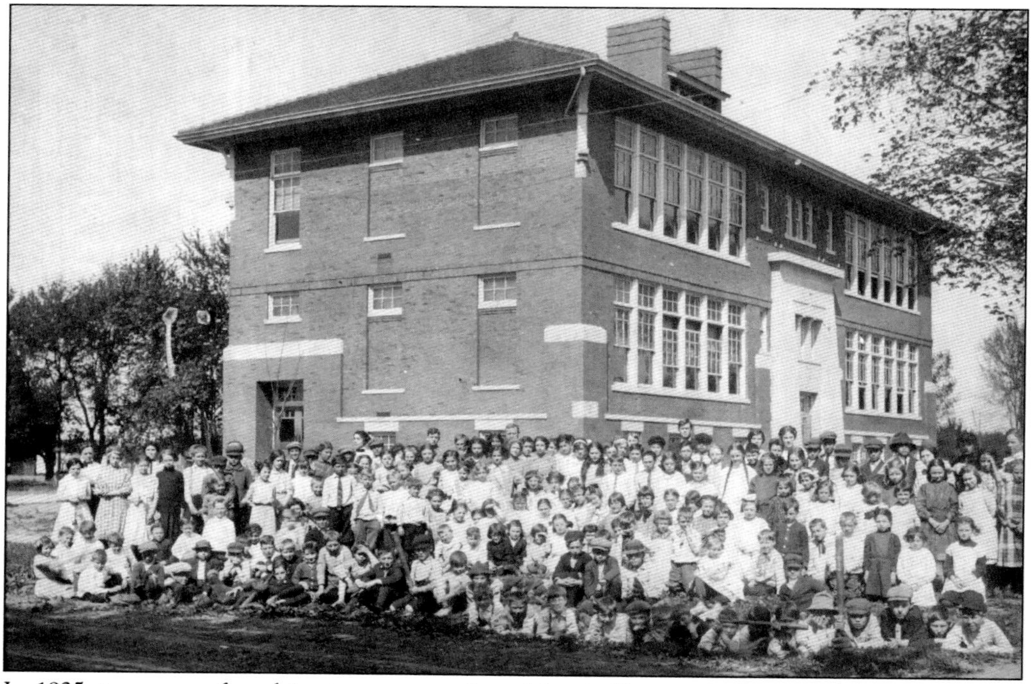

In 1935, ten years after this picture was taken, Monticelloans voted to pay $25,000 in bonds to enlarge Lincoln School. Until the school expansion was completed, each classroom held between 25 and 33 pupils, and all junior high students were grouped into one classroom together. Washington School junior high students were also overcrowding the school at the south end of town. (PCHGS.)

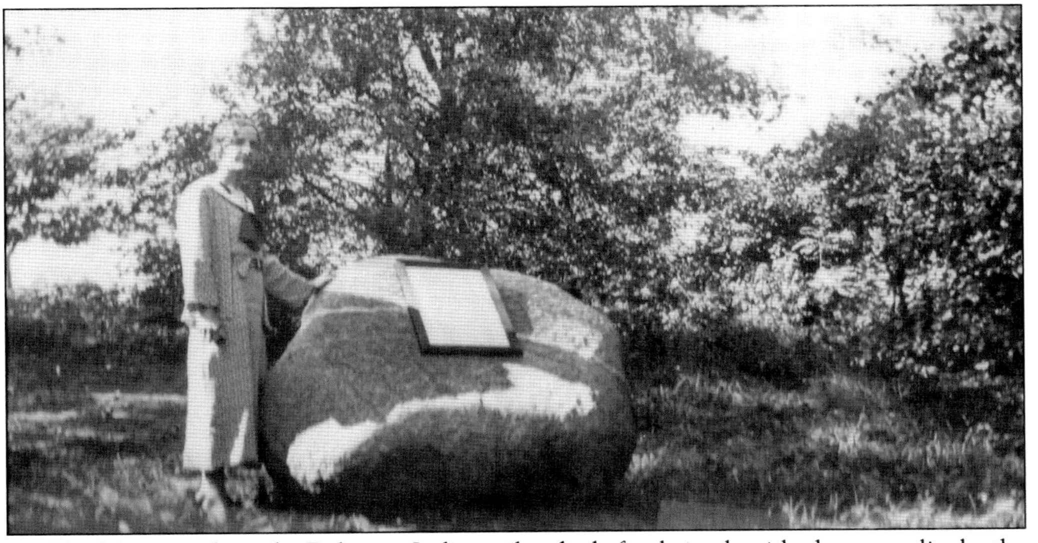

In 1834, Manasua, from the Delaware Indian tribe, died after being banished years earlier by the Lenni Lenapes. Her husband, Chief Buck, buried her by what is now Buck's Pond and left Illinois. After residents found her bones scattered, she was reburied on the hillside. In 1936, a boulder was placed above her grave in west Lodge Park. Another Native American, Danny Roscoe, was later buried alongside Manasua. The woman pictured is unidentified. (PCHGS.)

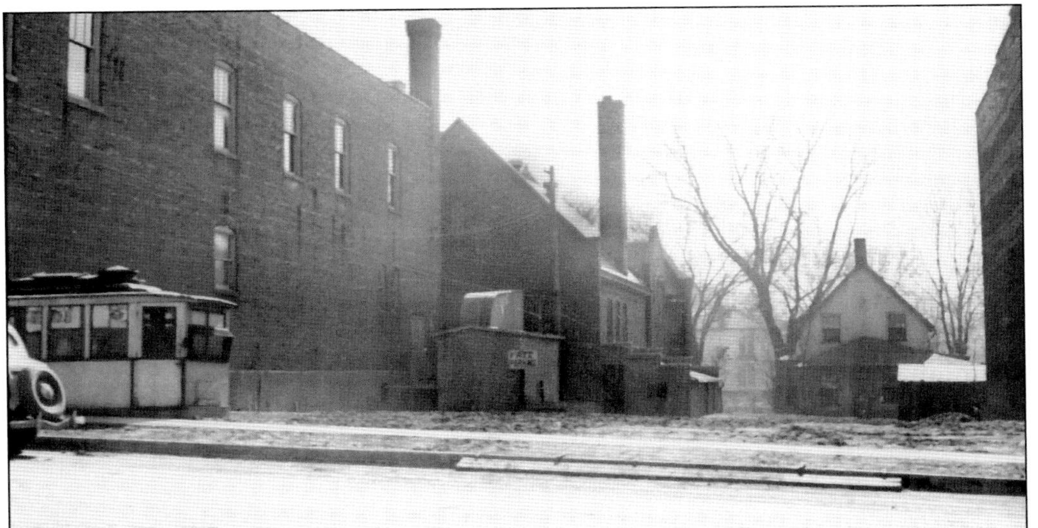

A rare empty lot is seen in the 1930s on Main Street, west of the Kratz Building where the First State Bank is currently located. The Presbyterian church is visible in the background. A small building for a peanut vendor sits opposite the car. The Lyric Theater was built on the lot in 1937. (PCHGS.)

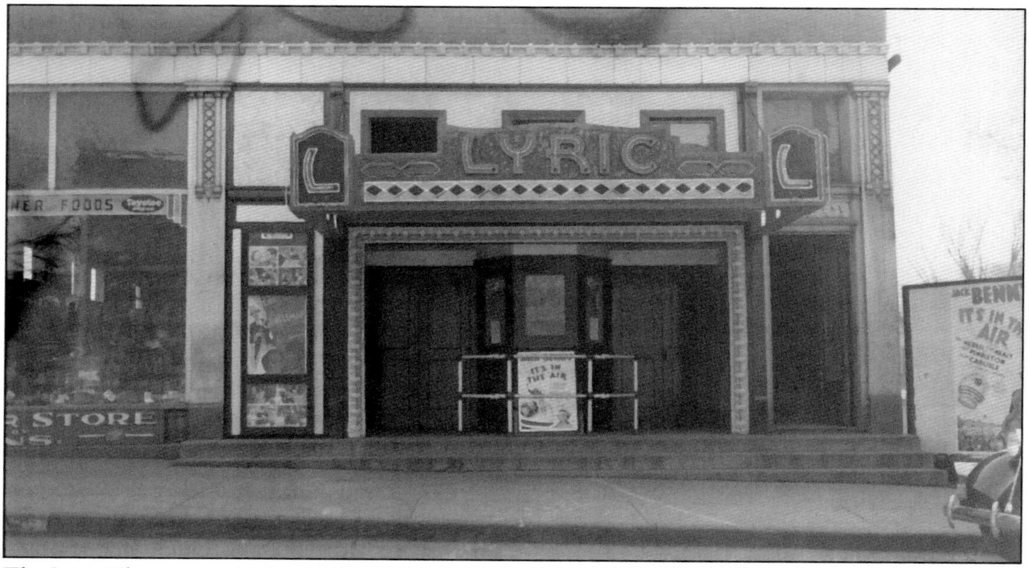

The Lyric Theater was built in 1937 at 203–209 West Main Street. Its Art Deco exterior incorporated black camera glass and a trim of stone and white metal. The feature at the time of the photograph was *It's in the Air*, with Jack Benny. As more movies became available in Champaign and Decatur, the Lyric's heyday ended. It closed in May 1979 and was demolished in 1981. (PCHGS.)

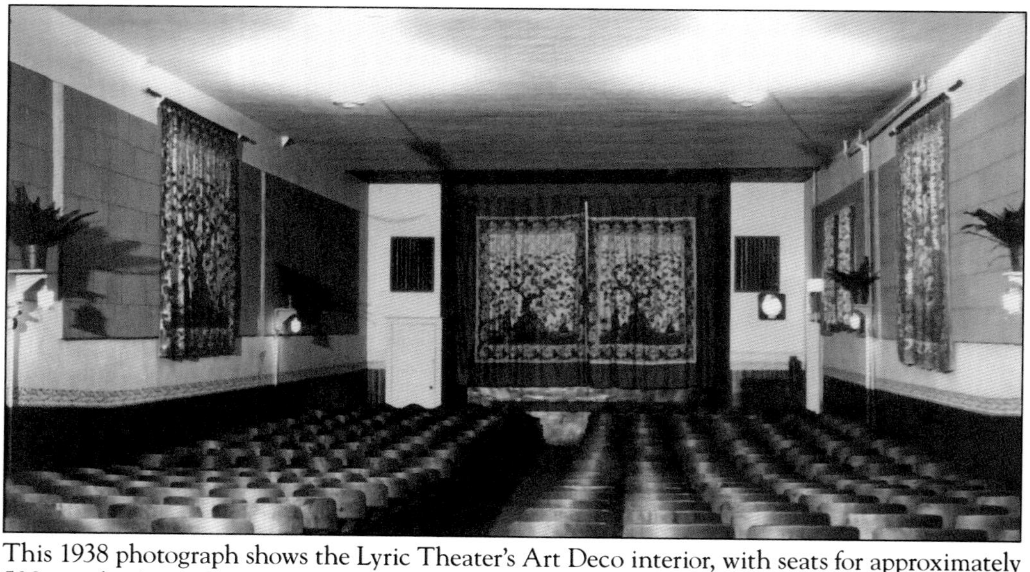

This 1938 photograph shows the Lyric Theater's Art Deco interior, with seats for approximately 500 people. An early movie theater, an open-air venue called the Airdome, opened around 1908 in an empty lot in the same location. From 1915 until 1921, the Princess Theater was established there. At one time, three movie theaters provided entertainment in Monticello. (PCHGS.)

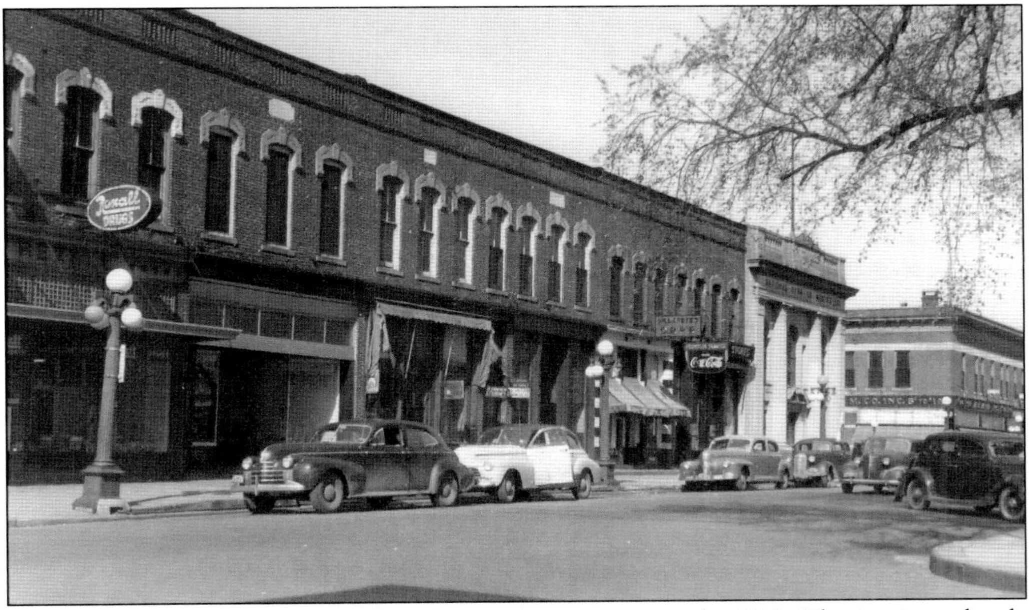

The north side of the square across from the courthouse in seen in the 1940s. The sign immediately in front of the Coca-Cola sign advertises Bill and Pete's Café, a building incorporated into the current bank building. The offices of attorneys N.E. Huston and Robert P. Shonkwiler were located above 110-1/2 West Washington Street. Raycraft's Rexall Drugstore occupied the next building. (PCHGS.)

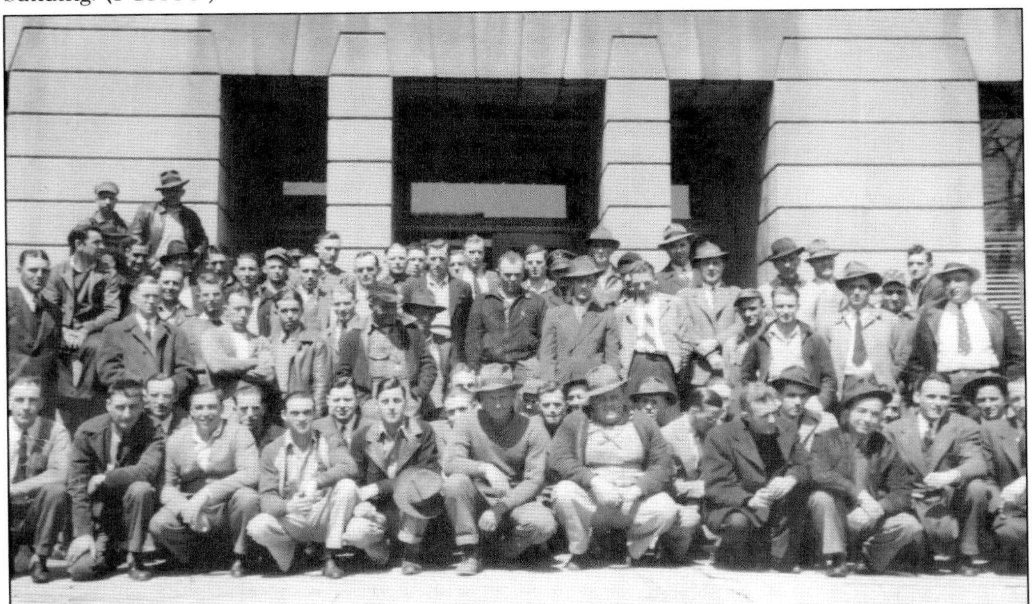

Ninety-two men smile for the camera prior to leaving Piatt County for World War II preinduction exams. This was the largest onetime group from Piatt County. During the war, local Selective Service Boards would draft the quantity required for each month. Piatt County's quota in April 1941 was 29 men. The newspaper would print the names of those men selected as well as the ones rejected. (PCHGS.)

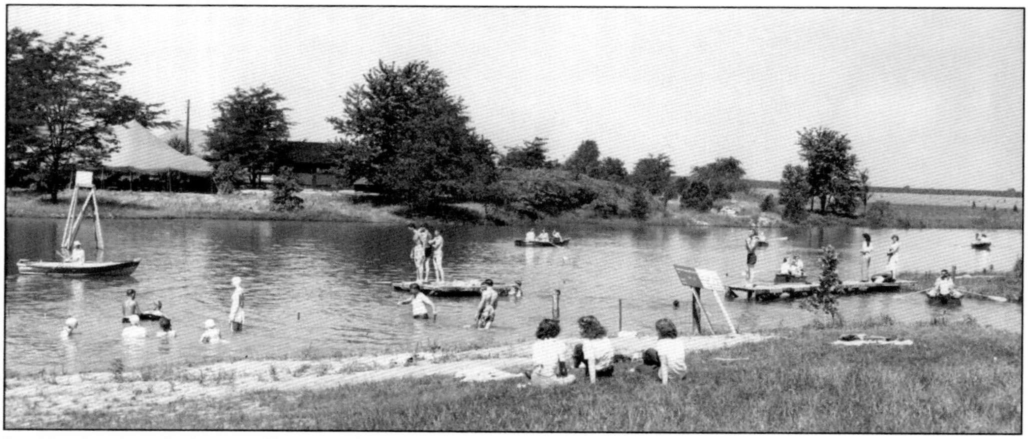

In 1946, after Robert Allerton decided to live permanently on his Hawaii estate, he donated approximately 5,500 acres of his mansion and gardens to the University of Illinois. He also gave 250 acres of his land across from the mansion for a 4-H Camp in honor of those members who served in World War II. Young people swim in one of the camp's two lakes in this 1948 photograph. (APL.)

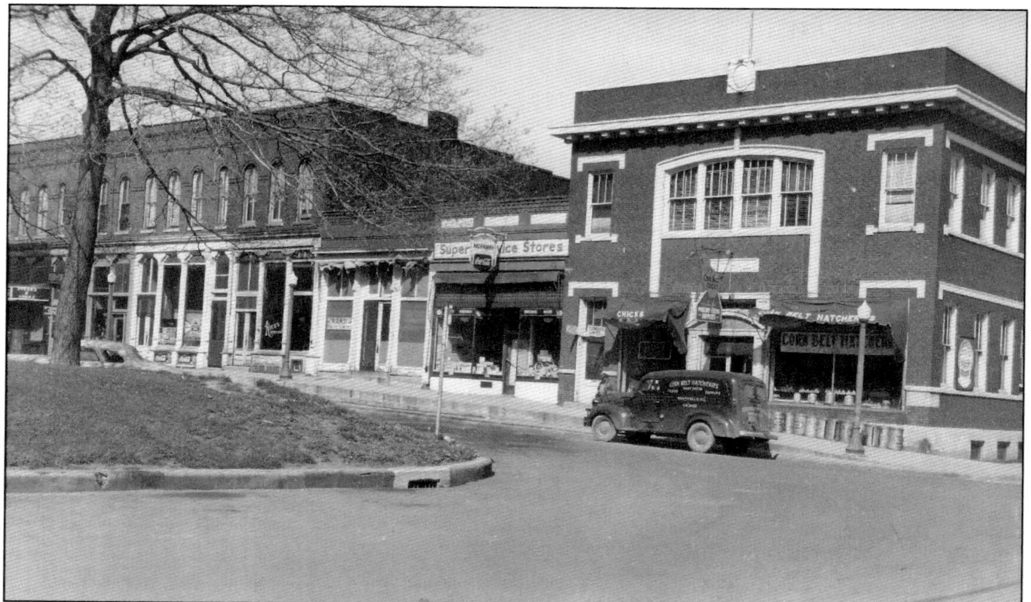

South State Street is seen in the 1940s. The businesses, from left to right, are Clodfelter's Restaurant, with the marquee advertising "Steaks" and "Chops"; Eshelman Tailor Shop, above the restaurant; Rice's Barber Shop at number 107; Geno Remedy Company; Kash-Karry Super Service Grocery Store; Corn Belt Hatcheries at number 113; and attorney E.J. Hawbaker, above the hatcheries. (SW.)

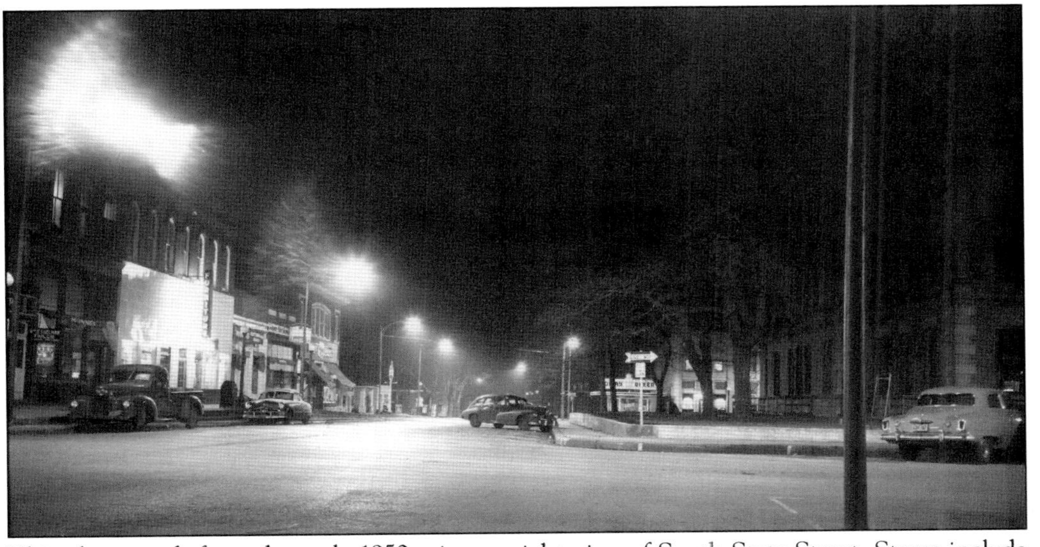

This photograph from the early 1950s gives a night view of South State Street. Stores include Clodfelters Restaurant at number 101; William Eshelman Tailor Shop above it; Ralph and Wilma McInnes's flower shop; Burgin Brothers Department Store at number 105–107, by the "Furniture" sign; Oehmke's Food Market; a gas station on the southeast corner of State and Main Streets; and the Dairy Queen opposite the station. (PCHGS.)

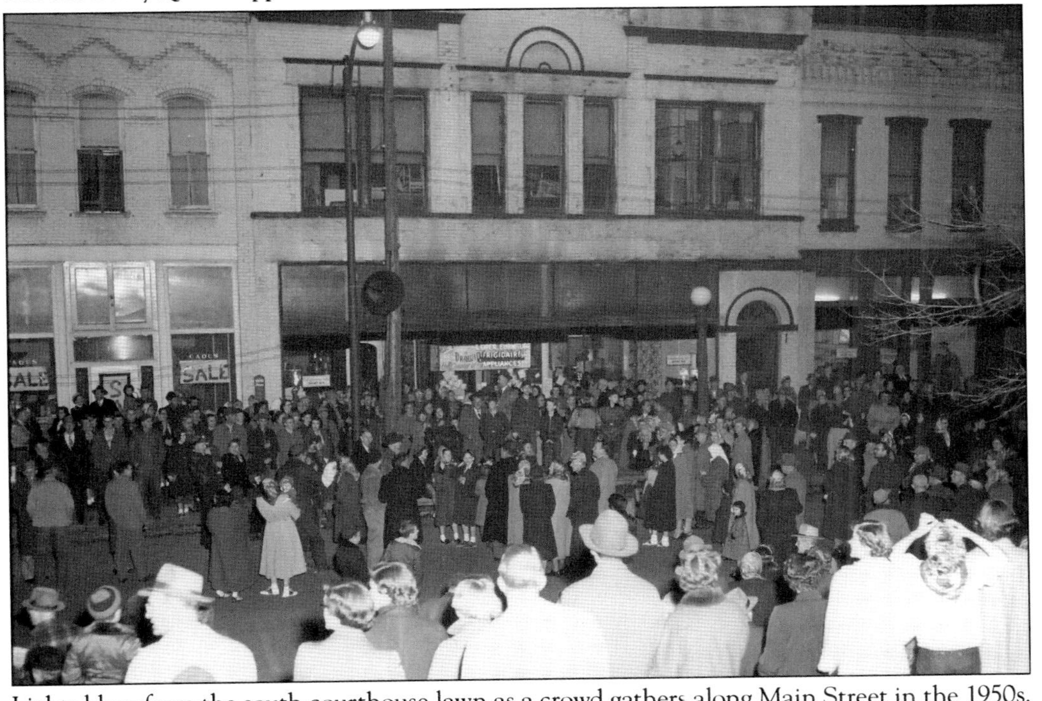

Lights blaze from the south courthouse lawn as a crowd gathers along Main Street in the 1950s. Mary Cade's Beauty Shop occupied 107 West Main Street (at the photograph's left). Leiper Furniture moved next door to the Beauty Shop in February 1952 from its Charter Street location. Window signs announce an "Enlightening Sale—January 30–31." Harris Drugs opened there in 1978, and the site is now home to Monticello Drugs. (PCHGS.)

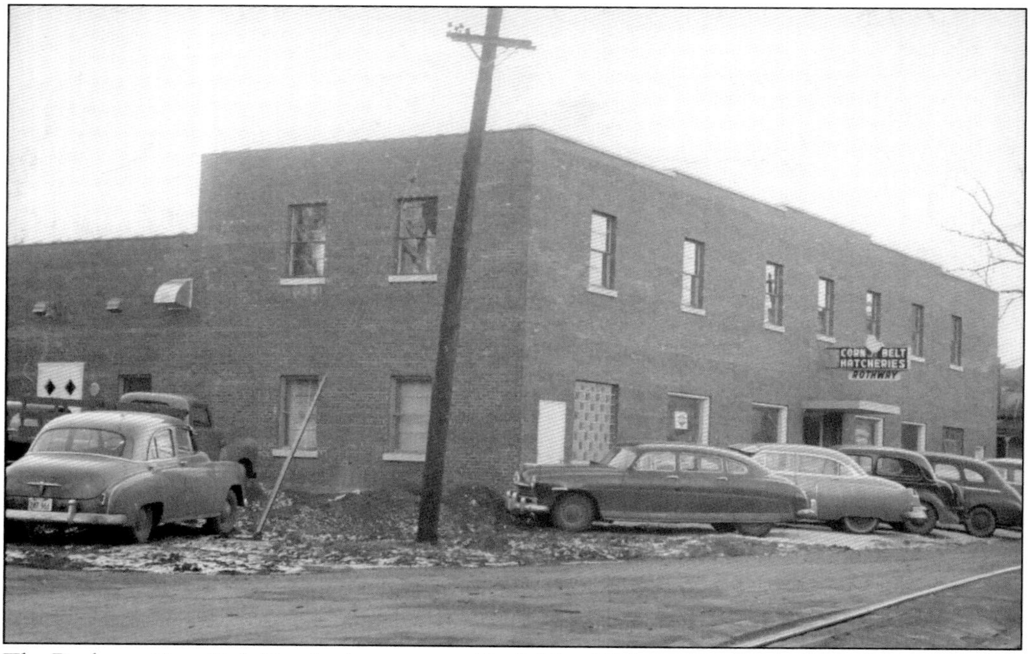

The Rothway Corn Belt Hatcheries, managed by Walter Williams, had been located on the square in the old city hall building at 113 South State Street. In January 1951, the business relocated to East Livingston Street, holding a grand opening with refreshments and entertainment provided by radio personality Red Blanchard and the WLS Barn Dance. The 96-foot-by-94-foot brick building included a brooder room on the second floor. (SW.)

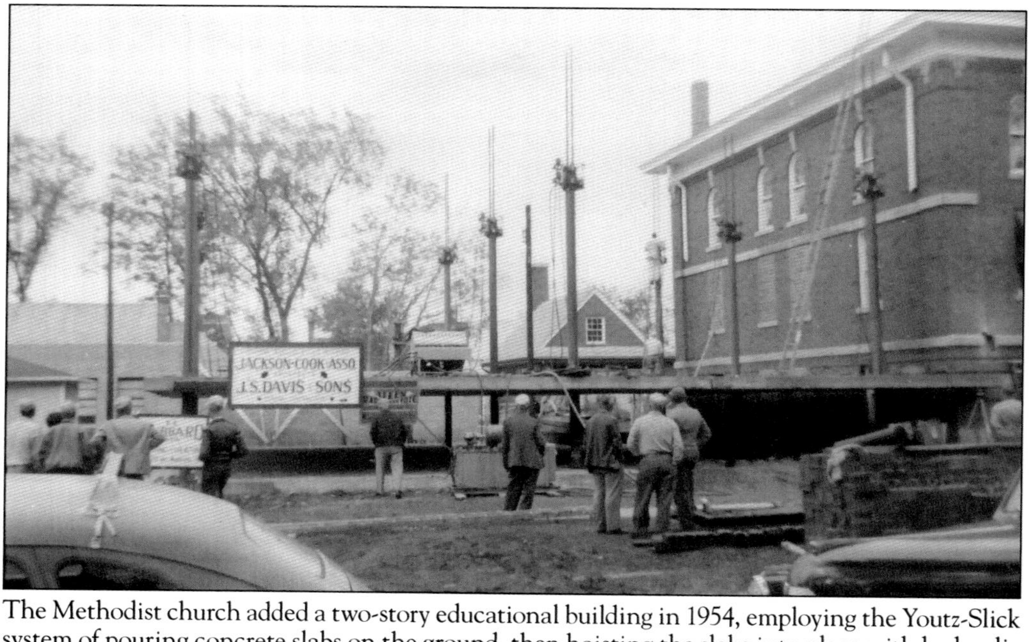

The Methodist church added a two-story educational building in 1954, employing the Youtz-Slick system of pouring concrete slabs on the ground, then hoisting the slabs into place with hydraulic jacks. The ground floor was poured first. The second floor and roof were poured on top of each other, with a special plastic coating separating them. (SR.)

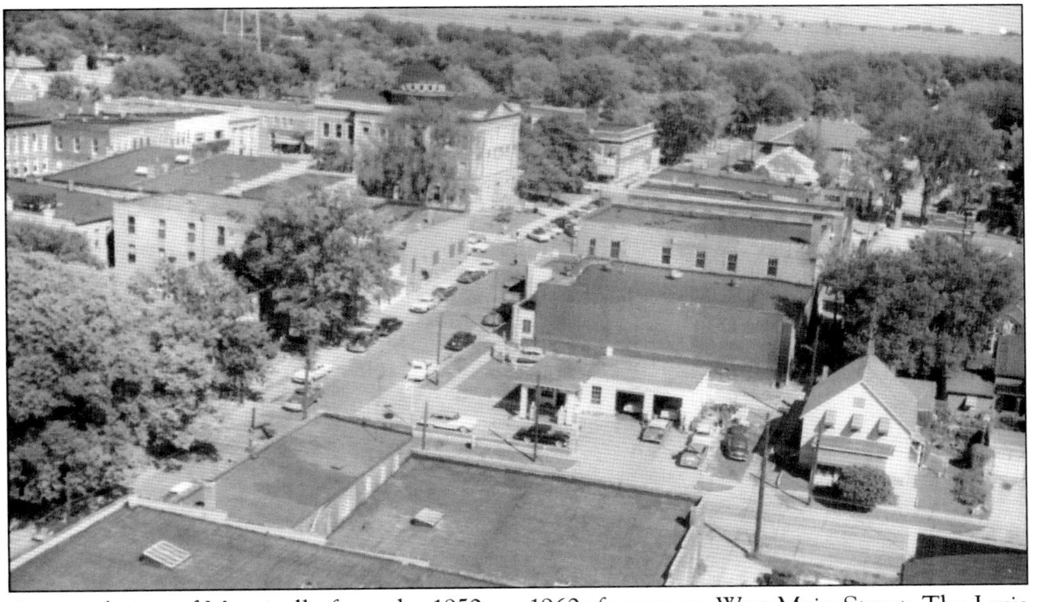

An aerial view of Monticello from the 1950s or 1960s focuses on West Main Street. The Lyric Theater sits directly east of a Shell gas station at the southeast corner of Main and Market Streets (211 West Main Street). Across the street from the station, trees obscure the front of the Sackriter Hotel. Drivers on Main Street are now only allowed to drive east, not west. (PCHGS.)

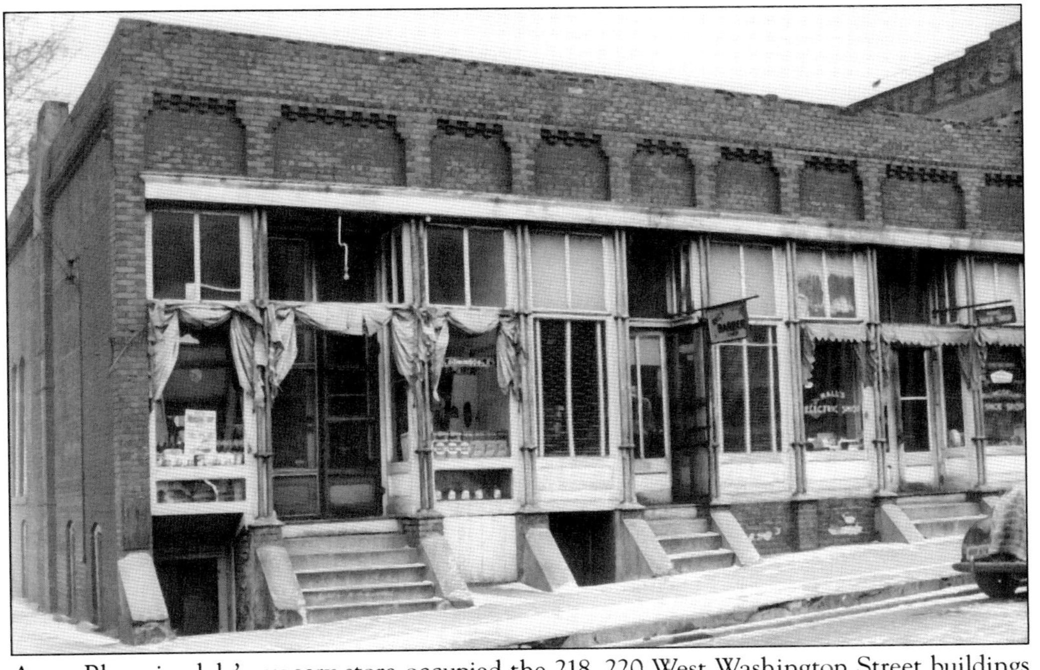

Amos Bloomingdale's grocery store occupied the 218–220 West Washington Street buildings during the 1940s. Bloomingdale sold the buildings to Eugene Kirby in 1967. At that time, Harmon Rice's Barber Shop occupied the storefront at number 218. Next to that was Hall's Electric, and the next store was the Model Shoe Shop. The site had been home to restaurants and groceries since the late 1800s. (PCHGS.)

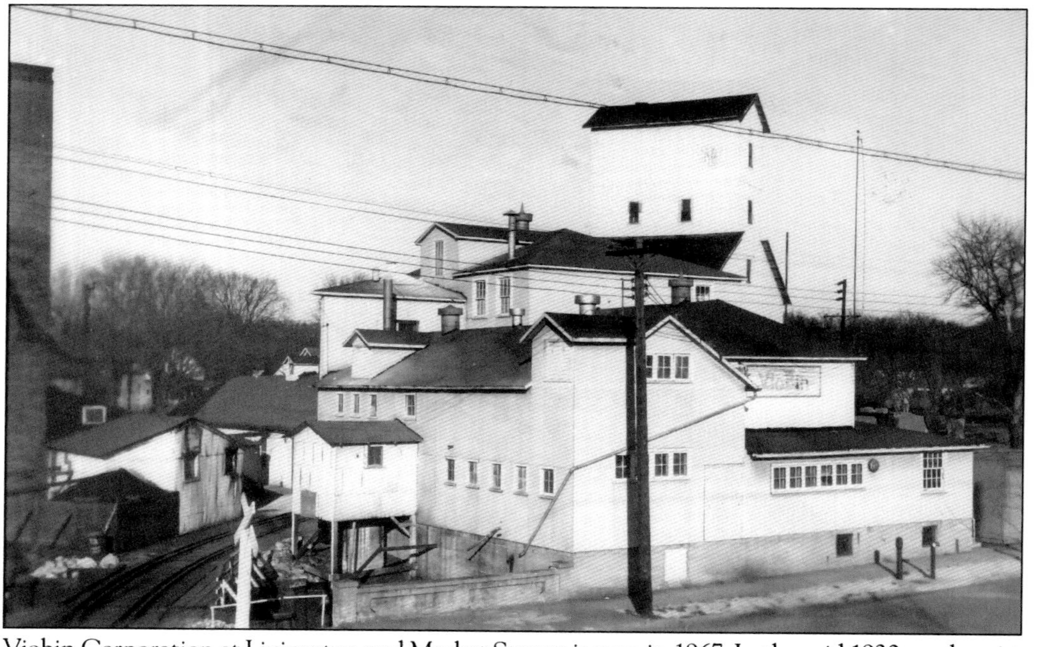

Viobin Corporation at Livingston and Market Streets is seen in 1967. In the mid-1930s, a chemist purchased an unsuccessful soybean-oil extracting plant from the Lodge family. The new company, Viobin, extracted oil from wheat germ. At one time owned by A.H. Robins Company but now a division of McShares, Inc., Viobin continues to offer wheat germ oil for use in hair products, cereals, granola bars, and animal supplements. (PCHGS.)

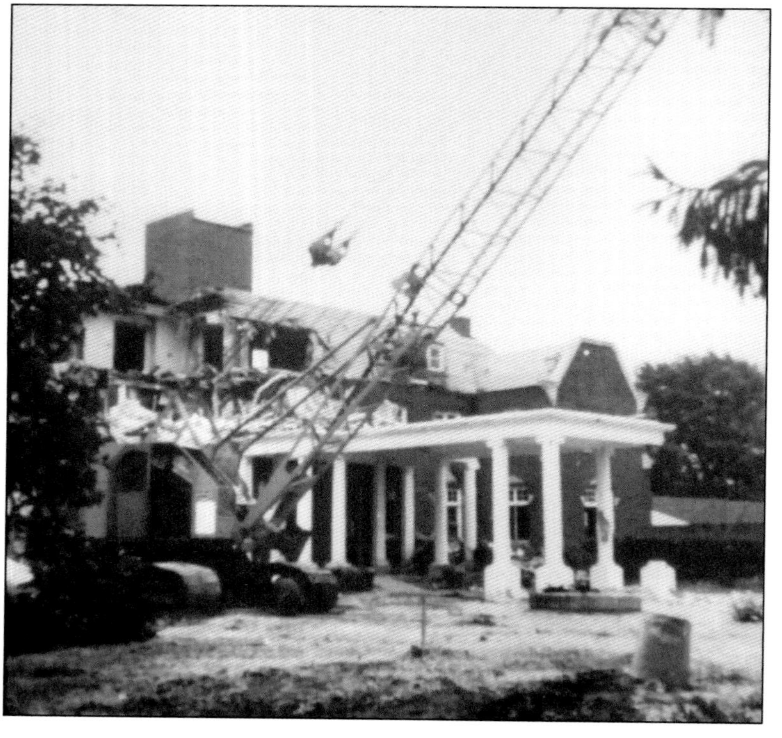

In the early 1970s, the Kirby Hospital Board of Directors learned that the facility could not fulfill the standards set forth by the State of Illinois and Joint Commission on Accreditation of Hospitals. The hospital, one of the smallest in Illinois, was given a deadline of December 1975 to construct a new facility or lose accreditation. Demolition took place in 1974, and a new one was built in 1975. (APL.)

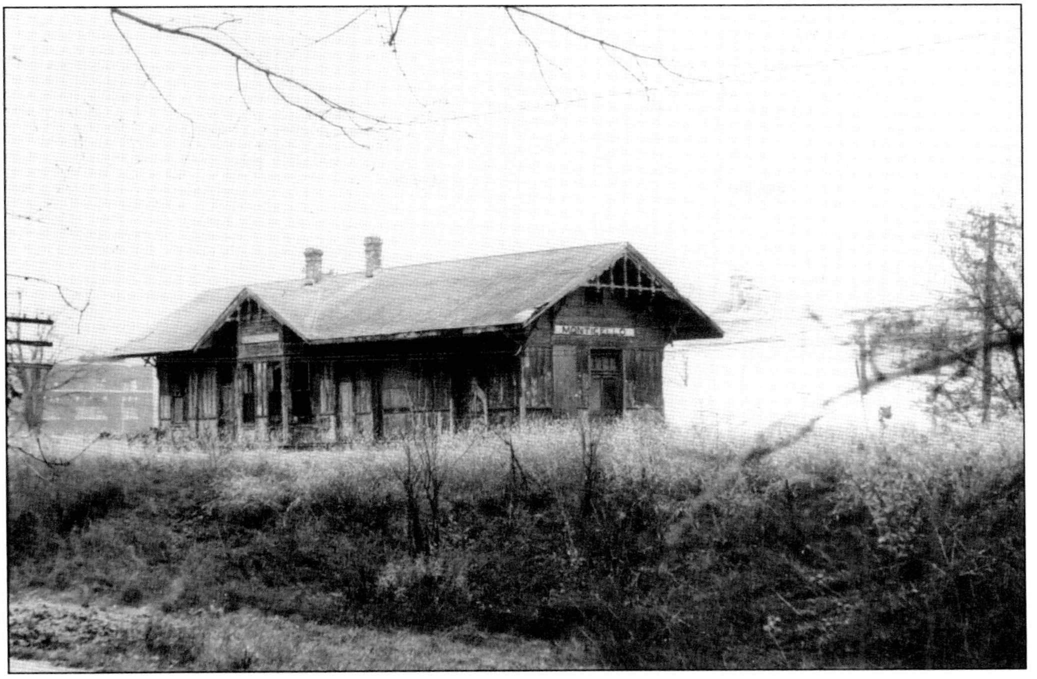

In this view facing east, one can see the shabby condition of the Wabash Depot, with the Pepsin Company to its left. Eventually, the Norfolk & Western Railway turned the depot over to Monticello's Railway Museum and then to the Monticello Depot Association. On May 29, 1987, the association moved it south of the Illinois Central track near the Allerton Library for later restoration. (APL.)

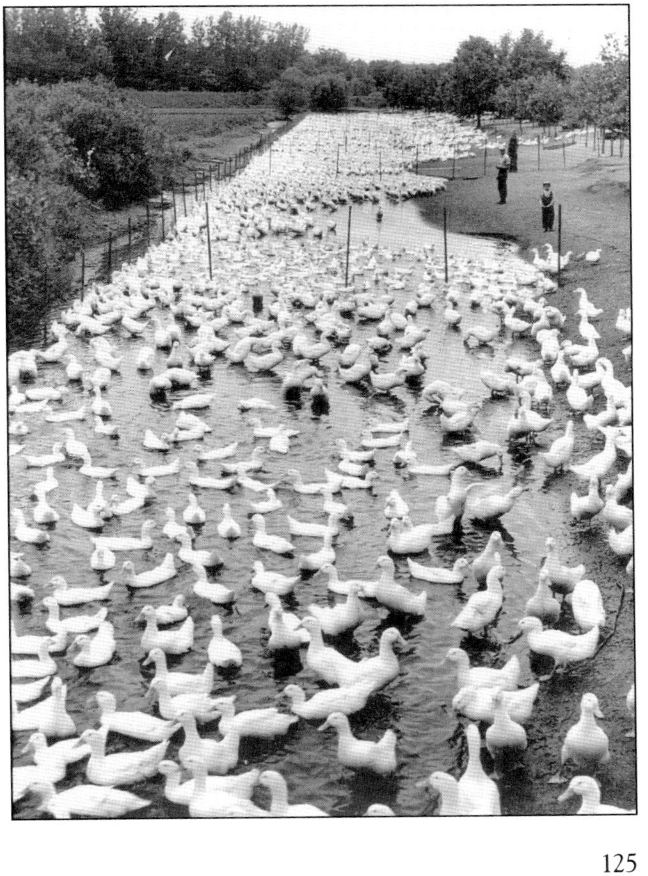

Camp Creek Duck Farm was situated north of Monticello's city limits between Route 105 and Camp Creek. Established in 1927, it consisted of 91 acres with a channel diverting part of the creek for the ducks. By 1930, it was one of the largest duck farms in the United States. Bradford Moore later sold it to the Galt family. This photograph shows the channel in the 1940s. (SG.)

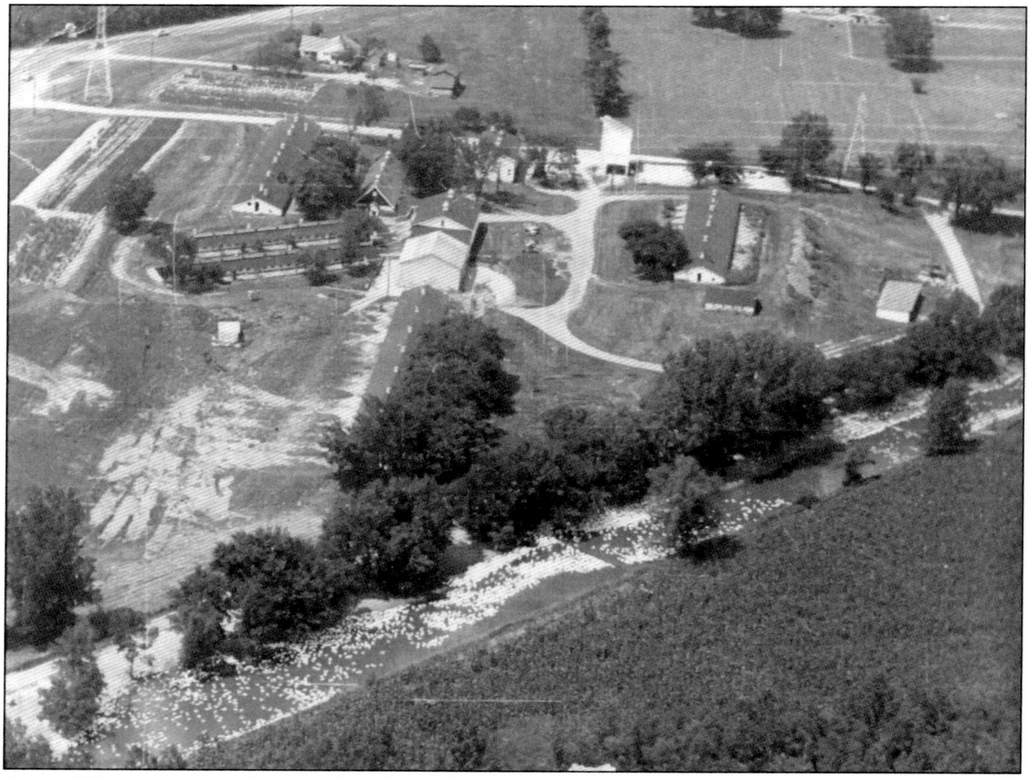

A c. 1970 aerial view of Camp Creek Duck Farm shows Route 105 running along the top of the photograph. The farm produced 20,000 ducklings in 1929, reaching 80,000 in 1934. Approximately 1,200 breeder ducks were kept at all times. Each duck laid about 125 eggs per season, with 75 percent hatching into ducklings. The farm closed in the 1980s. (SG.)

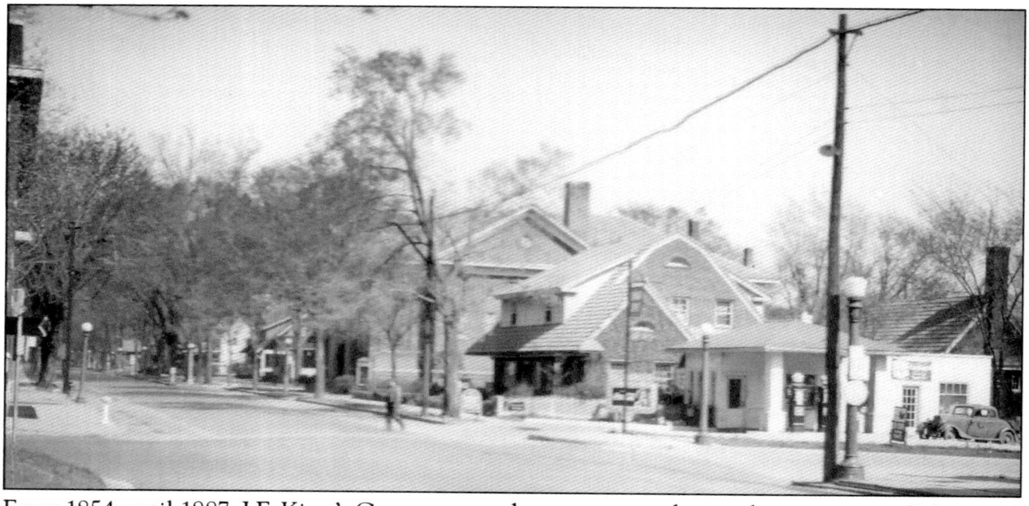

From 1854 until 1887, J.F. Kiser's Grocery served customers at the southeast corner of Main and State Streets. From 1926 onward, it became a sought-after spot for gas stations such as Bill Hook's Standard Oil Station, which operated from 1930 until 1968. Since 1977, a city park has given people a place to sit and enjoy the square and their Dairy Queen ice cream. (PCHGS.)

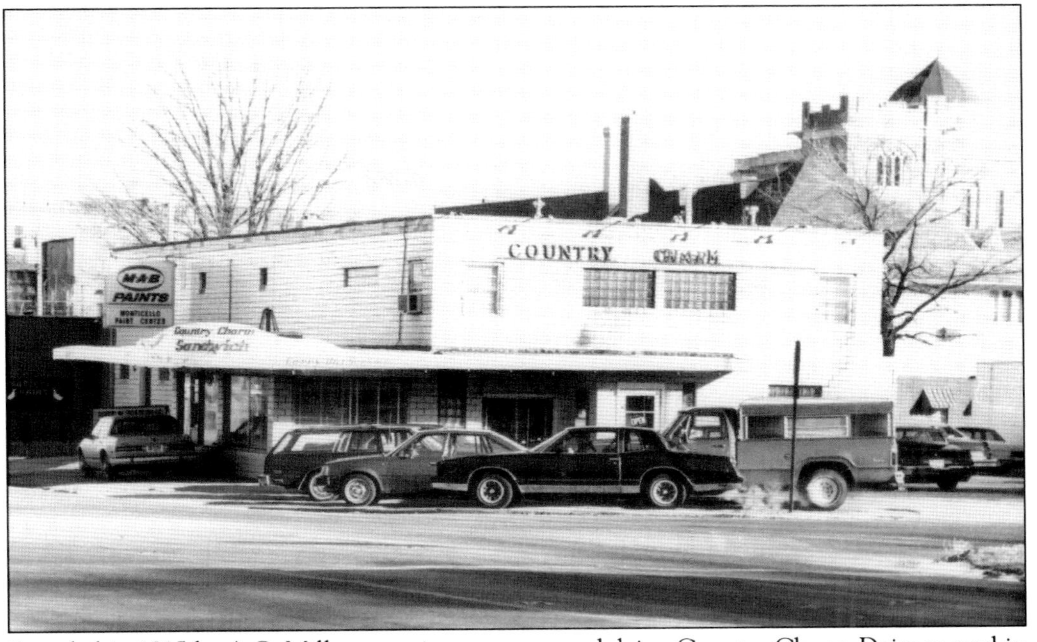

Founded in 1915 by A.C. Miller as an ice company and dairy, Country Charm Dairy moved in 1947 to the glazed tile building at the corner of Market and Main Streets. A special machine produced paper cartons for milk products and dipped them in paraffin, eliminating the need for bottles. The company later became the Country Charm Dairy Bar, a popular restaurant. It closed in 1987. (APL.)

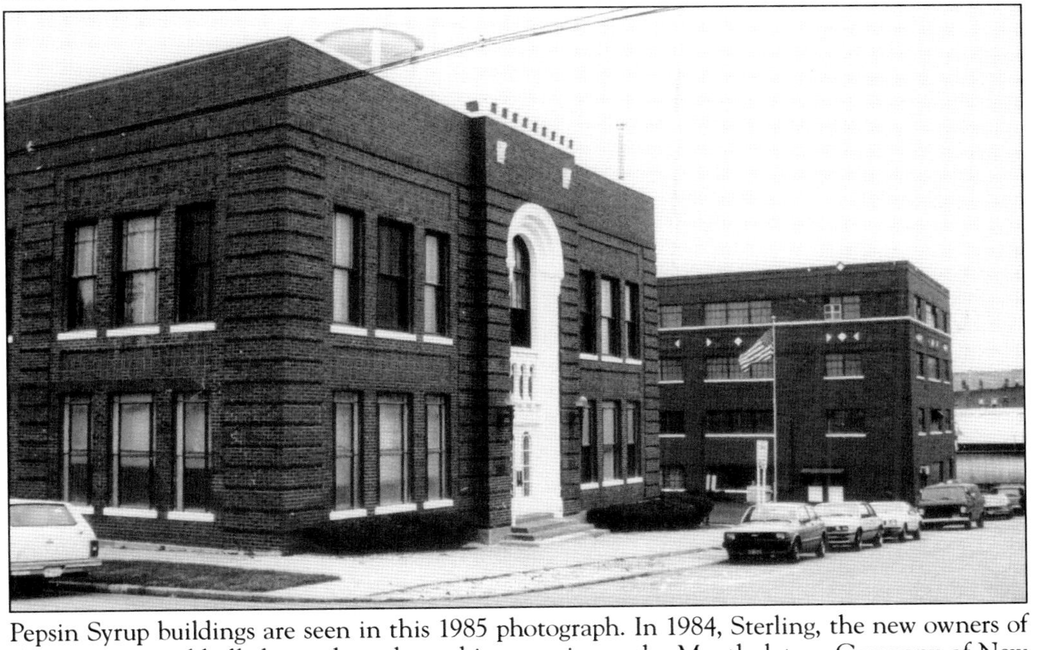

Pepsin Syrup buildings are seen in this 1985 photograph. In 1984, Sterling, the new owners of the company, sold all the trademarks and inventories to the Mentholatum Company of New York. On October 4, 1985, the Monticello plant closed after more than 80 years in business. It was demolished in October 2003. (PCHGS.)

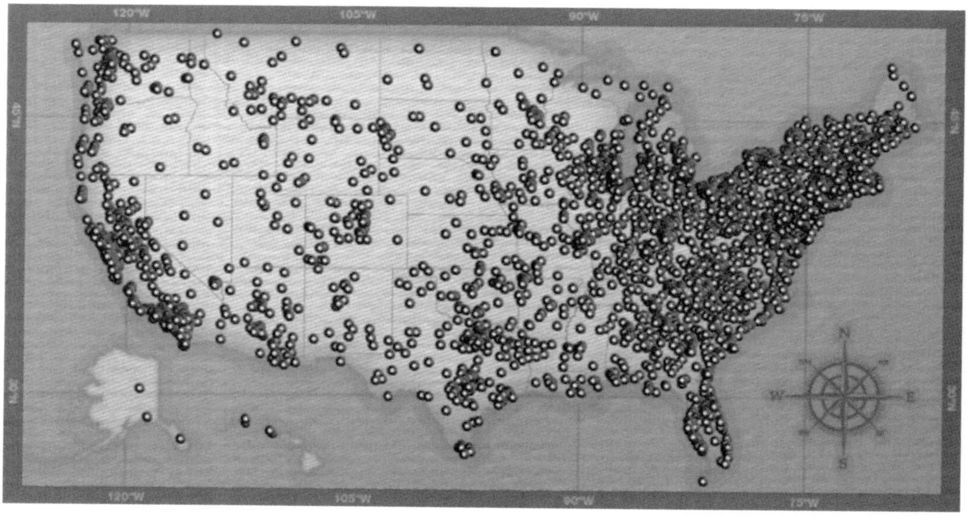